Remaking Horror

REMAKING HORROR

*Hollywood's New Reliance
on Scares of Old*

James Francis, Jr.

McFarland & Company, Inc., Publishers
Jefferson, North Carolina, and London

All photographs are from Photofest.

LIBRARY OF CONGRESS CATALOGUING-IN-PUBLICATION DATA

Francis, James, Jr., 1976–
    Remaking horror : Hollywood's new reliance on scares of old / James Francis, Jr.
       p.   cm.
    Includes bibliographical references and index.

    ISBN 978-0-7864-7088-4
    softcover : acid free paper ∞

    1. Horror films—United States—History and criticism.
    2. Film remakes—United States—History and criticism.
I. Title.
PN1995.9.H6F55 2013
791.43'6164—dc23   2012048422

BRITISH LIBRARY CATALOGUING DATA ARE AVAILABLE

© 2013 James Francis, Jr. All rights reserved

No part of this book may be reproduced or transmitted in any form or by any means, electronic or mechanical, including photocopying or recording, or by any information storage and retrieval system, without permission in writing from the publisher.

On the cover: Marion Crane (Anne Heche) reaches out for the shower curtain after being brutally stabbed by Norman Bates's mother in *Psycho*, 1998 (MCA/Universal/Photofest)

Manufactured in the United States of America

McFarland & Company, Inc., Publishers
  Box 611, Jefferson, North Carolina 28640
    www.mcfarlandpub.com

Horror has a place in my heart that most people would find quite strange, but I am glad such films continue to reflect our personal fears, strengths, weaknesses, and accomplishments—the monstrosities reveal we have not lost our human nature. Completing this project would not have been possible without the love and support of my family and friends. Thank you, Mom, for taking me to see *Twin Peaks: Fire Walk with Me* and watching me tear up at the end; Sis, for watching *Fear No Evil* with me as a kid and thinking it was kinda creepy; and Dad, for introducing me to a little show called *The X-Files*. Grandma gets the willies from *Gremlins*, and Gregory shall certainly inherit my DVD collection. Thank you all for believing in me.

Acknowledgments

David Lavery asked if I had given any thought to doing my PhD at MTSU at a Buffy the Vampire Slayer conference in 2004; it was my first conference. Within a year of starting my doctoral studies at the school, David accepted a position that required him to move to England; however, he returned later and became instrumental in the completion of this horrific text. Thank you, David, for pushing me in my writing. I hope I continue to live up to your expectations of me as a television and cinema scholar.

Before David and I teamed up, I worked with Martha Hixon in the early stages of this project. I cannot thank you enough for being a mentor in my exploration of children's literature—this base pushed me more than anything to understand horror's application to our everyday lives. Thank you for allowing me to vent in your office over the years and for being a true friend as well.

I am also extremely grateful to Drs. Linda Badley, Robert Bray, Jill Hague, Elyce Helford, Allen Hibbard, and Allison Smith for their support and educational teachings.

Cheers to my academic family, especially Becky Bobbitt for sharing half of my brain. Special thanks to Dan Lam, Christopher Ryan Bearden, and Phillip Ray for helping breathe life into the visuals on the pages.

This book is a work of study I was destined to write since I started watching horror films as a child. Again, I want to extend the biggest thanks to my mom, dad, and sister who helped form my love of horror films, and, of course, for standing by my side all these years while I considered the value of a good beheading on the big screen.

Table of Contents

Acknowledgments vi

Introduction 1

1 • The Value of Horror 9

2 • *Psycho*: The Last Bastion of Fear and Storytelling in American Cinema 19

3 • *Halloween*: When Holidays Gave Meaning to Horror ... 33

4 • *Friday the 13th*: Superstition Brought Universal Appeal ... 48

5 • *A Nightmare on Elm Street*: The Safety of Sleep Was Violated ... 60

6 • Remake Central 77

7 • The Interviews: Industry Professionals Riff About the State of Horror 146

8 • What's to Come 164

Conclusion 175

Remake Catalog, 1931–2013 183

Works Cited 193

Index 209

Introduction

U*nable to sleep, she decides a dip* in the hot tub will soothe anxieties about starting the new job tomorrow. She slinks out of bed, boyfriend still sawing logs, and heads downstairs in tank and panties. The summer house is full of windows, but there isn't a neighbor around for miles to peer inside; she loves the moonlight falling in hazy rays and beams over the furniture, off the walls, and onto her skin. The side door opens with ease, and within a few minutes the water simmers about her form. She hears the crack of a branch behind her; it's probably just a raccoon, but better safe than sorry. She was only going to stay in the tub for another minute, but before the time is up a forceful hand grabs her by the head and holds her underwater.

She can't breathe, she can't see, she gasps for air, her legs and feet and arms flail like a turtle on its back. Her right hand manages to grip a drinking glass left on the tub's outer rim and she crashes it into the assailant's head. Her body flies from the tub, water exploding in all directions, but when she looks around she sees … no one. In a flash she's back into the house, door locked behind her, and up the stairs crying out for the boyfriend; he doesn't respond. When she gets to the bedroom, her feet, dry from the carpeted staircase, are suddenly wet again. The bed is soaked around her boyfriend's limp body, his eyes wide open to the ceiling. She muffles a scream; her choked silence is offset by a huge figure bursting in from the second-story bedroom window. And the chase is on—down the stairs, past the carport, into the woods with no discernable path to aid in direction. She breaks through the trees into a clearing by the water and stops. A quick head turn to glance back at the woods reveals the menacing figure charging at her like a bull gone mad. He crashes into her with the force of a monster truck.

Once the killer tackles her, the fight is a blur—choking, scratching, punching, kicking, face grimacing. She reaches up, digs her thumbs into his eyes, and watches him fall away, but she's not done yet. In seconds the drill is in her hands as she straddles his moaning form. "This is for Ethan, you bastard!" she grunts violently, watching the bit crack bone and spiral into his heart. The man ceases movement. She removes her hands from the drill and stares at the blood dripping off her fingertips.

The girl, white tank-top drenched in blacks and reds, hair shellacked, body bruised and nipped by cuts from tree branches, face in anguish, throws her head back and cries out; the scream pierces the blackboard sky, breath escaping her mouth like steam from a hot spring in winter. She rolls from the killer's limp and mangled body, collapses to the ground, and begins to laugh hysterically. Her laughter is the only thing heard from across the lake. An expansive shot from the other side of the water shows her body rocking back and forth. She is safe ... until the camera zooms back to the killer's hand to show a finger twitch. The screen goes black. The credits roll.

But this is nothing new. The audience sees this scenario time and again. This is classic FGS (final girl syndrome: the innocent female protagonist as sole survivor who overcomes the powerful villain). And beyond this simple scene, the narrative becomes formula—redundant, repetitive, regressive ... remade. And we cannot get enough of it.

The horror film industry, once a pariah of filmmaking (and still considered not worthy of much respect according to mainstream critics), is in the process of becoming a giant remake of its genre film past. There have been minor adjustments, such as turning a final girl into a final boy, battling the happy ending by allowing the bad guy to win, showcasing African American characters who do escape slaughter, and even adding heady psychological and philosophical speculation to storylines. But the overall presentation of contemporary American horror films is now déjà vu. Classic film creations and modern-day B-movie exploits alike are being remade and cranked out quicker than an axe murderer beheads stalked prey. Although it is certain almost every film (no genre barrier) borrows from another (from camera angles to lighting to settings and a bit of storytelling), current American horror film production is snatching movies, domestic and foreign films from the 1930s to the 2000s, and remaking the titles.

Horror scholar Linda Badley, author of *Film, Horror, and the Body Fantastic*, partly attributes this wave of remakes to Japanese and Korean horror film successes near the turn of the 21st century. During the early stages of this publication, she observed:

> As the American horror industry devolved into sequels and remakes, a number of innovative foreign horror films achieved international success, and this (together with 1970s nostalgia?) helped fuel the current American horror film remake cycle. Specifically, this took off with the remake of *The Ring* (2002) and other Asian horror titles in the late 1990s and early 2000s. Other remakes, such as *The Haunting* [1999], were made earlier, of course,

but had only a so-so level of impact, and the *Godzilla* [1998] remake, while it made a lot of money, was more of a silly summer movie.

Although horror films of the '80s satiated the genre with sequels and prequels, those enterprises were considered new movies extended from an origin story; they gave filmmakers a chance to explore the villains in depth, develop the mystery, intrigue, and fear from the first films, and experiment with the genre's artistic capabilities. Sequels and prequels definitely helped solidify horror cinema formulas, and they have certainly assisted updated retreads of feature films previously released to be created.

The remake movement establishes careers for new directors and actors, makes money franchises out of castaway celluloid, and makes strong attempts to reinvigorate the element of fear in a field whose base subject is that primal emotion; however, it is anyone's guess whether or not the movement is helping progress the genre or retarding it by invoking films of yore. The art of horror has changed. The film industry will either continue to release remakes as its new standard of production, or rare, novel films (more than the two or three obscure gems at film festivals) will start to proliferate in the field and direct more attention to indie spirit.

Contemporary horror films are making a ton of money. Each new release is a cash cow for the film industry, at least for the production houses that are managing this development. Current audiences may not be aware that many of these movies are remakes, which enables studios to package them as completely new releases; the trailers do not advertise the films as remakes, nor do the opening credits or title sequences indicate such. These are the audience members who flock to see the new *Friday the 13th* (2009) or *When a Stranger Calls* (2006) or *The Hills Have Eyes* (2006). Many of them (typically the younger, teen audience) have no idea that each of these films date back to the 1970s and 1980s, and for those who do remember the originals, they often go to view the films to judge them against the original productions. Either way, the theater audience is packed with eager viewers who have purchased tickets and assure the film a profit. The companies manufacture remakes at a mere $10 million to 20 million a film on average, and the box-office return of ticket sales typically doubles, triples, or quadruples that, thereby allowing the film to be considered a success and guaranteeing a sequel, prequel, trilogy, and merchandise to market. The studios making the films partner with audiences in this phenomenon to make the remake movement possible.

New horror movie remakes are also giving unknown names career starters. No one really knew who Marcus Nispel was, outside of his music video creations, until he made *The Texas Chainsaw Massacre* remake in 2003. The same can be said about Alexandre Aja, creator of *The Hills Have Eyes* retread in 2006. Aja had previously directed the French film *Haute tension* (2003), but his name was not established in the United States. (With the way the remake wave is building, a redo of *tension* by Aja as an American film might not be out of the question.) Rob Zombie is able to take a seat next to Nispel and Aja as well. He made his directorial debut in 2003 with the innovative and nostalgic horror film *House of 1000 Corpses*. The follow-up, *Devil's Rejects* (2005), proved a welcome addition to horror, and then in 2007 Zombie played his hand with a remake of the John Carpenter classic *Halloween*. He was later quoted as saying he would not do a sequel; however, *Halloween II* found its way to screens in 2009 (Nix). Previously in talks to do a remake of the 1958 classic sci-fi horror film *The Blob* and eventually deciding against the venture, Zombie may not have started with remakes, but he is clearly on the path. Samuel Bayer, another music video aficionado, helmed the 2010 *A Nightmare on Elm Street*. The list of budding new talent goes on and on for such directors.

The actors in the films, too many to name, also have common ties. Almost all of the fresh faces meeting the monster's machete, chainsaw, or finger-knives are not exactly new to us. The men and women of remake stardom, portraying boys and girls typically of high school age, are an ensemble cast from *Gossip Girl's Supernatural Trip to 7th Heaven*. If that faux television series does not explain it all, the title alludes to the many faces from the former WB and UPN networks (now the CW) and other teen-audience programming networks who continue to appear in remakes. Teenage boys and girls (and quite a few adults) dedicate time to watch contemporary installments of *90210* (CW 2008), *Melrose Place* (CW 2009–2010), and scripted-reality productions such as *Laguna Beach* (MTV 2004–2006) or *The Hills* (MTV 2006–2010). They know the actors on these shows inside and out from watching the episodes, reading interviews with the cast, following their tweets, and stalking their celebrity profiles on MySpace and Facebook. But the actors want to be bigger household names, and a great way to fulfill such an enterprise is to take lead roles in horror remakes where the same CW audiences are sure to be found. Remakes give star power to both new directors and rising actors, while the film content seeks to offer new perspectives on older productions.

Audiences are excited to see Paris Hilton, Jared Padalecki, and Michelle Trachtenberg in horror remakes; but fear, not excitement for star power, has always been horror's key emotion. Yet another result of the remake machine is the complement of fear and celebrity anticipation within the movies. Fear inspires instinctual fight or flight; it activates anxiety and adrenaline, and provides a space for childhood terrors to be relived. When viewers are cowering in their theater seats, biting nails, shielding their eyes behind hands, and feeling the unmistakable prick of hairs rising on the backs of their necks, fear has found a home. Remakes work to provide this physical reaction with the bonus of presenting recognizable actors to fan bases.

Contemporary American horror, however, conjures fear among its audiences mostly via loud noises, red herrings (the cat jumps from out of a dark corner), and visceral attacks on the human bodies of characters. It is not typically moody and atmospheric like Japanese/Korean horror, quirky like Australian horror, or even maniacal and disturbed like French horror. American horror has seemingly always borrowed from the stories and technical presentation of international filmmakers, but it established cinema standards, and now it looks to its own films to reinvent itself. The remake industry continues to grow, and as it does, by recreating international cinema and movies here "at home," the intensity of fear mutates into a new creature. Fear diminishes as viewers watch horror movies more than once, and the same can typically be said for multiple viewings of comedies, thrillers, and so forth: emotions are not as strong as they are upon first contact. The horror remake presents fear anew with star power, directorial style, and memory of what scared audiences in the past. Audiences may not have seen the original or know the story, but the fear created and delivered in the first production never fades. Whether the issue is fertility drugs and their after-effects (*It's Alive*, 1974), the HIV/AIDS epidemic (*Aliens*, 1986), or the dangers of consumerism and wartime environments (*Night of the Living Dead*, 1968), most of the statements in fear that original productions made have to be updated in a remake. Fertility drugs, HIV/AIDS, consumerism, and international conflicts exist in contemporary society, but remakes have to approach the importance of these issues and the fear they generate from different perspectives by taking into account current cultural and social concerns, although some simple surface-level connections may work, too. With the number of remakes (and reinventions or reboots) being produced, the horror remake seems to be conducive to the genre's environmental health, stability, and future growth.

What horror remakes are *not* doing is regurgitating artistic expression, story value, or critical thinking. Director/actor starpower, the financial aspects, and fear are all interesting topics to examine, but there is more about the films being created to investigate. As for art direction, horror remakes are becoming more like action films. When people hear the name Michael Bay, they are interested to see what he has made because his style alters the genre's conventions. Over the past nine years he has produced *The Texas Chainsaw Massacre* (2003), *The Amityville Horror* (2005), *The Texas Chainsaw Massacre: The Beginning* (2006), *The Hitcher* (2007), *Friday the 13th* (2009), *A Nightmare on Elm Street*, and was previously in talks to make *Friday the 13th: Part 2* in the near future. Each film plays out like his *Bad Boys* movies from 1995 and 2003: a kaleidoscope of colors flashes across the screen when characters are in pursuit, sparks fly from weaponry as the killer stalks his prey, low-level camera angles achieve the "hero shot" of a character muddied and drenched in sweat with a blue sky backdrop, and the audience is presented with expansive establishing shots and tight-knit close-ups to show that no matter how far someone runs or how deep they hide, there is no escape. This action/thriller formula for horror films becomes more embedded with every remake. What is interesting about someone like Bay is that he is not directing the films; producers are stamping their personal styles on movies while the new directors are working on establishing their names in the market.

Screenplays, unlike production style, do not differ too much from the original content. Although it has been said that any good story is worth telling again, remakes typically follow two paths of storytelling. When these tales are retold, they are presented exactly as before, or they are altered to create a new vision. The new versions, however, typically do more than alter a storyline; they often change the original film's message to give viewers something new to think about. Fans of the original *Friday the 13th* (1980) and its sequels were shocked to find Nispel's production to be a mash-up of the first three films; message boards were filled with threads discussing the topic. Mrs. Voorhees is the killer in the first film, but her storyline is truncated into a five-minute opening sequence. Jason becomes the killer in the sequel, walking and stalking victims wearing a potato sack over his head, but the team behind the remake wanted him running through the woods wearing his famous hockey mask that wasn't acquired until the third film in the original series. The masked killer also takes a hostage in the remake and dies at the hands of a brother-sister team instead of a final girl. These changes highlight the original film's directive but showcase it differently to separate the remake from the past. It would probably be easier to make a completely different movie, but studios usually consider what fans want to remember from the original and mix that with a few contemporary changes; the nostalgic influences only help box office numbers. This is only one example; to catalogue all the changes that have and are occurring in horror remakes would exhaust even the most avid fan of the genre, but we will take a look at a variety of films in later chapters. These same fans who enjoy a good story also like to exit the theater with lingering thoughts of the film they just viewed. Remakes bring back memories of the original productions into a contemporary social consciousness.

Horror films are designed to inject fear into viewers, but they are able to inspire thought-provoking discussions as well. Remakes, however, cannot fully embrace this combined cinematic effect. The substantive research on or about horror films and elements of horror conducted by vital contemporary and formative critics like Julia Kristeva, Carol Clover, Sigmund Freud, Barbara Creed, and others does not apply to this current remake trend. Mainstays in the field, such figures offer rich evaluations of horror that guide discussions on abjection, final girls, the uncanny, feminist theory, and other revelations. All of these elements should be relevant to remakes in some shape or form: Zombie's *Halloween* offers genre commentary, but Carpenter's 1978 version helped initiate the slasher subgenre and gave rise to a substantial body of critical theory first; the remake came along long after the original cultural or social messages of fear had been evaluated. Contemporary horror remakes demonstrate their significance via financial gain to studio houses, celebrity status acquired by directors, actors, and producers, stylistic/genre alterations, and narrative reworkings. Each of the original films have already been received by audiences, celebrated or demonized by reviewers, and dissected by critics. This is where a remake theory needs to be constructed. Part of the goal of this book is to introduce discussions that lead to a working theory of remakes—something practical that critics, reviewers, and fans can come to terms with about the movement.

Some fans of horror bemoan remakes, while many others celebrate the enterprises, although both groups watch them diligently to see what changes have been made. They evaluate the cast, directing, production style, kill methods, and story alterations from original productions. The viewers who consider remakes to be inferior compared to earlier films cannot deny that the continuing support (going to the theater, renting/purchasing DVDs, streaming movies online, etc.) demonstrates that the movement is capable of being an effective phase in horror and worthy of study. Message boards from *IMDb* (*Internet Movie Database*), *Esplatter*, *Fangoria*, *Dread Central*, and a host of other horror networks light up with comments, discussions, and arguments every time a remake is announced, leaked, or rumored. Remakes do not have to be liked or disliked to create discussion. Although horror remakes are often labeled hollow shells in comparison to original productions, they cannot be dismissed as unimportant to academic research. In order to evaluate their place in horror it is vital to take a look at the films that precede their productions. One film in particular is the focal point of horror's popularity and in many ways has given birth to the remake movement.

Alfred Hitchcock's *Psycho* (1960) and Gus Van Sant's *Psycho* (1998) constitute the watershed moment in remake history: a time when the gates were officially opened, allowing any film—classic or contemporary—to face the remake machine and become a different creation for contemporary times. *Psycho*, as "a film that both resonated with and violated American cultural norms," is at the center of discussion because its remake constitutes the beginning of the remake trend (Phillips 61). "The film has been the subject of numerous books and hundreds of essays; indeed, the critical and academic attention to Hitchcock and *Psycho* played an integral part in the development of film studies" (Phillips 61). This type of reverence for a horror film is now extremely rare; studios are hardly ever up in arms about the subject matter of a film and the impact it may have upon its viewers. The *Psycho* chapter will focus on the film's altered storytelling (what was and was not kept from the original film, and a new representation of contemporary sociocultural fears), cinematography/art (changes in critical filmmaking technique), acting, and fear (emotional response). Consideration of the remakes of the three classic slasher franchises Hitchcock's movie gave birth to—*Halloween*, *Friday the 13th*, and *A Nightmare on Elm Street* (1984)—will follow, including a discussion of origin stories, fear, star power, and the poignant effects the films have had on the horror genre in comparison to their remakes. These three cinematic franchises are the heart of horror—seminal films—especially in the heyday of the 1980s. Ask anyone today "What is horror?" and s/he would probably say *Saw* (2004)—not because it is scary or made a certain way, but because its franchise flooded the genre. In a few years the answer might be *Paranormal Activity* (2007), as a fourth installment was released in October 2012. A critical analysis of each of horror's mainstays and the role they play in the remake arena showcases the current state and future trends of contemporary American horror in the genre's development.

Research will also show what effects the remake has had upon horror genre directors, actors, and producers (style and star power), and money and marketing (production value, MPAA ratings strategies, and theatrical/DVD releases). Discussion of the central films is followed by an in-depth exploration of horror cinema from the 1930s to present-day that demonstrate the remake movement in action. Personal interviews with industry professionals offering candid reflections on the current state of American horror cinema and the role remakes play in the genre make up the proceeding section. The penultimate chapter offers information about a showcase of horror cinema that exists outside American borders; these films are critical to any discussion of the current state of the horror genre. Although there are quite a few international horror movies making waves, French cinema is currently at the height of critical, original horror; a few notable films are discussed that demonstrate the cinematic levels of horror that the genre is still able to achieve in what many critics believe to be its current struggle to remain viable in the movie industry.

This book closes with a number of end remarks about the genre and its remake trend; it details a personal evaluation of the genre's future and demonstrates how rapidly the films are being produced. An exhaustive compilation of original horror films and their remake counterparts (in terms of ratings and box office revenue) is provided in the Remake Catalog, 1931–2013, at the back of this book. Although a great number of film critics, reviewers, and fans bemoan *and* celebrate remake endeavors, no one has given this genre movement critical, academic attention. *Remaking Horror* is a dedicated effort to begin formal discussion.

1

The Value of Horror

No one has written an academic treatise on the topic of horror remakes; there are no theoretical perspectives to reference. It is, however, first important to understand why horror movies are relevant and what values they exhibit. Badley writes about horror's connection to the body in her text. She writes, "Horror is ... the most physiological of genres—with the possible exception of pornography" (11). The genre articulates fear because it represents real-time terrors of the mind and body. Horror films may change directors, actors, producers, screenplays, cinematography, music, and locations, but they unify audiences in collective social fears.

Dramas and thrillers have scary moments, but horror films are different. Stephen Prince (*The Horror Film*) details why the genre is unique:

> Like other genre movies, any given horror film will convey synchronic associations, ideological and social messages that are part of a certain period or historical moment. One can analyze horror films in terms of these periods or moments, just as one can do with Westerns or gangster movies. But, unlike those genres, horror also goes deeper, to explore more fundamental questions about the nature of human existence, questions that, in some profound ways, go beyond culture and society as these are organized in any given period or form. Here lies the special significance of horror, the factors that truly differentiate it from the other genres and that make it conform most deeply with our contemporary sense of the world [2].

Horror films highlight human fears, and remakes remind audiences of the value of fear in cinema. Viewers may jump at a loud noise or turn their heads waiting for a loud noise to announce action on the screen, but the meaning of fear in a horror remake is twofold: it triggers memory of social and cultural commentary for viewers who have seen the original, and simultaneously situates a new experience for audience members to take home with them.

The original *Psycho* is a film that gave audiences authentic fears to think about beyond the frame of the movie. Caroline Picart and David Frank, co-authors of *Horror and the Holocaust: Genre Elements in Schindler's List and*

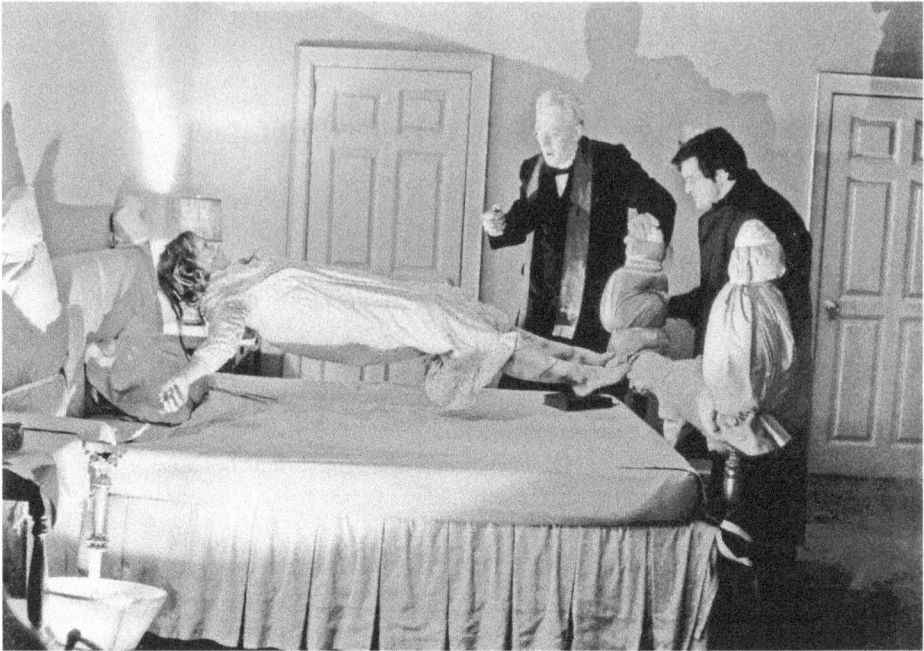

Regan (Linda Blair) hovers above her bed as Father Merrin (Max von Sydow) and Father Karras (Jason Miller) attempt to exorcise the demon from her body in *The Exorcist* (1973).

Psycho, remind viewers: "It is important to note that like *Schindler's List* [1993], Hitchcock's *Psycho* was based on fact: the real-life murder-mutilations committed by a Wisconsin man, Ed Gein, filtered through the novelistic lens of Robert Bloch" (208). Fifty years later, horror films are still utilizing the Gein story, which proves the staying power of social and cultural fears, and simultaneously the strength of reusable stories.

When Prince says horror goes beyond sociocultural boundaries, he wants readers to understand the manner in which horror frightens people more than reality. People are not afraid of Ed Gein in real life because he is a dark moment in history no one thinks about; however, they are frightened by films showcasing his brutal exploits. Gein cannot touch a viewer in a theater, but the fear generated by the production of a film based on his existence stays in the mind forever. Horror's unique ability allows fear to transcend the screen into the lives of its audience members.

Jonathan Crane's *Terror and Everyday Life: Singular Moments in the History of the Horror Film* explains this distinction further. Crane says, "Watching a horror film is a reality check; it is the entertainment equivalent of checking

CNN's *Headline News* for the latest tragedy or scanning monotonously bleak headlines over black coffee and an apple danish" (8). A slasher film depicting five deaths cannot measure up to the suffering experienced by people in natural disasters, wartime offenses, infection, or disease, but the everyday tragedies people experience are reflected in the perils faced in horror cinema. Critics and viewers become beside themselves at the thought that a new *Saw* movie is being released, but not many acknowledge news reports that inform the public that hundreds of villagers were slaughtered by a warring tribe or that thousands were killed in a landslide. A movie screen often has a more profound effect on the psyche than real tragedy. The horror genre exploits fear unlike any emotion that other genres try to elicit in viewers.

Horror's human factor should place the field in high regard across the spectrum of academic criticism and genre studies, but too often horror criticism becomes generalized, and statements made are accepted at face value because academic films like Fritz Lang's *Metropolis* (1927) or the comedic genius of Chaplin are labeled high-brow in comparison. Horror is often ostracized, but it is a field rife with bodies of work worthy of discussion.

Crane demonstrates that horror is susceptible to antiquated critical analysis when he discusses the roles of killer and victim. He stereotypes the roles by saying, "either you identify with the slasher—you'd like to have a razor-sharp, foot-long machete in hand as well—or you identify with the worthless victim whose spectacular dismemberment becomes the death you too merit" (3). This statement held more value in the 1980s and early 1990s when horror films followed binary formulas; viewers had to identify with the killer or victim in order to consummate the film-audience relationship. Crane's text was written in 1994, a time of reflection for horror critics because the genre was in limbo while the independent film found its niche in entertainment. Since that period of stasis, international horror films from France, Australia, Japan, and Korea have contributed to eroding the binary construction of killer and victim, while the remake seeks to establish its own contribution. Crane also states that "older forms of horrific imagery and storytelling have vanished.... In their place, we have films that reject the stories and stylistic devices of older horror tales in preference for inordinately simple narratives that seem to exist solely to showcase the latest leap forward in stomach-churning special effects" (2). Arguments such as this one demonstrate how quickly horror research can change when the genre shifts into a new phase. Only in the nineties could Crane say, "Unquestionably, contemporary horror films are infinitely more violent than their predecessors in the genre" (4). The films of the 1970s and 1980s have more violence in their opening scenes than many 21st century films contain by the time the end credits roll. Horror, as a genre and visual cinematic presentation, has transgressed many of its older contributions to the field; however, it seems to be the remake's goal to bring horror back to a simpler, more aggressive time of visual presentation—but without the same visceral depictions, as exhibited by the many PG-13 horror films recently produced or currently in development. This calculated and smart ratings game—releasing horror films in PG-13 format in theaters and later as R-rated or unrated on DVD—reaps financial gain by opening the movies up to a broader audience by lowering age restrictions.

Box-office revenue, not the biggest concern during classic horror, is now a driving force behind remakes, and it is necessary to look at who is buying tickets to the movies. Horror audiences are a mixed crowd. Most of the films have age restrictions that do not allow children under the age of thirteen into theaters to view them; some horror films restrict the appropriate viewing age to seventeen and older; and, in general, horror films typically do not appeal to the masses. Most critics argue that horror films attract a teenage/young-adult audience. James Twitchell, author of *Dreadful Pleasures: An Anatomy of Modern Horror*, contends that young viewers make it to the theaters out of a desire to become more knowledgeable: "Assuming an adolescent audience is the largest for horror art, how does this help us to understand the psychology of horror? Simply this: while we may not be able to locate what exactly it is within the horror myth that attracts its different audiences, we do know what is within this specific audience that keeps it interested. It needs information" (68). This is a reasonable point for original horror films, and it applies to remakes best via proxy of the older productions.

Young and old audience members remain interested in horror because of animal instinct. People have a fight or flight response within, and this response to stimuli makes the blood boil, provides an adrenaline rush, and prompts a call to action. When viewing a horror film, audience members fight with the protagonist or the killer and stick with the film to see how it all ends. Sometimes they shut their eyes, plug their ears, and threaten to (or actually do) walk out of the theater. Horror holds interest because no other genre provides such a kinetic viewing experience. Comedy makes people laugh, drama makes people cry, and action pumps people up, but horror takes all of these qualities, rolls them into an unstable ball, and shoves it into its viewers' faces so they turn away or beg for more. People have a favorite film of all time or a certain genre they stick with because that is a safe viewing condition. No one continually learns more "information" from watching the same kind of film all the time, not even a horror film. People are held captive by horror films that disturb complacency: their bodies and minds are stimulated, they talk to the screen to ridicule character dialogue, and they leave the theater in a different mood than when they entered.

When adolescent viewers from these audiences grow into adults, many of them remain avid viewers of the genre's films, but Twitchell disagrees:

> Like the fairy tale, the horror saga is remarkably rigid in prescribing behavior for its archetypes, but, unlike the fairy tale, the audience pays attention to them for only a few years and then seems to forget all about them. Once we stop listening to fairy tales we have to start telling them to our children and grandchildren, but when was the last time you thought about the vampire, Frankenstein monster, or werewolf? Are you still interested in stories about them? Do you want to read about them or tell your children about them? I would guess not. Like me you may be interested in learning about them, but not *in* them [66].

Twitchell's argument has to acknowledge viewers that are still interested in these archetypes; one only has to witness how many vampire and werewolf films/television series are currently in production (*True Blood* [HBO 2008], *The Vampire Diaries* [CW 2009], *The Wolfman* [2010], and the *Underworld* [2003–2012] and *Twilight* [2008–2012] films) to understand the phenomenon. His reasoning and stance separates horror audiences by age. Many adults are just as interested in horror as their kids, but too many seem to think that when the content of the movies features teens and young adults that only like-audiences will want to see the productions. Unlike Twitchell's assertion, fairy tales and horror films (slasher films in particular) are linked in storytelling, and they both capture audience interest throughout development from child to adult. The stories children read become life lessons to follow when they become adults or tales to transmit to their own children. Fairy tales and horror films have cyclical natures that allow their stories—villains, heroes, terrors, dreams—to link together through shared themes, motifs, and types, and the connection cannot be broken (as demonstrated by French and German oral tales that have mutated over centuries into written stories, theatrical performances, and film presentations). To answer Twitchell's questions: People think about Frankenstein's monster, vampires, and werewolves all the time; they read stories about them, and watch depictions of them in movies. This is another reason why remakes remain successful. Unlike Twitchell's argument, these films do not allow the social conscious to forget the tales. Audience interest has not waned over time, and the interested parties are both young and adult.

Mature audiences matter, but are considered irrelevant because they do not represent a room full of fearful children; however, some adults may be more frightened than children during a horror film because they know more of the world's evils than the "innocent" minds of the young. It is entirely too easy to forget that adults who watch horror films may not have been exposed to the genre when they were younger; they may have spent their entire lives watching romantic comedies, sports documentaries, or no feature films at all. These adults come to view horror films as novices and are able to experience fear with a similar level of shock as child viewers.

Critics continue to argue that children and young adults are more connected to horror films because they represent bodies going through scary changes; however, body development does not occur only in youth. Adults have similar fears because they are moving closer to stages of decay, rot, loss of mental faculties, aging, and death. Childhood is not completely innocent, and adulthood is not wholly learned or corrupted. Each viewer comes to a horror film with the chance to experience it (fear) and reflect upon it differently.

Twitchell says, "Essentially, horror has little to do with fright; it has more to do with laying down the rules of socialization and extrapolating a hidden code of sexual behavior. Once we learn these rules, as we do in adolescence, horror dissipates" (66). It is easy to talk about socialization and sex in relation to adolescents because the word "adolescent" represents growth, development, and societal assimilation. In post-pubescent stages of life, however, people do not stop growing, learning, acclimating to different environments, experiencing sexual encounters, and/or discovering new things about the body. In a dark theater, everyone is afraid of something, even if a laugh is sometimes heard with the screams.

Horror brings different audiences to the theater, and their reactions often blend terror and amusement. This leads into an interesting discussion about the genre. According to Crane:

> Contemporary horror films have broken ... dramatically with their predecessors ... in the altered connections today's films, as contrasted with earlier films, make between violence and humor. Earlier films made obvious which moments on screen were to be laughed at and which were to be frightening. Today's films do not draw clear distinctions between moments of levity and horror [37].

But it is not most important to recognize the demarcation between comedy and fear that separates earlier films from contemporary ones. The distinction is the result of viewer response. When a contemporary or classic horror film points to the audience to say, "Look, this is scary!" the element of laughter or fright depends on the response of the individual. Many people who find *Shaun of the Dead* (2004) to be unfunny may consider scenes in *The Exorcist* (1973) to be humorous. It is all a matter of viewer sensibility—different for each audience member—to what seems real or fictionalized, and how each of those presentations can stimulate or nullify a response. Verisimilitude tells a reader that it is less important that an event really happened than that it is told in a believable manner, and the same is true of all film. Audiences will typically be frightened by what is believable and laugh at what they consider ridiculous. Filmmakers often rely more on audience response to declare a movie successful than they care about delivering a message within the film. As long as the response is a positive experience (comedic or terrifying), a horror film resonates with audiences. Laughter and fear are both emotions of discomfort. In the theater, people laugh at themselves, mortality, and fictionalized portrayals of life terrors. Because of the cyclical nature of emotions, horror sometimes pushes people to a point that goes beyond fear and returns to humor. Simultaneously, people fear the terror depicted onscreen and laugh away any implications it has upon their own lives.

Fear is horror's most precious gem, and its value represents the genre's biggest export/commodity. It is sold in advertisements, trailers, books, television shows, haunted houses, and, of course, film. It is the foundation and formative element upon which all horror movies are based, and it is also the one thing slowly changing in the genre because of the remake movement. Besides the relevancy of fear, horror films have pedagogical and artistic values that are often overlooked.

Horror teaches audience members special codes, narrative formulas, and film techniques that are specific to the field, and these elements are relevant to understanding other areas of cinema. People often go to movies for escapist entertainment, but horror films teach as well. Crane suggests that horror fans, separate from other movie crowds, see the movies (especially repeated viewings or sequels) out of empty pleasure. He says, "Sequels are made not only because the audience for a horror film is preconstituted, the product presold; they are also made because that which returns again and again provides the audience with the greatest pleasure" (10). Crane mentions sequels, but his position can be extended to include the remake. A preconstituted audience, however, should not always be assumed. It is often argued that only horror fans see horror films, but at some point in life these viewers were virgins to the genre. People are exposed to their first horror film in different ways: they brave the cinema alone, tag along to a showing with someone else, or partake in a horror screening because another movie was sold-out.

When a person views a horror film, s/he comes to understand formula: the idea of a final girl, the cat that jumps out before the killer, or the scene where the killer is assumed dead but comes back for one last scare. Crane says, "What the audience knows, like that which the protagonist eventually acquires, has no value," but he ignores audience intelligence (10). The horror genre provides viewers with film knowledge of the highest standard. What audience members know is one of the significant reasons they watch horror films; they know what is to come, and that provides viewing power and possible instruction to those less learned. In the theater of remake presentations, this power becomes magnified. Horror audiences may not be film scholars on paper, but they have a strong understanding of theme, plot, character analysis, terminology, shooting techniques (camera angles and processes), special effects, star power (casting), and more. One of horror's most obvious attributes—audience knowledge—is invaluable to moviegoers.

Crane does understand that horror functions as a teacher, but he links the instruction to human socialization and not to art. He writes, "For those older members of the audience who still enjoy horror films, and who also have some understanding of what it means to be sexually active, horror films work as a refresher course in the instinctual: 'Yes, that is what we are all about, isn't it?' Returning to the horrible allows us to keep sight of the fundamental desires that rule the species" (28). Crane makes a statement that separates the horror audience in the same manner that Twitchell breaks it up by age group—that the sensation of watching horror films ceases as viewers grow older. He seems to assert that human instincts dull and need to be sharpened by watching horror films. It is a bit unclear, however, whether he is discussing the different stages of aging or horror films and their influences/ connections to viewership. Horror movies have artistic merit, but Crane privileges instruction:

> Horror is our vision/version of a primitive's dream. Never bemoan seeing the same thing on the screen time and time again, as what is important here is not artistic innovation but the revelation of our fundamental condition. Through the dark glass of the horror film we can learn who we are. Look elsewhere for cinematic innovation. A trip to the cinema is a valuable retreat to Plato's cave, and there many critics have enshrined the horror film [28].

Crane situates horror films as stimulus and response with no need for artistry, but the genre's ties to the human condition extend beyond those basic principles. In truth, horror has long held a close connection to theater arts with its display of makeup effects, setting, and attention to sound detail. "In the 1980s," Badley writes, "horror did not 'degenerate' into special effects; it returned to its wellsprings in the theatrical" (9). She connects horror films to productions in the Le Théâtre du Grand Guignol in Paris, which closed its doors in 1962, only two years after *Psycho* was released.

Prince discusses horror's early international art appeal as well:

> [Casper] Tybjerg examines horror output in Germany, Denmark, Sweden, and Russia [during the classical Hollywood period between 1910 and 1960] and shows how prolific it was. He also shows that, in many national cinemas, an aesthetics of "the fantastic film" was equated with the unique potential of cinema to be an art form. Horror and film art were relatively

synonymous. This fact makes for a striking contrast to the present period, in which horror is a rather debased and disreputable genre, in which no filmmakers of renown regularly work [5].

Prince's words support Badley's remarks about horror's tie to art, minus his final statement about the current state of cinema, which has changed in the nine years since his book was published. Many people still consider the genre as "debased and disreputable," but remakes are attracting new and established filmmakers to cash in on the movement's popularity. In either case, horror (classics and contemporary American horror) has artistic value, and its predecessors in theater and early films exhibit this notion.

Admittedly, a majority of horror movies follow formulas, but some of the films represent experimental art films, such as David Lynch's *Eraserhead* (1976), Dario Argento's *Suspiria* (1977), and Ken Russell's *Altered States* (1980). Formula has just as much, if not more, appeal in action films, romantic comedies, and dramas as it does in the horror genre. The field is lauded (and despised) for its creation of villains like Jason, Freddy, Michael Myers, and Pinhead, but it has also given cinema the obscure: *Martin* (1977), *The Beast Within* (1982), *Rawhead Rex* (1986), and *Castle Freak* (1995). Crane isolates the genre from other fields in terms of artistry, and says that the films should *not* be chastised for their repetitive nature, as they can evolve like productions in other genres, too. Horror is a field full of artistic endeavor; however, it will frequently be cast aside as an irrelevant cinematic enterprise because of its subject matter. But this view of the genre changes when more scholars, academics, and critics investigate its many reaches into cultural and social relevancies.

One criticism recently published about remakes comes from Kendall Phillips in *Projected Fears: Horror Films and American Culture*, but the opinions offered are only a paragraph or two in length. What is written, however, leads, as do these pages, directly into the discussion of *Psycho*. Phillips lists a few popular titles, such as *House on Haunted Hill* (1999), *The Haunting* (1999), and *Thir13en Ghosts* (2001) before making his argument:

> Horror is, once again, a moribund and all too predictable genre. Perhaps adding to this sense, or coming from it, has been the latest trend in horror films, the remake.... While these films were at the most adequate, their relatively low budgets made them profitable, and a bandwagon effect was created.... *The Texas Chainsaw Massacre* limped into theaters with much hype and nothing of the style or shock value of Hooper's original. A remake of Romero's *Dawn of the Dead* ... gave up any sense of the political commentary in Romero's 1978 classic [195].

Phillips is on target when he says remakes are made for little money in order to turn big profits, but *The Texas Chainsaw Massacre* (2003) and *Dawn of the*

Dead (2004) remakes do not lack cultural value, style, or fear that the original films first created (see "Conclusion"). Although not "original"—popularized by cast and director and made for financial profit—these are two exemplary remakes that have fulfilled promises to improve a previous endeavor or celebrate the memory of the original. This investigation is not about legitimizing or bashing remakes; it is a formal inquiry, critique, and discovery of the happenings in this current trend of contemporary American horror cinema. The trend first became a movement when *Psycho* was remade.

2

Psycho

THE LAST BASTION OF FEAR AND STORYTELLING IN AMERICAN CINEMA

In 1960 Alfred Hitchcock unveiled a stark work of filmmaking to the horror genre with *Psycho*. The film featured Janet Leigh and Anthony Perkins in roles they are remembered for posthumously today. As with most Hitchcock productions, the film is a combination of technical skill and artistic endeavor. Hitchcock created a movie that surprises viewers by killing one of its main characters (Leigh as Marion Crane) during the first act. Her death is also visually startling, as the montage tricks the viewer into seeing nudity that is not there. The film was labeled a mistake and a misstep in Hitchcock's career when it was first released, but it now stands as one of the most popular creations in American cinema. People were afraid to go into the water when *Jaws* was released in 1975; *Psycho* prompted the same fear in the shower.

The film was a sociocultural awakening, surprising audiences and critics. There was implied nudity, it was the first time a toilet had been shown onscreen, and the separation of public and private spheres was broken (Block). Phillips says:

> If Hitchcock set out to shock his audience, he clearly succeeded, though not to everyone's approval. Numerous contemporary critics blasted *Psycho*. *Time* magazine called it "a spectacle of stomach-churning horror," *Esquire* called it "a reflection of a most unpleasant mind, a mean, sly sadistic little mind," and the *New York Times* dubbed the film, "a blot on an honorable career." The film reviewer for *The Nation* was "offended and disgusted." The film was censored in a number of countries, and calls to boycott the film echoed from various religious leaders and psychiatrists [62].

Obviously *Psycho* was not an instant success with everyone, but the labels it garnered as being twisted or upsetting deserve unpacking. At the time of the film's release, the American public had already been exposed to monsters and oddities in horror and sci-fi, which are two genres typically linked by stories that exploit fear. There had been alien visitation in *The Day the Earth Stood Still* (1951), radiation exposure in *Them!* (1954), and catastrophic destruction in *Godzilla* movies. The viewing public had already been touched by an alien, controlled and devoured by mutated ants, and squished by the feet of a giant reptile. There are definite elements of fear present in these films, but the human factor is missing.

Psycho presents the viewer with "normal" people; there is no chemical spill, radiation leak, or spaceship involved to explain the death of Crane or the actions of her killer (Norman Bates). Uncovering this dark side to human nature and showcasing it on film gave the American public something to really be afraid of offscreen: themselves. Many horror movies display scary images that make audiences jump in fright or squirm uneasily in their seats, but few are able to have viewers leave the darkened theater and take the fear home. *Psycho*'s aptly-named title puts fear into the minds of audiences; it disturbed contemporary viewers and critics not ready to see the type of monsters humans can become. And with the film's ties to real-life killer Ed Gein, the depictions were simply all-too-real for some viewers at the time of its release.

Hitchcock understood the social climate and atmosphere in which he was producing the film. Phillips writes:

> For the present purpose, what is most interesting about *Psycho* is the way that the film resonates with cultural anxieties and violates audience expectations. The end of the 1950s was a time of both optimism and narcissism. While the Cold War still simmered under the surface, America was finally free from military conflicts, the economy was booming, and Americans were increasingly able to pursue their own individual pleasures. This cultural comfort and security was bought, in part, by the cultural logic of containment exemplified by *The Thing*: cultural and, indeed, global anxieties were contained within an optimistic veil of ignorance. As the 1950s turned into the 1960s, Americans turned away from the cultural problems rife in their society: racial injustice and unrest, the continuing danger of the Cold War, and a growing teenage rock and roll culture that was challenging notions of family and morality. In *Psycho*, Hitchcock revealed this thin veil of optimistic normalcy and then violently tore it open [65].

The director captured America's sense of prosperity to demonstrate that not everything in the country was perfect. *Psycho* showed audience members that they, too, could be victims because the most "normal" people they trusted could be the same people they needed to fear.

This is the private world of humankind revealed. Bates and Crane are everyday representations of the audience: middle class, working to make a living, tired of not getting ahead in life, and dealing with awkward, strained relationships. Crane and her lover share a secret affair, and Bates and his mother struggle in a battle of dominance and subversion. Audiences are able to identity with these realistic characters, unlike those in the fictitious storylines of *Village of the Damned* or *13 Ghosts* released the same year as *Psycho*. People regarded *Psycho* as a violation of the American public because films were supposed to be about escape, adventure, and thrills, not mirror reflections of society for the audiences viewing them. As if a secret had been uncovered, the film showed the American public the possibility for everyone to go "a little mad sometimes" like Norman Bates (*Psycho*).

Psycho crossed genres in its production. It is now labeled as a slasher, drama, thriller, heist or romance film, and its influence on remakes and inspired films ranges from the classic slashers (*The Texas Chainsaw Massacre* [1974], *Nightmare on Elm Street*, and *Halloween*), to contemporary productions like *The Silence of the Lambs* (1991), to current parodies such as *Behind the Mask: The Rise of Leslie Vernon* (2006) and television's *Family Guy* (FOX 1999), and even samples in music, like Busta Rhymes's "Gimme Some More" (1998). The film's reach from 1960 into contemporary cinema—big and small screen—and pop culture demonstrates the power it has as a production. *Psycho*'s storytelling is its strong point, and its relevance is like the longevity an oral tale carries into print centuries later. This is an element that is continually reappropriated in hopes of sparking a similar effect for current horror productions.

Marion Crane is unhappy in her current state of affairs (no pun intended). She is in a relationship with a divorced man (Sam Loomis) who is struggling to pay alimony to his ex-wife. Crane's middling employment and her desire to have a better life with the man she loves pushes her toward stealing a client's $40,000. She makes plans to drive to Loomis with the money; however, her one fatal mistake is stopping to rest at the Bates Motel. Bates (as his dead mother) murders Crane, which sparks an investigation into her disappearance involving a detective, her sister, her lover, the deputy sheriff and a host of other officials who soon uncover the madness within both the motel and Bates's mind.

In a word-association game, most viewers would remember "Bates Motel," "Norman Bates," or the catchy phrase "We all go a little mad sometimes," or would be able to imitate the screeching sounds made during the shower scene killing. But there is much more to the story than these surface elements. *Psycho* informs the viewer about the state of the middle-class worker and intimate relationships, and even offers a detailed definition for the term "transvestite" as it was known in 1960. Almost all of these aspects can be attributed to a kind of perversion of normalcy—if such a state of being exists. Bates's mind is perverted into a "split personality"; Crane's relationship does not represent moral standards of the 1960s; and the idea of Bates as a

Norman Bates (Anthony Perkins) and Marion Crane (Janet Leigh) talk outside Cabin #1 of the Bates Motel in *Psycho* (1960). After an evening snack with Norman, Marion is stabbed to death in the famous motel room shower scene by a shadowed figure in a dress with grey hair.

transvestite has to be explained by a psychiatrist who understands abnormal behavior.

These situations spark fear in viewers because they occur in everyday life. Although Bates is the "bad guy" and viewers should identify with Crane as the protagonist, it must not be overlooked that he is not the only person hearing voices in his head. Crane imagines what events will occur as a result of her theft. She thinks about what people would say at her office job, and what conversation she would later have with Loomis. Her onscreen face appears worried and frustrated, but the more the scenarios play out in her mind the more the viewer is afforded glimpses into her human perversion. She is happy with her decision, almost smirking like a deviant with the knowledge of the moral code she has broken. Before she is murdered, Crane decides she will go back to Phoenix and return the money, but it is the realization of her dark side that had the ability to scare audiences the most because they identified with her as the protagonist. We empathize with Crane wanting a new life and happiness in her relationship, but when she starts to smile when thinking about the money she has stolen, something changes. Suddenly the viewer understands that Crane is just as capable as Bates of committing misdeeds, and, along those lines, so is the viewer; her smile foreshadows Bates's deviant smirk.

This is effective storytelling. The writing for *Psycho* has a purpose and is not just a means to an end—the death of Crane and the capture of Bates. It exemplifies that technical filmmaking skill can be matched with a balance of screenwriting in order for a horror film to be successful, not solely in terms of box office rewards but in the manner of connecting with its audience. Storytelling and horror films are art forms that complement each other; however, the artistic vision of the genre's "heyday" quickly became a recognized formula. When Gus Van Sant announced he would do a frame-by-frame remake of *Psycho* in 1998, debates abounded. Did he think he was better than Hitchcock? Why not re-envision the film in his own style? Would the film be a shot-by-shot recreation of the original? But the biggest question was the most basic one: Why? Fans and critics questioned Van Sant for contemplating such a project. Van Sant's motives aside, the production of the remake represents the watershed moment for the remake machine. Its creation let filmmakers everywhere know that any movie was up for grabs to remake. It also marked fear, as the horror genre's foundation, as no longer being the basis for production but an integral part of a newly-forming group of dynamics that would shape horror into its current state of existence.

Already deemed a classic by critics and fans, *Psycho* was a unique enterprise. It has sequels no one usually discusses, but Van Sant's production chose the remake path. It could be argued that many remakes are forgettable and do not alter the status of the original; however, Van Sant announced he was making this film special by recreating it frame-by-frame in the original director's vision, thereby making a second "original" version. Van Sant, like other directors who have made remakes, could have had the original film re-released in theaters instead of attempting to make an exact copy of Hitchcock's production. It could have been a commemorative re-release with a special introduction by Van Sant where the director could have talked about the film's importance in cinema and American culture. But Van Sant took on the heavy challenge to remake *Psycho*, and the original was suddenly brought back in the limelight to be compared to the newer version's alterations and production considerations.

Van Sant's version offers many changes from the original film; the production team cinematography, narrative sensibility, acting, and casting have changed or been altered. These are production elements for which the film may be critiqued or measured against the original. Constantine Santas, author of *Responding to Film*, weighed in on the issue and declared there were people who supported the production amid strong opposition. "Patricia Hitchcock, who played a minor role in the original and was a consultant in this one, said her father would have been flattered by the remake of his movie forty years later; and Joseph Stefano, the screenwriter of the original *Psycho*, was more than eager to accept the job of re-writing the second *Psycho* script" (Santas). So the past came to revisit and support the new enterprise, a display that people felt gave credibility to Van Sant's vision; however, it cannot be overlooked that Patricia Hitchcock's involvement in the original was minor, and that Stefano, like any working writer, was probably happy to have a job and get paid. It is a definite trend to see cast, crew, and production members from original films work on remakes, but their support does not always guarantee a successful product by box-office standards or audience and critic responses.

Van Sant, as the film's director, holds the most responsibility for the remake's effect upon cinema. Santas writes, "Van Sant claims that his remake of *Psycho* should be seen as a creative rather than commercial endeavor," and that "one has to be fair to Van Sant and to his honestly stated motives—to attract younger audiences, and to revive interest in Hitchcock's classic work." Vant Sant clearly understood how much backlash he would receive by announcing his intentions; it seemed impossible for the film to make box office gold. Baz Luhrmann faced a similar situation concerning audience demographics, but he attracted younger audiences by casting Leonardo DiCaprio and Claire Danes in his *Romeo + Juliet* (1996). Seasoned thespians—Julianne Moore, Vince Vaughn, and Anne Heche—were unable to bring in the youth for *Psycho*. Luhrmann updated his film with guns instead of swords to comment on violence in contemporary society, while Van Sant's film avoided too much variance from the original. In this inception of the remake machine, Van Sant probably had not considered hiring actors from the television talent pool of *7th Heaven* (WB 1996–2006, CW 2006–2007), *Buffy the Vampire Slayer* (WB 1997–2001, UPN 2001–2003), or the film-to-television spinoff/adaptation *Clueless* (ABC 1996–1997, UPN 1997–1999) to attract younger audiences. His film stands at the forefront of the remake movement; all components for the trend had yet to be established.

What Van Sant filmed and removed from the original, and how scenes are acted in the remake, changes the original film's intent and audience reception. Santas mentions a few key points of difference between the original movie and its remake, including the switch from black-and-white to color, the difference in acting techniques, and how the original was seen as art. It is easy to see that the original film is shot in black-and-white and the remake in color. Both styles were chosen by the directors; they were not shot as such because of the time period or film stock availability. Santas says:

> It must be remembered that Hitchcock himself had already made several movies in color prior to 1960 (*Dial M for Murder, Rear Window, The Man Who Knew Too Much, North by Northwest, Vertigo*), and that his choice of black-and white was deliberate to mitigate the shock of blood swirling down the drain in the shower scene and to invest the film's gothic subject-matter with an aura of gloom.

Van Sant's film explodes onto the screen with the opening title-bar credit sequence in neon green and continues its pop art sensibilities in costuming and décor throughout. Unlike the stark and tense mood created by Hitchcock's black and white photography, Van Sant's style offers the viewer a palette of vibrancy and a quirky, upbeat tone. His vision removes some of the tension created in the original film in trade for a lighter presentation. Santas continues to say:

> This veritable deluge of oranges, pinks and light browns forces the viewer to notice the lapse of mood from the seriousness of the original to the light-hearted and essentially frivolous tone of the remake. Color and color tone affect the viewer's psychological disposition and help determine the emotions a film, and a violent film to boot, will evoke.

A simple change in format presentation (black-and-white to color) accounts for a large modification in how the film is received by audiences. Van Sant could have shot the movie in black-and-white, as other contemporary directors have done with films such as Spielberg's *Schindler's List* (1993), Jarmusch's *Dead Man* (1995), and the Coens' *The Man Who Wasn't There* (2001), but he chose color to update the movie to modern sensibilities; this possibly shows how audiences seem to have no patience for black-and-white on the big screen anymore. The intensity of fear and suspense become more of a tribute to technique and pop culture in Van Sant's kaleidoscope of color.

Acting in the remake goes hand-in-hand with the color implementation; most of the scenes play against the original content by separating emotions from the dark narrative structure. When the viewer first encounters Marion Crane (Heche) and Sam Loomis (Viggo Mortensen) in the unnamed hotel room, their interactions in bed and the sexual sounds from a neighboring couple through the wall give the scene an air of contemporary illicit behavior, not an impassioned love affair from the '60s. According to Santas, the dialogue,

> though copied almost verbatim from the original film, seems flippant, lacking the urgency of the original scene. These seem two casual lovers in a nonessential fling, and the scene elapses without establishing any real suspense, as Hitchcock's does. Their complaint of not being able to see each other except in her mother's house does not sound believable near the start of the 21st century, when this action takes place. They seem mature grownups not bound by the sexual inhibitions of their forbears 40 years ago.

Van Sant's opening establishing shots for his version announce the date as Friday, December 11, 1998. When Crane is driving in a later sequence, the viewer is also able to see a street billboard for the 1998 movie *Six Days Seven Nights* (starring Heche). It is a deliberate action to add the time period change and onscreen meta-commentary while simultaneously updating moral sensibilities for Crane and Loomis as a couple of the '90s. The added shot of Loomis's bare buttocks is in line with a freer moral code permitting nudity in the latter part of the 20th century, and shielding Crane's body from the camera places the scene in a post-modern presentation that allows the male form to be equally or more objectified than the female body.

This opening scene sets the tone for how the actors communicate with each other throughout the film; they recite lines with emotional detachment and come across as characters in search of motivation for the lives they have been provided. Even the highway patrol officer (played by James Remar) delivers the same original dialogue without much fervor. This is a representation of the times; people were disconnected from each other. No one ever knows what to say about the '90s because the decade felt unsure of itself—hence the presence of indie film and filmmakers trying to find a voice among the cinema crowd. Van Sant's time period update did not take contemporary rhetoric into account when the officer talks to Crane on the side of the road; the dialogue used in 1960 would probably not have gone over so well being told to a police officer in the 1990s. Santas comments on Van Sant's time adjustment between the two films in order to demonstrate how the director's attempt to remake the shower scene was unable to scare modern audiences:

> Times change, and so do people's outlooks. Most of the successful remakes have taken this factor into consideration, adjusting levels of violence and other aspects to meet contemporary audience sophistication. Hitchcock's audiences were relatively innocent and more susceptible to shock when violence erupted on the screen. Today's audiences are gorged with violent spectacle. The shower scene, though still shocking and frightening, can no longer traumatize them to the degree that it did then. Van Sant could have brought violence to a significantly more intense level, or delivered it with more innovation.

Always associated with its famous shower sequence, *Psycho* gives viewers more than one memorable scene or depiction of violence. The sequence, however, is too classic to be "new" to audiences in a remake; it was simply a given, like knowing what will happen at the end of James Cameron's *Titanic* (1997). A more in-depth discussion of acting in the remake reveals other prominent differences between the two films.

Perkins and Leigh will always be remembered for their roles in the original, so it is only fitting to focus a bit more on the portrayals by Heche and Vaughn as Crane and Bates. The biggest and most noticeable difference between the two films occurs in the most basic facial expression: a smile. Crane hits the road with the money she is stealing ($40,000 in the original and $400,000 in the remake). The remake amount changes the film category into a heist movie and not a horror-thriller about a desperate woman. Crane's imaginary conversations while driving are the same in both films, but in the remake her expression removes a sense of malice and conflict from the story. When Leigh plays Crane, "the smirk on her face when in voice-over she mimics Cassidy's surprise when he discovers she stole his money Monday morning indicates her vindictive spite against the male dominated atmosphere of her office to which she had said good-bye. Heche smiles a bit too broadly, showing more delight than fear, less guilt and more satisfaction, as she drives through the storm" (Santas). Heche's smile comes across as an afterthought in the scene; just as her lips begin to part to form the broad expression, the film cuts to a shot of rain hitting the windshield and then back to Heche with a furrowed brow—the smile is nowhere to be found. Her eyes also remain wide and unflinching in the scene (a complete twenty-nine seconds without blinking), which removes any sense of emotional mutation from worry to sinister delight akin to that in Leigh's performance. Heche's Crane is glad she did what she did. Her portrayal depicts a more independent woman with no regrets.

The appearance of Bates is important as well. Perkins plays Bates in 1960 with a squirrely, wired, gangly look about him. Vaughn, on the other hand, seems just as tall but looks like a linebacker with respect to body mass. The comparison evokes Jekyll and Hyde in physical appearance, demeanor, and action. Vaughn has a brutish physicality onscreen, from his prominent forehead to squared shoulders. Unlike Perkins's meek posturing in the parlor with Leigh, Vaughn seems more slovenly and dominant. His performance is certainly more "masculinized" than that of Perkins in three key scenes. In the original parlor scene, Bates displays two hand gestures that indicate frustration with his mother and submission to Crane's desire to end the conversation and go to bed. In the remake these gestures do not exist; Bates simply talks without stereotypical feminized hand gesturing. When Loomis and

Marion Crane (Anne Heche) reaches out for the shower curtain after being brutally stabbed by Norman Bates's mother in *Psycho* (1998).

Bates fight in the original office scene there's a close-body struggle of dominance and submission in what some deem as slightly homoerotic, but in the remake Bates whacks an unsuspecting Loomis over the head with a weapon from the leisure man's sport: a golf club. And in the final confrontation scene when Bates appears as his mother, there is an eerie element of suspended disbelief in his face; it lets the viewer know that Bates has left the room. The remake showcases Vaughn in scag drag, which cannot mask his large frame. This last fight scene alters a 1960s fear of sexual and mental difference in transvestitism and turns it into a killer in drag with no rooted motives, which can often be scarier to audiences since there is no reasoning provided; the psychiatrist's lines that explain transvestitism are also removed. Vaughn and Heche take on two iconic roles created by Perkins and Leigh and update the characters to '90s constructions of masculinity and female independence.

Other members of the cast spark interest, especially in connection to the remake's declared intent. Van Sant may or may not have been trying to capture young audiences, but he certainly benefited from the success of ensemble films like Paul Thomas Anderson's *Boogie Nights* (1997), released a year before *Psycho*. He hired Moore, William H. Macy, and Philip Baker

Hall—high-profile names from Anderson's *Boogie Nights* and *Magnolia* (1999), which was released a year after *Psycho*. Van Sant has never been a director of star-power ensembles. He once had a small collection of actors that he would work with (Keanu Reeves, the Affleck brothers, Matt Dillon, the Phoenix brothers), but never in such a high-profile status until *Milk* in 2008. Based on his previous films, it is doubtful that Van Sant tried to emulate Anderson, but he might have been subconsciously inspired by the character-driven work. It is clearly certain that he offered more celebrity status in the remake.

Van Sant's remake is not a complete copy of the original; it is not an exact shot-by-shot, frame-by-frame production, and the changes (additions and deletions) deviate sharply from the viewing and reception of Hitchcock's film, no matter how small the alteration. There are a few other changes that deserve mention because they modify meaning from the original to make the remake unique in comparison:

- Leigh is frantic and nervous in the car lot; Heche strolls about with a parasol.
- The trade-in car costs $700 in the original and $4000 in the remake. Leigh flips through seven bills while in the bathroom, which gives the film a mystic number (i.e., Seven Deadly Sins, Lucky Seven, and spiritual references).
- The first shot of Mother in the original is a shadow figure behind a drawn curtain; in the remake the viewer sees a bulky figure walk by a foggy window. Because it is clear that the figure in the foggy window could not be an aging woman, the tension and suspense is relaxed.
- The name Norman is a play on the term normal, but the last name Bates takes on a tongue-in-cheek meaning when Vaughn's version masturbates while watching Heche's Crane undress.
- Leigh appears frustrated trying to figure out where to hide the money in the motel room; Heche smiles and plays a solitary game of hide-n-seek with the money.
- The original Norman tells his mother to "shut up" twice, but the remake allows him to shout three times. The extended dialogue makes Vaughn's characterization more dominant and masculine over his mother's control.
- Leigh eats like a bird in the original, which allows the dialogue to match the action; Heche has more of a birdlike physical appearance, with a choppy, pixie haircut and sharp facial features.
- Leigh conveys happiness in the shower to show she is content with the decision made to return to Phoenix and give back the money; Heche is emotionless.

- The added masturbation scene and a few other additions queer the remake (detailed later).
- The shower curtain in the original is a dull plastic where no details can be seen through it. When Bates approaches the shower, the audience can only decipher the outline of a person. Fear of the unknown is heightened before the attack occurs. The curtain in the remake is see-through with patterns of sharp, geometric shapes. This adds to the idea that Bates is a fractured personality when his shadow figure appears in the bathroom.
- Perkins's Bates has birdlike eating habits. Vaughn's portrayal is more sexualized because he stuffs candy into his mouth, and with each piece his finger touches his tongue.
- A phone operator/dispatcher was technologically relevant in 1960. With an updated storyline, there is no need for a phone operator to connect the sheriff's wife to the Bates Motel in 1998.
- In the original, the psychiatrist asks if there have been any other missing persons, and he is told two women have gone missing. This information is removed from the end of the remake. Along with the extended/added shots of Crane's car being fully removed from the bog and all the police leaving the area, the remake wraps up the storyline and leaves nothing to be questioned, unlike the lingering, open-ended, more uneasy ending of the original. Fear lingers in the original; the remake operates on a closed narrative basis that implies "they lived happily ever after" ... after the tragedy.
- The last image viewers see in the remake, superimposed over a running shot of the vacant bog, is "In Memory of Alfred Hitchcock." The viewer is reminded that s/he is watching a remake of the original film and that this enterprise celebrates Hitchcock.

A final note—or the biggest change in the remake that no one really talks about: Van Sant queers the remake. This is a significant departure from Hitchcock's movie that Van Sant uses at key moments in the remake to give it contemporary social relevance. As previously stated, Mortensen's buttocks are shown during the opening but Heche's form remains hidden from camera. In Vaughn's masturbation scene the viewer is privy to Heche undressing, but again she remains turned from the camera. Sexuality in the remake privileges the male form and its actions. In a queer sensibility, the idea of the male gaze (a complement to Laura Mulvey's early theory) turns upon itself with a male director as the voyeur and androgynous/male bodies filmed for exhibition. (Gus Van Sant represents Vince Vaughn in that scene. As much as Van Sant directs the film, Bates directs actions that lead to Crane's murder.)

The scene is a product of Van Sant's style or auteurship which typically emphasizes youthful male culture that is often queered; however, this time it is a woman who happens to look boyish. (At this time, Heche was also known for her romantic relationship with Ellen Degeneres.) The scene—the added masturbation—is "safe" because it is a male figure voyeuristically eroticizing an unsuspecting female figure; the "danger" lies in Van Sant's other films where young males are victimized by the camera (i.e., the shower scene in *Elephant* [2003]). Also, with the dialogue about transvestitism missing, there can be no question that Norman Bates is a man; he gets no physical or mental gratification dressing up as a woman. Van Sant offers the viewer a masculinized queer spectacle, but he also queers Heche, Mortensen, and Julianne Moore (Lila).

The only time audiences see Heche's nude form is when she falls from the shower. Her buttocks are exposed, and two knife cuts with blood are shown upon her back. Heche's dying body position is queered submissively; the two knife cuts on her back are strategically placed to represent broken angel wings (angel wing tattoos and costume angel wings are popular GLBTQIA stereotype archetypes); she has visions of a cloudy sky while being stabbed; and when the camera leaves the bathroom to focus on the newspaper hiding the money, the word "Angeles" is prominent in the frame. Thus, Van Sant presents the viewer with a common theme in his films: the death of queer youth. Although Heche is a woman, the audience is not allowed to see body parts that "define" her physically as a female. Her pixie haircut and smallish frame align her with "twink" culture, a subculture in the GLBTQIA community commonly associated with youthful male and androgynous appearances and partying (including raves or other settings where wearing angel wings and imbibing in drug culture gives the feeling of flying in the sky). It is also fitting to imagine such a filmic (and real) figure in Los Angeles, the city of lost "angels" (queer youth).

The costuming for Loomis and Lila also help queer the film. Loomis wears a stereotypical ten-gallon cowboy hat and makes awkward expressions while handling a Judy Garland album. His character in the remake is stereotyped as "steer or queer," and his actions with Crane and sexual advances to Lila make him a perfect candidate for rough trade, which is another motif of some of Van Sant's productions. Lila is, for lack of a better phrase, lesbianized to counter the queer Loomis portrayal. She is another stereotype: shirt, jeans, lug shoes, keys attached to her belt loop, and a sporty walkman she cannot seem to leave behind. Her only concern is her sister as she constantly puts off Loomis's advances. Moreover, it is Lila who subdues Bates in the final fight scene when she kicks him in the face; this allows Loomis to wrestle Bates into submission, which is something he seemingly could not do on his own (compare Vaughn's massive body to Perkins's lean build in the original). If these changes to queer the original were more deliberate throughout the entire film, Van Sant's signature style and content would have been more overt; however, these limited (but poignant) instances of queering slightly open the door for the film to be read in such a manner.

Hitchcock's *Psycho* has had enormous influence on film history. Its remake did not have the same impact. Remakes reflect cinema trends. They show that nostalgia for past productions is popular and that American horror cinema is now facing an era where star power, money, and genre-bending are at the forefront of societal demands. *Psycho* redone by Gus Van Sant forever changed horror filmmaking for the American public; it altered the principles of centrality of fear and storytelling in horror. The original "had a director who could penetrate audience's inner fears, irrational desires, and mad urges, and actors who could simulate these feelings perfectly. Hitchcock, above all, wanted to communicate with his audiences; their pity and fear mattered to him" (Santas).

Van Sant made a grand attempt to celebrate a classical film text by reproduction. In other words, remaking *Psycho* is comparable to Whitney Houston's 1992 cover of "I Will Always Love You" by Dolly Parton (originally recorded in 1974). The song cover was a massive undertaking by someone whose prominence in the field came years later, and the result fueled interest; and although Van Sant garnered interest, his endeavor did not fare better financially than that of Houston's.

The idea of a remake is not new, and it is not allied with filmmaking only. Songs are covered by artists; television shows are revamped on different networks; and paintings are recreated by hobbyists. When someone takes on the responsibility to redo a "classic" in an artistic field, the dam breaks and a wave of others rush in to try their hands at some of the same. In music, this would pertain to the number of covers for Rihanna's "Umbrella" (2007), which are almost innumerable. Van Sant's *Psycho* is the only remake (so far) of the original, and this production will remain the breaking point in remake history because the implications it holds for other films being remade are groundbreaking and influential. In the realm of horror, fear and storytelling (the art of the genre) are changing, while starpower (actors, directors, producers) and money/marketing campaigns continue to hold great value.

3

Halloween
WHEN HOLIDAYS GAVE MEANING TO HORROR ...

It was the boogeyman. —Laurie Strode

The sleepy town of Haddonfield, Illinois, is about to receive a rude awakening from one of its former residents. He was only six years old when he murdered his sister and was subsequently sent away to a mental health facility for rehabilitation. But after fifteen years he escapes during a transfer and emerges as an adult hell-bent on returning home to kill his other sister. This is the story of Michael Myers and Laurie Strode, two estranged siblings who engage in a horrific game of cat and mouse on Halloween night.

It was 1978, and John Carpenter's now legendary horror film *Halloween* made its debut. The attention to detail—a masked killer, a sharp kitchen knife, an eerie soundtrack, and the bloodcurdling scream of a heroine—pays homage to Alfred Hitchcock's *Psycho* (1960) and historicizes real-life bad guy Ed Gein. The film spawned seven sequels through 2002 (including the debatable *Halloween III: Season of the Witch* [1982]). *Halloween* is typically credited as the original slasher film, although recognition is always given to *Psycho* and *The Texas Chainsaw Massacre* (1974) for exhibiting early elements that paved the way for the development of the subgenre. This was the start of a new era in horror involving multiple kills, bloody death scenes, gratuitous sex, drug and alcohol abuse, an unseen terror (until too late), and the final girl (an element *Psycho* brilliantly lacked, because it was ingenious and shocking to kill the protagonist early in the film). *Halloween* is the bridge to the '80s, home of the slasher decade. Moreover, it was an unveiling of American society's strengths and downfalls, its dreams and night terrors.

A recap of the original franchise demonstrates that Michael Myers was a terribly busy man. In the first film he returns to Haddonfield to stalk and kill his sister, but is thwarted by her and Dr. Loomis, his psychiatrist, who shoots him six times, causing him to fall over a balcony to certain death. The sequel continues events from Halloween night as Strode is taken to the hospital. The now not-dead Myers picks off victims one by one but again is stopped by Loomis and Strode when they work together to burn him alive.

Halloween III: Season of the Witch is unrelated to the franchise; it was meant to start a wave of films that focused on scary things happening on Halloween nights, but was quickly dismissed when *Halloween 4: The Return of Michael Myers* (1988) brought back the infamous killer. Myers returns to Haddonfield ten years later after terrorizing Strode; this time he aims to kill his niece Jamie, but Loomis does his best to avoid that situation from becoming a reality. Myers is gunned down by the police, falls into a mine shaft, and is presumed dead by everyone. But the final kill belongs to Jamie, who dons a clown mask and stabs her adopted mother in imitation of Myers's first murder at age six. *Halloween 5: The Revenge of Michael Myers* (1989) takes place one year later. Myers awakens from a coma in the refuge he discovered after finding his way out of the mine shaft in the previous film and continues on his journey to locate and kill Jamie, who is now mute and psychically connected to her murderous uncle. It is at this point that the original franchise takes a turn toward the supernatural, as most horror films seem to do when they have exhausted explanations as to why a killer comes back so often in sequels. This chapter in the franchise ends with Jamie and Loomis luring Myers back to his old house. Loomis tranquilizes Myers, and he is taken to a holding cell to await transfer, but some unknown person creates an explosion which leaves the holding cell empty when inspected.

Halloween 6: The Curse of Michael Myers (1995) has the most complex plot of any sequel in the franchise, and to describe what happens could fill the pages of a novella. In short, the story involves a pregnant Jamie six years later, Laurie Strode's adoptive parents, Tommy (the kid Strode is babysitting in the first film), a Druid curse, human sacrifice, genetic engineering, star constellations, and, of course, Loomis. Myers kills Jamie, but her baby survives in hiding with Tommy, and in the end a host of characters find themselves fleeing from a sanitarium after Myers is tranquilized. Loomis goes back into the building only to discover the infamous mask on the floor before he lets out a final scream. (Donald Pleasance [Loomis] died three years later—the same year another installment in the franchise was released.)

Halloween H20: 20 Years Later (1998) is basically a showdown between the cowboy in white (Strode) and the cowboy in black (Myers). Twenty years into the storyline Myers tracks down Strode in California where she lives under an assumed name after faking her death in an auto accident. She is dating someone, has a teenage son, heads up a boarding school, and is happy. But Myers destroys that happiness and in the process kills close friends.

Annie (Nancy Kyes/Loomis) talks to her boyfriend while Michael Myers (Tony Moran) lingers in the shadows outside in *Halloween* (1978).

Strode attempts to kill Myers by pushing him off a building and running him over; her success comes when she decapitates him in the end, thus ending the *Halloween* franchise—at least that is what audiences were made to believe.

In 2002 the final film in the original series, *Halloween: Resurrection*, hit theater screens. The production marked the end of an extremely long, winding narrative, as the story is set three years after the previous film. Strode resides in a psychiatric ward, incarcerated for beheading a paramedic she mistook for Myers. She patiently waits for Myers to come after her again, and when he fails to disappoint she is ready for him; however, he tricks her and throws her off the roof to her death. After 24 years two members of the *Halloween* character trinity (Loomis and Strode) are dead, but Myers lives on. He heads back to his home only to find winners of a reality television contest sleeping over to prove who can survive the Myers household. Myers uses his usual modus operandi to claim his victims one by one until he is bested by two characters who electrocute him. In conventional horror fashion, the audience is taken to the morgue where Myers's remains are in a body bag. When the bag is unzipped, his eyes open and a piercing scream ends the original franchise; however, this still leaves room for more sequels.

Michael Myers walks a strange path throughout the original series of films; there are notable inconsistencies in the storytelling and/or characterization. He is mentally incapacitated, but can drive a car, steal Strodes's personal file to find out where she lives, and switch clothes with a victim's body to escape capture. However, horror franchises in the '80s became more about the kills, and his improbable evolution from child to adult to demonically-possessed shell of a human being does not diminish the fact that he is a killing machine. The mystery surrounding Michael Myers remains throughout the films and solidifies his character as a horror icon. Laurie Strode labels him "the boogeyman," but Dr. Loomis, the one person who knows Myers inside and out, describes him in detail:

> I met him, fifteen years ago. I was told there was nothing left. No reason, no conscience, no understanding; even the most rudimentary sense of life or death, good or evil, right or wrong. I met this six-year-old child, with this blank, pale, emotionless face and the blackest eyes—the devil's eyes. I spent eight years trying to reach him, and then another seven trying to keep him locked up because I realized what was living behind that boy's eyes was purely and simply—evil.

This personalized character analysis represents Myers from the original film through the last in the franchise. The number of sequels alone demonstrates his power and celebrity in the field of horror, but Myers shares his fame with Carpenter, Curtis, and Pleasance, who all helped give the films a place in horror history.

Although the franchise has a rich history because of its serialization, the original film stands as the most celebrated. It introduced the horror genre to one of its most recognized villains, founded the slasher subgenre, and created a new sense of fear in American cinema. What began in *Psycho* filtered into *Halloween*, and because of this connection the face of horror changed once again.

When *Halloween* appeared there was nothing else like it. *Psycho* frightened many audiences in the 1960s, but *Halloween* is more visceral: the killer is a shadow of a man with an unrecognizable face; the film is painted in colors people see every day; the kills are explicit; the music is iconic and relative; and the mood/atmosphere is confrontational. Michael Myers (also credited as "The Shape" on the *25th Anniversary Edition of Halloween*) is a masked killer; his visage is protected by the legendary William Shatner *Star Trek* costume cover. It is this mask, which may sound completely ridiculous, that heightens the fear and makes him the monster people cannot see. Fear of the unknown turns thriller into horror when danger is not obvious. The viewer is told that Myers is the brother of Laurie Strode, a regular teen girl, but that does not change his monstrous presence in the film. Without the mask Myers would be an escaped mental hospital patient who needs to be gunned down or re-institutionalized. The mask helps Myers blend in with trick-or-treaters and walk among society as an individual who fits in. Kids dress up for Halloween by wearing scary costumes and/or makeup that covers their faces, but beneath it all they are kids trying to have fun and fill their sacks with the most candy possible. Behind Myers's mask lies the true terror. It is a role reversal for the celebration of Samhain, but the masks serve to demonstrate that a deadly stranger walks among "normal" members of society, which can be the scariest thought of all. Tommy Lee Wallace, production designer and co-editor, credits the film's crafty use of unseen fear to Carpenter's own knowledge of the genre:

> From childhood, from earliest days, one of his [Carpenter] passions was scary movies, and when he got his turn he drew from the lessons he had learned watching these movies, and one of the cardinal rules is don't, don't show too much of the monster. One of the oldest tricks in the book is to understand that it's not what you see it's what you don't see that gets you scared. It's about knowing something's in there, and when your character for some compelling reason must go in there it's about anticipation. Where's it gonna happen? [*Halloween: A Cut Above the Rest*].

Carpenter's horror knowledge-base established the unseen terror rule as a guideline to atmospheric horror; however, most American films today seem to bypass this earlier concept.

Throughout the original franchise the idea, persona, and spirit of Michael Myers became one symbol: the mask. American society relates to symbols because symbols (such as the cross, a rainbow flag, or a white hood) are imbued with collective power. Such symbols instill fear or generate welcome familiarity when viewed, and the same is true for the mask of Myers. Movie posters simply have to show the Shatner mask for fans to identify the film, or for those who do not know the connection to recoil in fear. The unknown has this effect—to attract or repulse. *Halloween* started a trend for masked horror villains the same way that *Psycho* influenced horror movies to film scary shower sequences. Once the iconic symbol has reached mass appeal and/or fear, the monster behind the mask becomes legendary in cinema. The fear factor of Michael Myers will not diminish.

Like *Psycho*'s remake, *Halloween* is shot in color. People do not walk around in everyday life viewing the world in shades of black and white; sighted people see in color. Suspending disbelief thus comes a bit easier when the colors on the screen match what viewers see while sitting in the theater or in front of a television. Of course, as exemplified in *Psycho* and *Night of the Living Dead* (1968), black-and-white films can be just as frightening as color, but color adds a realism that black-and-white removes. Black-and-white continually reminds the viewer of artifice, and even if audiences get scared, they only have to look around to see the standard colors of reality. When night falls on Haddonfield, viewers experience that time of day as if it were the same outside environment they would walk into from theater or home. Although the rain and gloomy setting of *Psycho* resonates with audiences, the more natural/standard colors of *Halloween* succeed in providing viewers with tangible fear. In a slasher film, however, there is only one color that seems to matter most: red.

The *Psycho* shower scene is historical film art, and nothing can be taken away from its creation; however, the blood audiences see on the body of Marion Crane and running down the drain is a dark grey because of the black-and-white filming. The audience is somewhat distanced from the scene because the blood does not appear to be "real." In color, *Halloween* is able to bridge the distance between viewer and visual. People bleed red, not black or grey (unless they are demons, zombies, or some vampires and werewolves). This simple color connection makes injuries and/or death more frightening, and creates more pathos in an audience. This comparison extends beyond these two films and the horror genre. There is massive destruction and high body counts in any of the *Lord of the Rings* trilogy films (2001–2003), but most of that blood is greenish black from slaughtered orcs. The reaction is not as strong as it would be if the monsters were doing most of the slaughtering of humans, elves, hobbits, and others whose blood runs red. It is the color viewers know flows through their own veins and pumps rapidly while watching horror films; greenish black fluid does not get the same reaction.

Kill Bill: Vol. 1 (2003) also illustrates this point with the fight scene between Beatrix Kiddo and The Crazy 88. When the fighting commences, Kiddo begins to slay her attackers left and right; blood from sword wounds spills to the floor and spews about. Suddenly the film switches to black-and-white and the fighting continues, but now the blood is less immediate because grey fluid fills the screen. Tarantino easily shows how viewers can be desensitized to blood when it is not filmed in color, and many people who saw the film complained about that section because they wanted to see the blood; they wanted to be more immersed in the fight. Although an homage to early Kung Fu/martial arts films, Tarantino achieves the indirect result of letting audiences see how they relate differently to onscreen blood in color versus black-and-white. Black-and-white filming also allows the MPAA to pass judgment less harshly for explicit depictions of violence.

Halloween digs deep into its audience with displays of red blood; its original sequel, which has to be mentioned since the events that occur are on the same night, goes so far as to show one of the characters (Jimmy) slipping on a pool of blood drained from a victim, landing on the floor, smashing his head into the tile, and blood splattering upon him. The film demonstrates the importance of red blood in many horror films; its onscreen depiction incorporates the viewer into the narrative. Blood also functions as a symbol. While it represents the bond between Myers and Strode, and highlights the important and traditional theme of family in the horror genre, it is simultaneously vital and dangerous. *Halloween* is not the first horror film to use color, nor is it the only one to use color effectively, but with its connection to *Psycho* and the discussion of fear, it is important to understand its relevance. It is arguable that no film exploits color better than Dario Argento's *Suspiria*, but American cinema is the focus of our discussion.

In addition to its masked killer and blood depiction, *Halloween*, like *Psycho*, makes use of visual space and setting to maintain a high level of fear. Marion Crane leaves the big city, stops at a roadside motel, gets a room, and dies in the confines of a shower; her body spills out of the space as life fades. Laurie Strode, in similar fashion, strolls the sidewalks of Haddonfield, babysits in a house, and finds herself fighting for her life from the enclosed space of a closet; however, Strode, unlike Crane, survives. Visual space in film controls viewer emotions; it can make audience members feel larger than life and embodied with power, or make them feel small, insecure, and vulnerable. The nighttime setting in *Halloween* strengthens fear of the unknown and makes perception of space difficult. (Carpenter does the same in *The Fog* [1980].)

Viewers never feel completely in control of their bodies or emotions during the film because they identify with the protagonist (Strode) and her struggle to survive. Audience members take the journey with Strode and find themselves metaphorically running around the dark streets of Haddonfield and hiding in a closet to avoid death by a deranged psycho killer. As the sequels grow in number, moviegoers often take sides with the killer because it becomes a cinematic game, or even find it funny if the franchise has lost some of its fright appeal, but the original film puts those same patrons in a place where they can do nothing but identify with the lead (typically a final girl) whose only desire is to escape from harm. *Halloween* came about when the steadycam had only been in circulation for a couple of years, and the filmmakers used the new technology to their advantage. Viewers were afforded point-of-view shots from the perspective of Michael Myers as a child, an onlooking presence stalking the babysitters, and a fly on the wall listening to conversations. Some people (mostly critics) thought the idea of a POV shot from the killer represented a crude or immoral decision on the part of the filmmakers, but it should be understood that using the camera to show Myers's perspective as a child killing his sister simply unnerves audiences and generates more fear; viewers do not take any enjoyment from "being" the killer in such a scene. The varied use of the steadycam allows fear to generate from all sides within the film and not just the perspective of the killer. It is merely another manner in which the film uses visual space presentations to inflict terror upon its audience.

The audience, however, always has the advantage over the protagonist, and not because viewers know the film is entertainment; they are always able to stay one step ahead because the nondiegetic theme music announces the killer's presence. The music from *Halloween* is known worldwide, akin to that of *Jaws* and *The Exorcist* (1973). Signature musical themes announce when Myers is getting back up after being attacked, when he is stalking his prey, when he is chasing victims, and more. All of these musical accompaniments relate to the action of the story and help fuel tension, surprise, anxiety, and fear in the audience. John Carpenter made sure the music for the film would befit the story by composing the soundtrack himself. The title theme is now one of the most recognized musical creations not only in horror but in music in general. Daniel and Seth Nelson discuss *Halloween*'s appropriate use of music in "Killing His Contemporaries: Dissecting the Musical Worlds of John Carpenter":

> One of the most poignant variations of this main theme takes place in *Halloween II*.... The Shape, better known as Michael Myers, follows Laurie Strode (played by Jamie Lee Curtis) to a hospital, where Laurie is recuperating from wounds suffered in a previous encounter with Myers. While hiding in the hospital parking lot, Laurie realizes that he is in the lot with her, and as she frantically pounds on the hospital's front doors, the variation of the main theme smashes into the film. The simple repeating melody that delivers fast and immediate pulses of sound is created by a high pitched synthesizer. The unending theme matches what is taking place not only in this particular scene, but the overall storyline: Michael Myers cannot be stopped! This stripped-down version of the main theme does not have the low bass tones that the film's main theme starts out with in the beginning of the movie. Instead, Carpenter replaces this bass sound with the hypnotizing breathing from Michael Myers and the shrieked screams from Laurie.

The piano, synthesizer, and other instrumental sounds give weight to the onscreen action, but Carpenter also uses key sound effects, such as heavy breathing, screaming, whimpering, gasping, potted plants breaking, and car tires screeching, to achieve a film in which music and sounds are as important as story and equal in the creation of fear.

Fear is easy to recognize in horror films because it always represents a binary of actions: to die or not to die, to kill or be killed, to run away and hide or confront. *Halloween*, although formidable and contributory to developments in the genre, is not immune to this system of fight or flight / survival or death. In a slasher film, one of the main concerns for a viewer is who dies and who lives, which is directly linked to the fascination of "the kills."

The first death in *Halloween* occurs when young Michael Myers mortally wounds his sister with a kitchen knife. The action follows through the eyes of a clown mask shrouded in shadows around the oval-cut holes. Viewers see the sister turn to her brother before the knife is raised and then brought down to initiate the first stab; however, no blood and no contact between knife and flesh are depicted. If this sounds at all familiar, it is an homage to *Psycho*. Debra Hill, producer and co-writer who passed away in 2005, said Carpenter wanted the film to be scary, not gory (*Halloween: A Cut Above the Rest*). His use of shadow, implied injury, screams, and a stalking camera sensibility demonstrate such skill.

The shock of the kill in *Psycho* comes at the expense of the film's protagonist, and the only other character seen murdered is Milton Arbogast. Bates's mother is long-dead, and any other crimes he has committed are not shown. What *Halloween* does to solidify itself and proceeding films into the subgenre of slasher is up the ante by killing more victims. Five people die in total, most notably two of the three babysitters and Myers's sister in the beginning, but the kills are not splatterfests, as the field of slasher films has come to represent. *Halloween* eases its way into the subgenre with simple, clean kills by a common kitchen knife, minus the telephone cord strangulation of Lynda (P.J. Soles). The film acts as a precursor to other movies in showing that the category of slasher does not simply rely on numbers (although *Halloween* sequels raised the number, with at least thirteen dead in one film); slasher films can have well-developed stories, strong acting, relevant soundtracks, and atmospheric fear.

Another factor that *Halloween* indirectly helped formalize for the subgenre is the characterization of the victim. The two babysitters and one boyfriend are all teenagers killed in the film. These are young adults who engage in acts of sexual intercourse, nudity, marijuana smoking, and other social ills parents are supposed to warn against; however, the slasher film is never about parents, and viewers rarely see any adults in typical adult positions of authority until the end of the movie. *Halloween* did not promote the idea that promiscuous teenagers should be killed, but its depictions of teens having sex and smoking marijuana became a central motif in slasher films. This victim stereotype helped popularize the slasher subgenre and became one of the staple reasons people frequented the movies in the 1980s.

Tony Timpone, former editor of *Fangoria* magazine, says academics have always read too much into the film and that Carpenter simply wanted to make a good horror movie to scare audiences (*Halloween: A Cut Above the*

Rest). *Halloween*'s success turned its solid filmmaking effort into a clear candidate for remake production:

> It was the, you know, the new indie sensation that everyone had to see. What set *Halloween* apart from other horror films of that time I think was just a skill that John Carpenter brought to the material. Subjective shots from the killer's point of view really hadn't been done that much before. He came up with a very memorable score that had you on edge right from the beginning, he had good actors, and the victims were also sympathetic.... So many of the slasher films that came out after *Halloween*, you know these characters are just set up to die, but you cared about the characters in *Halloween* [*Halloween: A Cut Above the Rest*].

There were stories behind the victims in *Halloween*; they were not shells of characters meant only as slasher fodder. Carpenter also defends his characters and their kills. He says the film holds no Christian moral testing or punishment for the teens who are having sex and/or engaging in other debauched activities. "The movie's about the revenge of the repressed. And Jamie Lee has a connection with the killer because she's repressed, too. To me, these kids are just engaged in normal teenage behavior. They get killed 'cuz they're not paying attention; they're involved with their boyfriends and they don't think anything's going on" (*Halloween: A Cut Above the Rest*). Despite Carpenter's cautions, critics continue to dig deeper into the meaning behind teenage characters getting killed by horror villains. Drugs were popular in the 1970s, 1980s, 1990s, and into the 21st century, and rates of teenage sexual activity have not diminished over the years. Sex sells, and audiences like to see onscreen depictions of things they can identify with in their own lives from the past, present, or future. It does not take a scholarly point of view or critical analysis to understand that audience members invest more in stories that resemble personal experiences and/or recognizable sociocultural climates. Intimate connection to a film is what makes the element of fear strongest for a viewer.

Carpenter acknowledges the centrality of audience fear in relation to watching a horror film. He says, "Fear is an interesting thing 'cuz we all are afraid of the same things. That's what makes these movies so universal, that makes them play in every country. We're all afraid of death, loss of identity, loss of a loved one, disfigurement; all the horrors of humanity we all have" (*Halloween: A Cut Above the Rest*). Although *Halloween* is classified as one of the first slasher films, it contains a story with characters and situations viewers can all relate to through personal fears. Sometimes the scariest thing of all is the end of a horror movie because there is typically an open ending that refuses to offer any sense of hope or alleviation of fear. Carpenter details the ending:

The ending means he's not only gone, he's everywhere. This guy is a human but he's not, he's more than that. He's not exactly supernatural, but maybe he is. Who knows how he got that way. It makes the ending more surprising if you don't say he's been, you know, cursed by some ... you don't give much of an explanation so your imagination works much more; it's much more terrifying [*Halloween: A Cut Above the Rest*].

Fear lingers on, and so does Michael Myers in the franchise sequels; however, he is not the only person or thing from the film that gains popularity or achieves a notable status.

Halloween helped launch the careers of directors, producers, and actors; original films function just like remakes in this respect. Carpenter had worked on several monster movies prior to helming the 1978 film, and his recognition was limited to the overseas success of his 1976 movie *Assault on Precinct 13* (remade in 2005). After *Halloween*, he went on to make memorable films of the 1980s such as *The Fog*, *The Thing* (1982), *Starman* (1984), *Big Trouble in Little China* (1986), and then a host of other movies with high-profile actors like Christopher Reeve, Pam Grier, and Kurt Russell. In 2001 he took a four-year hiatus from directing only to return to horror in the Showtime series *Masters of Horror* (*Cigarette Burns* [2005]), which featured short films by some of the world's most respected horror creators, and he continues to work in horror as director, writer, and producer. *Halloween* established Carpenter as a master of horror, which can often be more of a curse than a celebration, but he focuses only on the benefits received from the film. He says, "*Halloween* got me branded as a horror director, and it sent me down a career making fantasy, science fiction, and horror, but hey, I got to become John Carpenter. How cool is that?" (*Halloween: A Cut Above the Rest*).

Jamie Lee Curtis was a fresh face in 1978, but also Hollywood royalty as the daughter of Janet Leigh and Tony Curtis. Her role in *Halloween* evokes her mother's pivotal scream queen role in *Psycho*; Hitchcock had his protagonist in Leigh, and Carpenter had his in Curtis. Prior to her feature-film debut, Curtis was a television actor for almost two years, appearing in series such as *Columbo* (NBC 1971–1990), *Charlie's Angels* (ABC 1976–1981), and *Operation Petticoat* (ABC 1977–1979). Post-*Halloween* she found herself in the same horror blessing/curse as Carpenter when she popped up in *The Fog*, *Terror Train* (1980), *Prom Night* (1980), and, of course, *Halloween II* (1981) to reprise her role as Laurie Strode. Carpenter never returned to direct another segment in the *Halloween* franchise, but over the years Curtis kept Strode going strong in *Halloween H20: 20 Years Later* and *Halloween: Resurrection*, where her character finally met death at the hands of Myers. Curtis's debut film catapulted her into horror, but she found time to avoid typecasting by doing movies such as *Trading Places* (1983), *True Lies* (1994), and *Freaky Friday* (2003). Laurie Strode, much like John Carpenter, Michael Myers, and Dr. Loomis (Donald Pleasance possessed a strong acting portfolio for almost twenty-five years before he accepted the role), lives on in the horror history annals.

Debra Hill and Nick Castle also benefited from the film, as both ventured off into successful careers in producing and directing, but the movie itself holds another special mark in slasher history. Studios that initially turned down *Halloween* as a film project began making their own imitations of the film. Tony Timpone sheds light on how much *Halloween* influenced other movies by title alone:

> It created a whole industry of slasher films from *Friday the 13th* [1980], and any holiday wasn't safe anymore. You had *New Year's Evil* [1980], *Silent Night, Deadly Night* [1984], *April Fool's Day* [1986]. It should also add that a lot of mainstream movies I think imitated the slasher tropes; films like *Fatal Attraction* [1987] and *Sleeping with the Enemy* [1991], you know films like that where they took, you know ... sure they dressed it up with big stars and big production values but those are really slasher films under the surface, and again they also owe a debt to *Halloween* [*Halloween: A Cut Above the Rest*].

Other holiday and/or celebration films—*My Bloody Valentine* (1981), *Mother's Day* (1980), *Happy Birthday to Me* (1981)—also followed in *Halloween*'s footsteps, with the cult parody film *Student Bodies* (1981) opening the field to comedy long before the *Scary Movie* franchise (2000–2006) was created. In 2007, Robert Rodriguez and Quentin Tarantino released *Grindhouse*, a flashback double-feature reminiscent of the drive-in era, and between the two movies (*Planet Terror* and *Death Proof*), rising directors contributed fake movie trailers for intermission. The *Halloween* influence was showcased in the trailer for the holiday horror film *Thanksgiving*, directed by Eli Roth. In the same year, only four months later, Rob Zombie became a remake director.

Zombie made his way into horror films directing the fan-favorite *House of 1000 Corpses* in 2003 and the critically acclaimed *Devil's Rejects* in 2005. Both films show a respect for the genre, offering homage to traditional themes, motifs, storytelling and visuals, and they were both original films written by Zombie. He also filmed a trailer (*Werewolf Women of the S.S.*) for *Grindhouse* that evoked both classic cult women-in-prison films and mad scientist movies. Zombie became a hot ticket in horror, but when he announced a remake of *Halloween*, fans and critics took a step back to question his decision. It was a scenario reminiscent of Van Sant's announcement in the '90s. With the success of Zombie's previous films, it prompted curiosity about the fact that he would not be making another original film but instead remake a classic. Fans asked Zombie to speak out on why he would do a remake, and he replied, "I wouldn't even go near this project if I didn't feel like I had a fresh, worthwhile approach to the material. Besides, I'm not touching one single frame of Carpenter's classic. That film will remain as it always has" (*HalloweenMovies*). Although Zombie's project is a re-imagining of the original and not a full remake or a shot-for-shot recreation, "fresh" and "remake" are words that seem oppositional. It is important to look at the film itself to find out what changes were and were not made, and how they alter the reception, innovation, spirit, and impact of the original film and its full franchise. What the remake offers cinema is also important to understand.

There are three main changes between the original film and the re-imagined vision: the beginning sequences, Dr. Loomis, and Laurie Strode's fight with Michael Myers. The first two-thirds of Zombie's *Halloween* is the most original aspect of the remake. The film separates itself from Carpenter's production by showcasing Michael Myers as a child, his homelife, troubles at school, and four murders (a bully, his sister, his sister's boyfriend, and his mother's boyfriend) that get him committed to a sanitarium. Instead of the opening sequence of six-year-old Myers murdering his sister in Carpenter's film, Zombie makes his character a ten-year-old boy suffering from severe depression and psychological problems. His mother is a stripper, and his home life is less than ideal. The remake provides visual social commentary to depict how a child can be affected by his environment, thereby offering some rationale for his behavior and murderous actions. Zombie's explanation and presentation of the killer as a child is ambitious. When the audience is presented the history of the young Myers, an effort to understand the killer lessens the aspect of fear in the production and storytelling. Zombie manages to change the film's original genre. He turns shock and fear of the unknown into a drama that attempts to explain psychopathic, murderous behavior. Instead of the audience's fear of what lies behind the mask in the original production, the remake pushes viewers to see the monster as just a boy who was picked on as a child and had a family life that forced him to strike out against others. *Psycho* previously showed audiences the fear of "normalcy," which makes Zombie's attempt a continuation of that tradition.

In the *Halloween* remake, Myers almost kills Loomis and leaves him for dead. This is a huge divergence from the original film, which made the doctor's character a staple of its many sequels. Zombie said in countless interviews that this was one of the changes made to ensure studios would not ask him to do a sequel. (He made a sequel unrelated to the original sequel.) The act of wounding Loomis (the viewer sees Myers squeezing his head), who is a clear father figure for Myers, is relevant for the story. The beginning of the remake acknowledges Loomis as the only stable male figure in Myers's life (minus rare interactions with a mental health institution employee). Loomis visits Myers every day for several years to talk to him and watch over him like a surrogate. When Myers attacks Loomis, the act represents the struggle between him and the father figure he never had in a family consisting of a mom who strips and her deadbeat boyfriend.

The director's other notable change comes at the end of the film. Before the showdown between Strode and Myers, the viewer witnesses a few reenacted scenes from the original, such as the memorable scene where Myers appears in a sheet pretending to be Lynda's boyfriend. At the end, Myers and Strode engage in a battle royal that pits his brute strength against her smarts. More of an action film than the original, in the final sequence Myers charges Strode, and both fly out a window off the second story balcony (the original film depicts Loomis shooting Myers until he falls off the balcony to his death, disappearing moments later). Strode regains consciousness on top of Myers's body; she is beaten, battered, bloody, and covered in dust. She straddles him, points a gun at his face, and fires three times, but the gun is empty. In the last twenty seconds of the film, Myers grabs her arm; Strode shoots; the gun fires a single bullet to his face; she drops the gun and begins to scream uncontrollably. The camera closes in on her bloodied face, and the screen dissolves to a shot of Strode as a baby being cradled in the arms of her mother. Zombie changes the film's genre from drama at the beginning to action inside the house, and at the end to 1970s rape-revenge exploitation, which many critics now label as a form of torture porn. This final change in genre informs the viewers that the world is a mad, mad place, but leaves the storyline somewhat neat and tidy when the credits roll. Loomis is apparently mortally wounded; Myers can only be presumed dead after being shot in the face; Strode is enduring a mental breakdown; and sirens heard in the distance announce the eventual arrival of the good guys. This ending offered more narrative closure than the original—until Zombie made a sequel.

Zombie's remake accomplishes more kills, offers a psychological backstory that removes the monster's shroud, changes genres, recreates original scenes, and features an ending that kills main characters in an effort to provide closure (until the production of a sequel). It is definitely a remake that demonstrates the current state of the field—starpower (Zombie as a noted entertainer and director, and his recognizable acting troupe from his previous films) and money, which will be discussed momentarily.

Zombie literally has a name befitting horror, so clearly he would take on the job of re-imagining a film he loves. Zombie was given the ultimate green light when he contacted the original film's director. "I talked to John about it and he was very supportive. He basically said, 'That's great Rob, go for it and make it your own.' What more do I need?" (*HalloweenMovies*). This is also a trend in the proliferation of remakes: when the original directors, producers, actors, and/or production houses offer support for the films to be created; some even work with the new teams on the remake. Horror remakes appear more plentiful each year, and these collaborations between the new and original creators help fuel their productions and interest from fans. But we cannot forget the money. Carpenter says he did not want to make the original *Halloween II*, and when he was asked to reunite with Curtis for *H20*, he was happy to be consulted but turned down the project; however, he remains content with the serialization of the franchise, remake included, because he is a working director and certainly enjoys all the residuals he receives from the continual efforts to keep Michael Myers alive in more films (*Halloween: A Cut Above the Rest*).

The original *Halloween* had a production budget of $325,000 and grossed $47 million ($60 million worldwide); Zombie's remake cost an estimated $15 million to make and earned over $58 million (over $80 million worldwide). There is no clear winner if there were a battle in box-office sales, but the original film was designated as one of the most successful independent movies of all time. It was also selected by the National Film Registry to be preserved as a "culturally, historically, or aesthetically significant" work of filmmaking (*Halloween [1978 film]*). America is, of course, a capitalist society; when a director remakes a film that is classified as art, preserved by the Library of Congress, celebrated as a production that changed a film genre, and viewed as an historic cultural marker, and he does so with the approval of the original film's director, everyone wins.

4

Friday the 13th
SUPERSTITION BROUGHT UNIVERSAL APPEAL ...

You see, Jason was my son, and today is his birthday. —Pamela Voorhees

Camp Crystal Lake is a woodsy retreat for kids and young-adult camp counselors. The participants get to swim, hike, tell ghost stories by campfire, make new friends, and join in a host of other summertime events The mother of a kid who drowned at the camp while the supervising counselors were preoccupied does not find the activities any fun since dealing with the death of her son, Jason Voorhees. In 1980, *Friday the 13th* made its way to theaters to do for camping what *Jaws* did for boating, swimming, and other water sports. Sean S. Cunningham directed a film portraying a mother's revenge for the accidental death of her son—a mentally challenged young man who drowns while no one is watching. The film has nine original sequels; however, Jason was not the killer in the original film or its fourth sequel, *Friday the 13th: A New Beginning* (1985).

Friday the 13th is the ultimate cautionary tale for campers and sexually-active teens going out into the woods to explore their newly-developed adult bodies and hormones. With its masked killer, recognizable theme music, and final-girl syndrome, the film represents the offspring of *Halloween* and the grandchild of *Psycho*. All the elements are there, most notably a knife for killing and teenagers in jeopardy, but this time the mother is the killer. This twist shows what life might have been like had Norman Bates's mother been alive before her son took over the business of killing. *Friday the 13th* was not the only slasher film to emerge post–*Halloween*, but it mastered the elements of the subgenre to become one of the top three alongside its *Halloween* precursor and before *A Nightmare on Elm Street*.

The franchise traveled a road similar to *Halloween*'s. In the original *Fri-*

day the 13th Pamela Voorhees exacts revenge on unsuspecting young camp counselors whose only fault is working at the same camp where her son drowned. These teenagers know the story of Jason, but none of them were working at Camp Crystal Lake when the event took place. Pamela takes it upon herself to punish the new counselors who are oblivious to their surroundings because they are too involved with sex, drinking, and/or drugs. John Carpenter says teens died in *Halloween* because they were not paying attention, not directly because of sex or drugs, and the same is true here. Before Pamela is beheaded by the last girl standing (Alice), she tells the story of the boy-who-would-be-killer:

> Did you know a young boy drowned the year before those two others were killed? The counselors weren't paying any attention. They were making love while that young boy drowned. His name was Jason. I was working the day that it happened, preparing meals ... here. I was the cook. Jason should've been watched every minute. He wasn't a very good swimmer. We can go now, dear [*Friday the 13th*].

After the legendary battle by the lake, Alice wakes up in a hospital after a supposed dream of Jason attacking her from the water, but the police have no idea what she is talking about, and so the time of Jason begins.

It is never revealed to viewers how Jason came to be, but speculation dictates he never drowned and Pamela had been caring for him, *or* his mother's death brought him to life to carry out the killing. He takes

Jason Voorhees (Steve Dash/Daskawisz) bursts through a window in *Friday the 13th Part 2* (1981). Voorhees does not acquire his infamous hockey mask until *Friday the 13th Part III* (1982).

Pamela's place in the 1981 sequel and sports a potato sack over his head while stalking victims, until he, too, meets his match in a final girl (Ginny) who uses a machete to slice into his shoulder. Ginny and her boyfriend race back to a cabin where Jason attacks again, but that scene cuts to her waking up like Alice in the first movie, with memory loss and no knowledge of what happened to Jason. By the time this sequel came out, horror films had already set in stone the open ending to leave room for its killer to return in later segments, and the final girls in *Friday the 13th* were seemingly mystified by Jason's presence because they always seemed to be disoriented about the murderous events and the killer's whereabouts in the end. *Friday the 13th Part III* (1982) again picks up where the previous film ended: Jason removes the machete from his shoulder and begins killing teens at a home not far from the lake. He is bested by another teenage girl who brings an axe down upon his head, and again the survivor's mental capacity is injured after being taken away by the police. The importance and significance of *Part III*, however, is that this is the sequel where Jason acquires the infamous hockey mask from one of his victims. This sequel solidified the character who had been developing into a monster since his mother talked about him as a darling boy in the original film.

Friday the 13th: The Final Chapter (1984), *Friday the 13th: A New Beginning*, and *Friday the 13th: Jason Lives* (1986) offer a mid-franchise trilogy that chronicles the life of Tommy Jarvis, a young boy (and one of the original "final boys") who "kills" Jason in the third sequel after Jason escapes the morgue. Tommy is committed to a mental health facility in the fourth sequel where he faces Jason again, only to discover it was a copycat killer seeking revenge for the death of his son at the institution. Tommy appears a final time in the fifth sequel where lightning strikes a rod impaled in Jason's body and revives him. This is the first time the killer returns through some form of extraordinary or supernatural means. Tommy, however, chains an enormous rock to Jason and leaves the killer to drown in the lake where it all started.

The franchise seemed to follow in the footsteps of *Halloween*, which by this time was wandering into the land of intricate storytelling; however, *Friday the 13th* made choices to go the way of inconsistent and arbitrary Jason resuscitations—storytelling took a backseat to bringing Jason back to kill and be killed again. This point is illustrated in *Friday the 13th Part VII: The New Blood* (1988), where telekinetic Tina accidentally revives the monster and has to use her powers to defeat him at the end, sending him back into the water yet again. He is brought back by an electrical cable in *Friday the 13th Part VIII: Jason Takes Manhattan* (1989), and chases after teens in the Big Apple (a long journey from home, akin to Michael Myers's trek to California). At the end of this sequel Jason is killed by raw sewage washing over him, but his remains reveal the innocent boy he was at the time of his drowning in the original film. And before the sludge hits him, a young voice emerges from his mouth to say, "Mommy! Don't let me drown, Mommy!" The sequence baffles fans and critics alike because it is completely foreign to the storyline to think that Jason was a mature, monstrous shell hiding the body of a small child within, but that is how it was filmed.

Jason Goes to Hell: The Final Friday premiered in 1993. People thought the films had nothing new to offer, but this sequel proved otherwise. There is no explanation for his resurrection, and he begins to possess people by having them devour his heart. In order to regain his physical body, Jason needs to find a family member, and the story proceeds to reveal he has a sister and a niece (reminiscent to, and borrowed from, *Halloween*). After he reconciles with his body, his niece stabs him with a magic dagger, and giant hands come out of the ground to take him to Hell. The story does not relate to the original film, but fans ate it up (pun intended). As disconnected as this sequel was in relation to the franchise—everyone knew that the word "final" had been used in a title before and did not stop the serialization—*Jason X* hit theater screens in 2002. In this final sequel of the original franchise, Jason boldly goes where no horror villain had gone before (other than *Critters 4* [1992], *Hellraiser: Bloodline* [1996], and *Leprechaun 4: In Space* [1997]). In short, Jason returns (no one knows how) and is cryogenically frozen, awakening over 400 years into the future. The technology that brings him back resurrects him as an indestructible cyborg that the team aboard a spaceship must try to defeat. After an arduous and somewhat comical struggle, Jason's body is hurtled toward the planet "Earth Two" like a meteor in flight. A couple of teenagers at a lakeside setting witness what they think is a falling star and head in that direction to investigate, while the camera shows Jason's mask sink to the bottom of the water.

The *Friday the 13th* franchise began in 1980 as a clear offshoot of *Halloween*, but by the time it came to an end, the sequels were less about Jason or his victims; they were slasher films relying on the kills. Continuity issues were evident throughout the series; startup writers, directors, and actors worked on the productions and assembled sequels in rapid fashion; and the idea of a legacy narrative like *Halloween* faded as every new installment distanced itself from the original concept.

In its inception, the film carried over clear mirror markers from *Psycho*: the knife as murder weapon, and Pamela Voorhees as the overbearing, controlling mother of Jason in a relationship not unlike that between Norman Bates and his split-personality mother figure (Pamela channels Jason to kill; Norman channels his mother). *Friday the 13th* did not, however, carry with it the critical support *Psycho* achieved. Roger Ebert slammed the film and called it an "immoral and reprehensible piece of trash" (*His Name Was Jason*). Ebert was joined by his reviewing partner Gene Siskel, but the bad publicity simply made audiences more curious about the film and brought in more viewers.

It is a unique horror franchise because the killer in the original story is not the iconic masked villain of its sequels. It also features a sequel in which a copycat killer does all the work. This situation is the same as the unrelated second sequel in the *Halloween* series, which shows that the serialization of slasher films is never a road of certainty. Seth Grahame-Smith, author of *How to Survive a Horror Movie*, supports the notion that *Friday the 13th* remains a unique film in a sea of slashers because of its iconic star. He says, "Jason started as a drowning victim—that's as simple as you can make it. And he's just a little boy who was ignored by his camp counselors and couldn't swim very well and drowned. And no matter what movie you're talking about, he's still a victim" (*His Name Was Jason*). Although Jason's origin seems markedly different from Michael Myers and other figures that followed, his status as victim seeking revenge is not as different as Grahame-Smith purports. The *Halloween* films demonstrate that Myers is a troubled kid, somewhat influenced by society, a mental-health disorder, and a ritualistic curse; and in a movie like *A Nightmare on Elm Street*, Fred Krueger is a sinister villain, but one seeking revenge on his fellow citizens who killed him via vigilante justice rather than letting law enforcement personnel do their jobs.

Jason, like Michael Myers, did not become a horror icon because of his origin story. A large majority of people watch movies in the *Friday the 13th* franchise for the kill factor. The film series outnumbers its *Halloween* predecessor and *Nightmare on Elm Street* successor, and throughout the series the tone of *Friday the 13th* became humorous during its sequelization. Instead of audiences being afraid of Jason, viewers came to celebrate his inventive slayings as horror entertainment; frightening moments in the series became— appropriately—camp.

The fear in the original *Friday the 13th* comes from storytelling, not killing and not a masked villain. Michael Myers starts his killing spree with five victims in the first *Halloween*, and his numbers climb into the teens by the production of the third sequel. Jason starts with nine victims, and his numbers climb to almost thirty in *Jason X*. The more victims slaughtered in the films, the more aware audiences become of the voluminous carnage. *Halloween* relies on collaborations between music, masked fear, and stalking, even when the kills became greater in number. The *Friday the 13th* series, on the other hand, has always hooked audiences into seeing the films by offering more kills and more creativity to the kills. Joe Lynch, director of

Wrong Turn 2 (2003), says the movies in the series are "really about watching Jason do his thing; he was the protagonist in these films" (*His Name Was Jason*). The innumerable death counts, however, make some of the murders comedic, expected, and celebrated by an almost audience-participation agreement. Fans have been known to count the death scenes as a sequel would play on the big screen, and this attention given to the number of violent deaths replaces the element of horror with a more active viewer response too attentive to scorekeeping to allow defenses to drop for fear to take over.

Jason's hockey mask is as iconic as the Shatner mask of Myers and should be able to inspire the same amount of dread, but the element of fear does not reside in his hidden face. Throughout various sequels the audience is allowed to see his face when the mask is knocked off somehow, and although it is a disfigured appearance, Jason's malformation is more about shock than fear. There is also a clear difference between the two masks: a hockey mask is easily recognizable as equipment in a sporting event, but a Shatner mask that has been altered—eyes widened, sideburns removed, eyebrows removed—creates a Freudian *unheimlich* reaction, where viewers are torn between the recognition of a human face and the fear of its alien appearance. If Jason had not picked up the hockey mask in the second sequel it is possible that the films would have relied more on fear of the unknown rather than fear of an iconic mythology. He wears a potato sack in the first sequel, hence he is shrouded like a Grim Reaper figure, and the mystery created by that sack can certainly be scarier than a hockey mask. But the mask is a recognizable symbol for horror entertainment. The element of fright emanates mostly from the origin story told in the first film.

Friday the 13th utilizes the campfire tale. Such a story, told at night around a roaring fire in the open air while a circle of friends listen intently, is presented by one camp counselor to the others as a joking way to break the ice of newfound or reconnected camaraderie. The story extends beyond the circle into the movie theater or living room where viewing audiences become a part of the listening group. Characters and viewers become so engrossed in the storytelling that they all jump or scream when the quiet, whispered tale is interrupted by another counselor who appears from nowhere to make a loud noise or act wildly. The first three films make storytelling the trademark of fear. Counselors tell the stories with such honesty that the other characters fall into the trap; however, none of them know the story is true within the scope of the film. Audience members realize this is storytelling contained in a fictional presentation (known in narratology as a frame tale), but they are scared, too, because almost everything in life is "based on a true story"—the phrase that seems to always bring intrigue, mystery, and fear.

Pamela Voorhees uses the same aspects of storytelling to frighten and reveal the truth in her final encounter with the counselor who claims her head. Her flashback tale informs the audience she is the killer, and the shocking information turns to fear when she says, "You let him drown! You never paid any attention. Look what you did to him," before attacking Alice. From campfire tale to confession, *Friday the 13th* effectively uses rhetoric to scare its characters within the action and audiences looking in on the film. As the sequels continued to be produced, the storytelling aspect became shorter, more rapid, and less frequent; the abundant, creative kills became the focus.

Jason simultaneously decapitates three paintball players standing next to each other in *Friday the 13th: Jason Lives*; he slices a machete into the face of an unsuspecting character whose wheelchair rolls backward and bounds down an enormous flight of stairs in the rain in *Friday the 13th Part II*; and in *Friday the 13th Part VII: The New Blood*, Jason grabs a sleeping bag with the female victim struggling inside, slings her into a tree trunk, and kills her instantly. These kills are never about fear; they are a representation of Jason's methodology. These kills are about anticipation, which is an adrenaline rush much different from fear. They make audiences question, "What is he going to do now?"

The storytelling within *Friday the 13th* extracts fear from its viewer, and much like the telling of a tale, the emotion is cyclical and returns when triggered. Anticipation, however, leads to relief, usually in the form of laughter. It is not unusual to find viewers laughing at the *Friday the 13th* films because the franchise is a celebration of innovative and often impossible kills. Audience participation is present throughout the entire series, but fear comes in second place behind the kill factor.

Friday the 13th does not offer much star power in its series of films. Compared to *Halloween*, the cast and crew are quite different: Sean S. Cunningham, Steve Miner, John Carl Buechler, and Joseph Zito are the only directors whose careers received a boost from the franchise. Cunningham recently found a home producing remakes such as *Friday the 13th* and *The Last House on the Left* (2009); Miner directs television episodes on such popular series as *Smallville* (WB 2001–2006, CW 2006–2011) and *Psych* (USA 2006); Buechler is currently developing a remake of the 1986 cult horror flick *Troll* set for future release; and Zito found some exposure directing the '80s action movies *Missing in Action* (1984) and *Red Scorpion* (1989). But none of these directors have gone on to achieve the success of Carpenter from his work on *Halloween*. It is easily argued that the big splash (or slash) that *Halloween* made in the horror genre was difficult to repeat by an offshoot like *Friday the 13th*. The directing skills were there, but the original film and its sequels were unable to match the impact of *Halloween*.

The actors have encountered the same fate. Jamie Lee Curtis became an overnight sensation because of her role as Laurie Strode, but no female or male actor from the *Friday the 13th* franchise enjoyed the same outcome. There are a few actors who appeared in the films that have continued to work in the entertainment industry, but most of their names or achievements have not been able to reach or surpass Curtis's success. One of those actors is Corey Feldman, who had been acting for six years before he appeared in the third sequel at age 13. He went on to act in high-profile projects like *The Goonies* (1985), *Stand by Me* (1986), and *The Lost Boys* (1987) to attain teen heartthrob status, but his career never hit the big leagues even as he continued to work in film and television. Now a mature man of 40, Feldman uses his former teen status to reprise the role of Edgar Frog in the direct-to-DVD sequels *Lost Boys: The Tribe* (2008) and *Lost Boys: The Thirst* (2010). He is probably the most recognized actor from *Friday the 13th*, alongside Shevar Ross from *A New Beginning*, who went on to work in the acclaimed television series *Different Strokes* (NBC 1978–1986), *Magnum, P.I.* (CBS 1980–1988), and *Family Matters* (ABC 1989–1998). Ross is also able to say that his character broke the African American racial stereotype in horror films by surviving the onslaught of Jason. Kevin Bacon, Crispin Glover, and Miguel A. Nunez, Jr., also appeared in the films and went on to bigger careers, but all of their characters were kill strikes for the masked villain; none of them survived in the movies to have future considerations for the storylines.

The biggest star from the films is, of course, Jason Voorhees. Jonathan Crane is surprised by Jason's star power: "With nothing more in his favor than gutting teens in enormous multitudes, Jason has become an American institution. What is exceptionally interesting about Jason's stardom is that it is the persona who is popular and not the actor or a combination of actor and character" (142). There's no denying the character's popularity, but Crane should also realize that the actors/stuntmen playing the character *are* also widely-recognized by supporters (fans) of the genre, especially at horror and comic-book conventions. To devout horror followers, the men who have stood behind the mask of Jason are just as famous as the character. The figure was portrayed by various actors and/or stuntmen throughout the series until the last four films, in which Kane Hodder became the masked killer. Taking on the role of Jason in four consecutive films provides Hodder with a huge fan base all over the world, even if audiences never see his true face, and he shares this fame with the makeup effects artists who each got to stamp their own creative visions in constructing different looks for Jason's disfigured face.

Outside the film franchise, Jason enjoys constant cultural appreciation in the form of Halloween masks (ironically) and collectible figurines and dolls. Michael Myers and many other horror villains have been merchandized, but in terms of star power, the *Friday the 13th* series celebrates this as more of an accolade than the unrecognized accomplishments of its actors, directors, and producers. Jason's iconic status also lends influence to other film and television productions. He appears animated in cameos for *The Simpsons* (FOX 1989), *Family Guy, South Park* (Comedy Central 1997), and *Robot Chicken* (Adult Swim 2005). Jason remains a masked killer, but the shows portray him in a comedic light. When *Friday the 13th* became serialized, Jason became overexposed and his fear-appeal turned into wide-scale marketing projects.

In film, his influence was felt immediately after the original movie and its first sequel when *The Burning* (1981) and *Just Before Dawn* (1981) were released; both movies employed the scary camp killer motif. The same year also saw the release of the horror spoof *Saturday the 14th*, which took liberties with the horror film's title and themes of superstition. Jason also manages to stay current in music with rapper Eminem dropping the character's name in several of his songs. In addition, the franchise spawned a television series of the same name about cursed antiques, established the final girl syndrome en masse, inspired Nike commercials, *MadTV* (FOX 1995–2009) episodes, and lunchboxes and thermoses. Jason even accepted a lifetime achievement award at the 1992 MTV Movie Awards and also appeared on *The Arsenio Hall Show* (Paramount 1989–1994). His celebrity extended into a haunted house attraction at Universal Studios and a published book detailing memories of Camp Crystal Lake (*His Name Was Jason*). Star power for *Friday the 13th* relies on branding, merchandising, and cultural awareness. Both brand and merchandise were rebooted seven years after the ninth sequel in the series.

The interesting aspect of *Friday the 13th* returning in 2009 as a remake is that it represents another remake receiving support from its original production team. Sean S. Cunningham served as producer for the *Friday the 13th* remake, directed by Marcus Nispel, a man previously known for his remake of *The Texas Chainsaw Massacre* in 2003. Cunningham says, "It's made by people who love the franchise, but who are going at it with many more resources than we ever had or ever dreamed of" (*His Name Was Jason*). Resources, as with most remakes, means money, and the people working on these films use big money in hopes of creating better films to pay homage to or even replace the originals. Cunningham, like Carpenter, had few resources to create his original horror vision, but that lack of funding for actors, locations, equipment, and special effects forced the production teams to be creative about how they would make the movies (and these are the stories they all celebrate on DVD extras, in interviews, and in retrospectives made about the heyday of horror). Contemporary, bigger production budgets utilize computer-generated imagery, hire well-known actors, attract high-profile producers, and create aesthetically pleasing sets or travel to lush locales to make sleeker, glossier horror films than the gritty fare of yesteryear. Horror was never a "pretty" genre because the films of the 1970s and 1980s were visceral in subject matter, and that content was matched in production value and presentation. As indicated before, the newer, polished remakes turn horror films into blood-drenched action movies, and these days there is one man in particular to credit for such a development: Michael Bay.

Bay, known for his pulse-pounding action productions like *Bad Boys* (1995), *The Rock* (1996), *Armageddon* (1998), and the *Transformers* series (2007, 2009, 2011), served as producer on remakes for *The Texas Chainsaw Massacre*, *The Amityville Horror* (2005), *The Texas Chainsaw Massacre: The Beginning* (2006), *The Hitcher* (2007), *Friday the 13th*, and *A Nightmare on Elm Street*. For each of the these remakes he teamed up with a relatively unknown director, or, in the cases of Dave Meyers, Samuel Bayer, and Marcus Nispel, the directors all had a history of music video directing experience working with top talents such as Green Day, the Cranberries, Janet Jackson, Dave Matthews Band, Missy Elliot, Britney Spears, and Cher. Bay also directed a couple of music videos in the early 1990s. In this manner, the horror wave of remakes offers a growing number of highly-produced, big-budget films with blood, young Hollywood actors, contemporary music soundtracks, and CGI components for mainstream American audiences. Video may have killed the radio star, but those who make videos are working in the horror genre to spice it up. The box-office numbers do not lie; audiences cannot get enough.

The new *Friday the 13th* is different from the *Halloween* retread because it is part of a specific remake machine component led by Bay that always features teens or young adults cast from popular television shows. The storytelling has also been altered, and Jason's actions are not as monstrous (more humanized) as they were in the original series. Previously-mentioned remakes produced by Bay feature popular actors like Jessica Biel, Ryan Reynolds, Sophia Bush, and Eric Balfour from hit TV series *7th Heaven, Two Guys, a Girl, and a Pizza Place* (ABC 1998–2001), *One Tree Hill* (WB 2003–2006, CW 2006), and *Six Feet Under* (HBO 2001–2005). These actors were well-known as television stars before jumping onto the remake machine, which enhances their mass audience appeal and recognition for film projects. *Friday the 13th* features Amanda Righetti from *The O.C.* (FOX 2003–2007) and *North Shore* (FOX 2004–2005), Danielle Panabaker from *Shark* (CBS 2006–2008), and Jared Padalecki from *Supernatural* (WB 2005–2006, CW 2006) and *Gilmore Girls* (WB 2000–2007). They are all recognized actors with large television audience followings, and are cast in remakes in the hope that viewers will follow them into the theaters, thereby helping to create film careers for the actors and revenue for the films. The actors also find themselves doing more than one remake to secure popularity and a name in the film industry. Padalecki appeared in *House of Wax* (2005), and Panabaker acted in *The Crazies* (2010). It was definitely an intelligent move on both parts for stardom and box-office numbers (the original *Friday the 13th* had a production budget of $550,000, with over $39 million made in the theaters; the remake cost $19 million, with a box-office pull of almost $65 million).

The story of *Friday the 13th* also changes. Nispel turns the remake into a mashup of the first three films in the franchise. His film opens with a short sequence that plays while the credits roll. Audience members see a recap of the events that take place at the end of the original film; the sequence was reshot in the rain with new actors. After the actor portraying Pamela Voorhees is decapitated, the final girl runs off, and a young boy walks over to the lifeless body. This is Jason, depicted as witnessing his mother's death in order to give explanation and reasoning behind his killings. It is a scene not shown in the original, and the audience had to use its power of imagination and deductive reasoning in order to figure this out in the 1980 production. After the audience is presented this sequence, viewers are also able to witness the young Jason pick up the machete his mother's attacker used and walk off into the woods to become the legend he is today. It is understandable that filmmakers of remakes want to dive into the story of iconic figures like Jason, Michael Meyers, and Freddy, and there is something to be said about contemporary audience expectations; more elements are presented onscreen for viewers so they do not have to make too many connections about how the narrative proceeds. Audience participation in the moviegoing experience becomes more about the physical viewing pleasure in the theater.

Once the opening sequence is complete, the formula of young adults camping, nudity, drug use, and Jason killing ensues. Five campers are slowly picked off one by one by Jason (sporting a potato sack over his head and later acquiring the infamous hockey mask to bring the 1980s-film mashup full circle) because they have stumbled upon his homeland. The first is killed while trying to obtain marijuana, which seems to imply Jason is growing the plant around his home and kills the victim for attempting to steal. Next, a female victim and her boyfriend are killed, but the boyfriend's death is prolonged because he is first snagged in a bear trap. This implies Jason is a hunter-gatherer or a forest child who has grown up to depend on the land to live (humanized instead of a killing machine that cannot be stopped). Another couple is also attacked while rummaging through Jason's home. They find a locket Pamela Voorhees carried when she was alive that contains pictures of herself and Jason, and it is suggested that the girl (Whitney) resembles Pamela. The boyfriend is dragged beneath the floorboards where he meets his maker, but Whitney escapes and Jason gives chase. These are classic slasher film themes and motifs for Jason (minus the human factor), but there is one situation with the girl who escapes that changes the narrative design behind the *Friday the 13th* franchise.

Jason takes Whitney prisoner; he abducts her and shackles her to a bed underground. Many slasher films, the original *Friday the 13th* movies included, have moments where the killer becomes humanized by a victim trying to reason with him/her in order to stay alive. Victims often call the killer's name to make him remember his humanity. Typically the killer stops mid-attack, tilts the head to show understanding, and for a moment listens to what the victim has to say. But soon some action takes place to break the moment—a vase shatters, another character stumbles into the scene, or, as in *Friday the 13th Part II*, a slight movement reveals the severed head of Pamela Voorhees and Jason realizes the girl standing before him is only impersonating his mother—and the killing resumes.

The remake, however, goes beyond a moment of recognition, and Jason takes Whitney underground to live with him. It is uncertain what would have happened to her had she not been rescued, but Jason keeps her with him for at least six weeks before she is discovered. Jason is one of slasher films' most formidable killers, but he keeps this teenage girl captive because she is wearing his mother's locket and bears a slight resemblance. This is another effort to humanize a serial slasher from the '80s, who has never before acted in such a manner. Our contemporary consciousness makes viewers want to see the human side to monsters from the '70s and '80s. For six weeks he would have had to care for his victim—feed her, allow her to relieve herself, and take care of her in possible sickness—but we are not privy to such scenes. Jason is more of a homemaker and a father figure in the remake than the masked killer who claims the life of anyone who dares set foot on his property or around Camp Crystal Lake in the '80s production. The original film franchise is iconic because Jason is a killing machine that cannot be stopped, but its historical standing in the horror genre is given a new perspective when filmmakers turn the villain into a forest dweller who misses his mother and is protecting private property.

Monsters and other horror villains who have humanistic qualities can be scary, but that is how those characters are created in their origin stories. This is not the Jason that Cunningham created thirty years ago, but contemporary sensibilities (not explicitly connected to franchising, money, merchandise, etc.) have humanized him. It may seem like a small alteration in order to make the new film show a different point of view, but every change made to a movie that revolutionized the horror genre is another reflection of how significant the remake trend has become in cinema.

5

A Nightmare on Elm Street
The Safety of Sleep Was Violated ...

Whatever you do, don't fall asleep. —Nancy

When people sleep, they allow themselves to slip away from the harsh realities of the real world into a landscape of dreams. They fly, make love to celebrities, relive good times with friends and family, and sometimes find themselves naked in a classroom unprepared for a final exam. These dreams can bring physical and mental pleasure; even the awkward birthday-suit dreams give people something to laugh about when they wake up. But not all dreams are pleasant—a sunny day turns into a dark tunnel, weddings become funerals, body gratification becomes injury, and a multitude of other oddities, scares, and emotional downfalls present themselves. These are nightmares; they are still the stuff dreams are made of but nothing anyone ever wants. It is during the occurrence of dreams and nightmares that people are at their most vulnerable. All over the world people experience the dream of falling down stairs or off a building and into an endless abyss of black, but they wake up before hitting the bottom and wonder what would have happened had the dream continued.

The age-old question of whether death during sleep correlates to death in reality is answered in *A Nightmare on Elm Street*. The film's premise centers on Fred Krueger, an accused child molester, rapist, and murderer who is burned alive in Springwood, Ohio, by a group of neighborhood parents concerned for the welfare of their children. Krueger returns from physical death to invade the dreams of his attackers' children on Elm Street and, out of revenge, kill them one by one. As the sins of the parents are revisited upon their teenage kids, it is up to the victims to band together in an effort to survive the mortal dangers during sleep.

Wes Craven established a pivotal moment in horror history by writing and directing *A Nightmare on Elm Street*—much as John Carpenter (with

Debra Hill) did with *Halloween*. Unlike Carpenter or Sean S. Cunningham, however, Craven was a well-established director before he created *Nightmare*. His previous films, *The Last House on the Left* (1972), *The Hills Have Eyes* (1977), and *Swamp Thing* (1982), gave him a name in both science fiction and rape-revenge/exploitation horror films. These were not genres most people celebrated; in fact, exploitation films, especially of the rape-revenge subgenre, typically made people see these directors as immoral human beings. But *The Last House on the Left*, Craven's first feature film, demonstrates his focus on the human spirit and the importance of story. *Last House* is basically a remake of Ingmar Bergman's *Jungfrukällan* (*The Virgin Spring* [1960]), a film derived from a 13th century medieval ballad. Craven's early movies depict the resilience of humankind, and *Nightmare* is no different. The slasher elements—teenagers, sex, drugs—are present (along with more parental figures than *Halloween* or *Friday the 13th*), but the film sets itself apart from others by using dreams as its killer's stalking grounds.

Other horror movies, like *Friday the 13th*, have presented viewers with dreams, but those sequences are typically daydreams by the protagonist or scenes intended to fool audience members into believing they are witnessing the appearance of the killer. Although other films had previously utilized the concept of mind control and psychic abilities (*The Fury* [1976], *Carrie* [1976], *Scanners* [1981], and *Firestarter* [1984]), none of them used the idea of the dream format as a new frontier in which to attack unsuspecting teenagers. *Dreamscape* (1984) premiered a few months before *Nightmare*, and although its main villain killed people in their dreams, the film was more of a science fiction production involving government experimentation and psychic abilities, and it was not a commercial success. *A Nightmare on Elm Street*, in comparison, preyed on the natural sleep patterns of teenagers, and allowed its killer to terrorize and surprise victims supernaturally.

The film appeared during a time when the slasher subgenre was inundated and satiated with knockoffs from *Halloween* and *Friday the 13th*. It seemed a new slasher movie made its way into the theaters every weekend in the early 1980s. Both filmmakers and audiences were being surrounded by the same masked killer story, naked teenagers dying gory deaths, and a decline in production budgets and casting choices. *A Nightmare on Elm Street* revived the slasher film. Wes Craven and Robert Shaye (producer) found themselves in the same spot as Carpenter with *Halloween*—no studios wanted to take on the project because they all felt people had seen slashers before, and no one would be interested in a movie about dreams (*Going to Pieces*). *Nightmare*, however, took some of the slasher subgenre conventions and retooled them to energize the spirit of horror again. The film succeeded in ways that many others had previously only attempted, and the original spawned six sequels.

The *Nightmare* franchise was more stable and distinctive than its two main predecessors. The *Nightmare* movies have no break in storyline, like *Halloween III: Season of the Witch* or *Friday the 13th: A New Beginning*, and they did not venture into unchartered territories like space or demonic possession. Freddy is always the killer, and in the land of dreams and nightmares anything can happen. This is the franchise that brought narrative importance back to the slasher subgenre with a clear story, solid filmmaking, and endless creative possibilities in the new arena of dreams.

In the origin film, Nancy (Heather Langenkamp) is the final girl who must atone for her parents' (and their neighborhood associates') transgressions against Fred Krueger (aka Freddy). Freddy kills all of Nancy's friends (and mother), which leaves her alone to try to bring him out into reality where she can do him the most harm. Nancy discovers she basically has to wish "there's no place like home" to make everything normal again. The ending—a mix of reality and dream, happy ending and ambiguity—is not a masterpiece of horror filmmaking, and Craven has said before that it is not an ending anyone could decide upon; however, the movie marks the beginning of a rejuvenated slasher film period.

A Nightmare on Elm Street is the long-lost child of *Psycho*, via *Halloween* and *Friday the 13th*, because it owes its creation to the 1960s classic but sur-

Nancy (Heather Langenkamp) falls victim to an attack by Freddy Krueger when she slumbers during her nighttime bath in *A Nightmare on Elm Street* (1984).

vives on its own merits. Freddy is known as "the bastard son of 100 maniacs," which is a fitting title because his film reached audiences after *Halloween*, *Friday the 13th*, and a mass of copycat movies that featured prolific onscreen killers and carnage. The knife that passed from *Psycho* to *Halloween* to *Friday the 13th* becomes Freddy's finger-knives in a reinvigorated slasher subgenre.

Nightmare continued to set itself apart from its inspirations in the first sequel, *A Nightmare on Elm Street 2: Freddy's Revenge* (1985). In the follow-up film, Freddy returns to terrorize teenagers, specifically one who has moved into the house where Nancy lived in the original film. This plot sounds like a typical slasher sequel, but in this one Freddy makes the teenage protagonist do the killing for him. His proxy also happens to be a male (Jesse), which ignored the slasher tradition of having a female protagonist. Freddy invades Jesse's body and uses him to kill a victim or two before becoming corporeal and tackling the job on his own. In the franchise this production became known as the "gay sequel," because the filmmakers presented the audience with a final boy scenario that adhered to final girl rules. In a reversal of conventional gender roles, Jesse wakes from his nightmares screaming in a high-pitched voice, his clothing is feminized (tight jeans, colorful shirts, ornate accessories), and his would-be girlfriend (Lisa) plays the supportive and strong boyfriend role. He dances to cutesy pop music and visits his best male friend (a fit, muscular guy clad only in tight briefs) in the dead of night with the request that he watch over him while he sleeps—in the same manner Nancy petitioned Glen in the original film. Jesse takes Nancy's role as the final "girl," and the script befits a female protagonist. Some viewers say, "It was the '80s," and that is how guys and girls were during that decade. Either way, the sequel goes against type and represents a departure from the other classic slasher franchises (including the Tommy Jarvis trilogy in *Friday the 13th*, because his character was kept masculine throughout). In the end, Lisa helps Jesse break away from Freddy, and the dream killer is defeated again.

The second sequel, *A Nightmare on Elm Street 3: Dream Warriors* (1987), reunited Wes Craven as writer, Robert Shaye as producer, and Heather Langenkamp as Nancy. The franchise's original final girl returns to help teenagers who are suffering terrifying bad dreams in a mental health facility. Nancy learns that the teens are being terrorized by Freddy, so she steps in to help them rid their dreams of the monster. She harnesses her powers from the first film to teach the teens that they, too, have powers in their dreams to use against the killer. Kristen, the strongest of the teens, works with Nancy to defeat Freddy, but not before Freddy is able to kill the original film's heroine. The two also receive help from Dr. Gordon, who meets Freddy's mother Amanda, who informs him that her son's bones must be buried in hallowed ground in order to stop the killer for good. This sequel represents the start of the "dream series"—three consecutive sequels that all focus on the idea of a dream world landscape where Freddy lives and in which the teenage victims must learn to control their dream personae to survive. In these films the franchise began to resemble *Friday the 13th* by delivering inventive kills audiences wanted to see.

Kristen reappears in *A Nightmare on Elm Street 4: The Dream Master* (1988). Freddy kills her and the other survivors from the previous sequel, but she transfers her knowledge and power to Alice, a school friend, before dying. Alice indirectly pulls friends into her dreams where Freddy lies in wait to kill them. She does not kill for Freddy—like Jesse does in the first sequel—but her dreams supply victims for him. Alice, who does not fancy herself strong enough to defeat Freddy alone, absorbs the strength of her fallen friends and uses their combined powers to become a master of the dream world and defeat him.

As the franchise closed out the '80s, Kristen lingered on into another sequel, *A Nightmare on Elm Street: The Dream Child* (1989). This time she is pregnant, and Freddy begins using her unborn child's lifeforce to revivify himself and kill more unsuspecting teenagers. Viewers witness the return of Freddy's mother, who manages to trap her son in the dream world while Kristen and the manifestation of her unborn baby (Jacob) escape to freedom. The audience learns that Freddy was conceived by Amanda, a nun working in a mental health facility who was inadvertently locked within its walls and raped repeatedly by "100 maniacs." The dream series of sequels established more about Freddy's character—how he was conceived and the many ways he can manipulate the dream world to take victims—and let the audience see his development from scary killer in the original to a more wise-cracking, sinister villain crowds have come to love.

Two years later, *Freddy's Dead: The Final Nightmare* (1991) was released. It is revealed that Freddy has a daughter, and he needs her in order to go beyond the boundaries of Springwood and be able to kill even more teenagers. Freddy, it seems, has plans for nationwide death and destruction. In a quick succession of flashbacks, the killer's homelife and childhood is visualized for the audience: a broken home, abusive father, animal cruelty, peer ridicule, loss of wife, and the moment he is given immortality in dreams by spirits of the nightmare landscape (or a version of hell); however, it is not an exploratory sequence like that of Rob Zombie's *Halloween*. Freddy's daughter (Maggie) is a smart cookie and picks up various dream manipulating skills to help fight off his attacks, bring him into the real world, and defeat him as a man, much like Nancy tried to do in the first film. Maggie's last words in the sequel are meant to solidify the closing of the franchise. She says, "Freddy's dead," which simultaneously reminds audience members of the title and assures them they have just witnessed the end of an era with the obliteration of Fred Krueger. But Freddy is dead in the original film, so Maggie's announcement is a somewhat tongue-in-cheek hint that in death Freddy lives.

Four years later that life was realized. *New Nightmare* (1994) breaks from formula completely to create an entirely new kind of slasher horror film. Wes Craven returned again to write and direct this sixth sequel, which reprised the role of Nancy and her father, Lt. Thompson. Nancy's three-time appearance in the franchise comes close to matching multiple appearances by Laurie Strode in *Halloween* (four times in the series with Michael Myers, and one time as an uncredited announcer in *Halloween III*) and the three-film sequence of the Tommy Jarvis character in *Friday the 13th* (although Tommy was portrayed by different actors). Tommy lives after his third appearance, Strode dies in her final (fourth film) meeting with Michael Meyers, and Nancy dies the second time she encounters Freddy, but Craven devised a way to bring his original final girl back and satisfy a fan base that wanted another *Nightmare* film.

Craven uses a meta-fictional approach to deliver this final sequel in the original franchise. The setting for *New Nightmare* takes place in Los Angeles, where Heather Langenkamp, Robert Englund, Wes Craven, John Saxton, Robert Shaye, and others live as actors, directors, and producers. Their lives (friendships, loves, and business dealings) are chronicled for the audience in a way that shows what they go through every day in the film industry. It is almost a documentary production until they start to realize that upon the tenth anniversary of the original film, all of the previous *Nightmare* films they produced have created an evil entity that has taken on the form of Freddy Krueger in an attempt to break into the real world. Langenkamp's husband (Chase) is killed in a freak auto accident, her son (Dylan) starts to have bad dreams about a man with a knifed glove, Englund begins to paint creepy artwork with apparitions of Freddy, and constant earthquakes demonstrate something odd is happening between the boundaries of dream and reality. Craven reveals he is writing a new *Nightmare* film, and Shaye wants Langenkamp to star in the vehicle as a tribute film for the fans and as a movie to put the character of Freddy to rest once and for all. The terrifying events and deaths force Langenkamp to portray Nancy one last time in an effort to travel into the dream world of the *Nightmare* films and defeat the sinister presence.

This sequel defied all other "final" franchise movies by stepping outside the fiction in order to give audiences a glimpse into the lives of the real people playing the roles. Of course the "reality" is itself scripted, but the blend of fiction elements and faux real-world happenings make the film a unique gesture of horror in the slasher subgenre. In fact, *New Nightmare* would be wrongly labeled a slasher film; its innovative design breaks from standard formula. Craven gave audiences a fan-friendly sequel in which moviegoers could revel in once again seeing Nancy, Freddy, the Elm Street house, the infamous glove, and a few kills, but he complicated (in an intelligent manner) the film by stripping off the cinema façade—or breaking the fourth wall—to reveal the actors, makeup, special effects, script writing, producing, promotional advertising, and industry professional lifestyles behind the scenes. Fans, however, were accustomed to tradition, and their reaction to something "new" in a well-established slasher franchise was demonstrated at the box office. The film cost approximately $8 million dollars to produce, and its box office yielded just over $18 million. Although it earned back its budget and then some, the movie represents the least successful entry in the original franchise. It offered a new approach to a slasher series that had been focused on formula, but the originality did not spark much interest in theaters. This was also the 1990s, a time period in which many considered the horror film to be dead or nonexistent, and although that is a strong statement to make, the lack of offerings during the era made it apparent that horror films were no longer on the front lines of cinema. Other franchises—*Warlock* (1989) and *Child's Play* (1988) at the close of the '80s, and *Leprechaun* (1993), *The Prophecy* (1995), and *Tremors* (1990) in the 1990s—tried to become box office success stories but were lost in the shuffle as American independent film began its ascent.

Only two years after the release of *New Nightmare*, Craven partnered with Kevin Williamson (writer), Marianne Maddalena (his executive producer on *New Nightmare*), Bob and Harvey Weinstein (executive producers), and a host of popular young acting talents to direct *Scream*, the film that changed the face of horror and slasher movies in one box-office swoop. The film cost an estimated $15 million to produce but became box-office royalty by taking in over $100 million in six months. The formula that Craven was developing in *New Nightmare* is fully realized in *Scream*: the characters are self-aware about the horror genre; rules for survival are provided to the audience; and viewers are able to participate in the film (answering trivia questions and playing whodunit) in a way that *New Nightmare* helped make possible.

The *Nightmare* series interrupted the traditional slasher productions that had become so common after the releases of *Halloween* and *Friday the 13th*. Themes, motifs, and other elements of the slasher were evident, but the productions took into account that audiences already knew not to go into the water, or go camping in the middle of nowhere, or even babysit on an ominous holiday. There was a new killer in town, and his name was

Freddy. Craven's killer wears no potato sack, hockey mask, or altered William Shatner face. His appearance is not shrouded, and the films hold nothing back in letting the viewer get to know the villain. In the origin story it takes some time for characters and audience members to know who the monster is, but once his story is told, his menacing presence is not reduced; it is his confrontational actions that create much of the fear, and unlike the silent killers of *Halloween* or *Friday the 13th*, he can talk, taunt, and play tricks on his victims. The overt human factor makes fear more tangible because it lets characters and viewers know how dark the human spirit and heart can get when seeking revenge. Until he is named, Nancy echoes the thoughts of the audience when she says, "I don't know who he is, but he's burned and he wears a weird hat and a red and green sweater, really dirty. And he uses these knives, like giant fingernails." The monsters that scare audiences on the screen, the ones moviegoers know do not exist, are nothing compared to those that scare people in real life because they have seen them before on the news, in documentaries, and in history books.

Fred Krueger was a monster before he became Freddy. He molested, raped, and killed children, and this is not a scenario that had to be made up for the film because such despicable crimes do and have occurred in the past entirely too often. Freddy is the embodiment of those fears in a heightened form for entertainment, but the meaning behind his creation is quite easy to understand. Craven says, "With some slasher films I think it's just, it's just blood and guts and torture and things like that which are pretty reliably upsetting, but I think kind of a cheat, and to me it's much more about the social, economic zeitgeist of what's going on in the culture at the time that I try to get at" (*Going to Pieces*). Under Craven's direction, *A Nightmare on Elm Street* achieves social and cultural relevance. Everyone, no matter what culture, race, age, or religious background, has an emotional response to the destruction of a child's innocence. Audiences must connect with a film in order to have a physical or mental response to the material, and Craven achieved the ultimate repulsion in his creation of Freddy.

Because the power of imagination in a darkened theater is much stronger than anything a script, recap, flashback, or dream sequence can provide, the audience never sees Krueger interact with children or commit crimes against them. *Freddy's Dead*, however, does attempt to show snippets of Krueger's life from child to adult, but after a handful of sequels the audience probably had its own construction of Freddy's early life already mapped out in the imagination. Freddy, somewhat of a mixture of Michael Myers and Jason, is fear personified without need of a full back-story. The title "child murderer" is enough.

His face is burned, his hand is clad in a glove with knives that extend and cover the fingers, and his language is less than pristine. Viewers (and characters) fear him for the many reasons we fear physical harm. People are afraid to be burned alive, and no one likes getting poked in the eye accidentally, certainly not with a sharp object; these are acts in which the soft tissue of the body is being inflicted with pain. Freddy also represents social fears of death or dying and experiencing the rot and decay of the body. His presence is that of a social degenerate encroaching upon the safety of suburbia from a sleazy dark alley. Craven took the temperature of America and incorporated the rational (to a degree) fears of the 1980s into his film.

An even more universal element of fear is the vulnerability of sleep. Freddy represents a dangerous sandman character, and in a sleep state there is no escaping the killer—he cannot be run from like Jason—unless someone understands the difficult art of controlling dreams. In dreams, people like to let go and let the imagination run rampant, but in that freedom also lies the possibility of nightmares or worse—the realization that something could happen to the body outside the sleep state. People pray, "If I should die before I wake..." to seek protection during slumber, hoping nothing comes near the body to do physical damage, but the fear is magnified when the harm may come from within their minds while cut off from the waking world.

When the first sequel in the franchise is considered, Wes Craven's social commentary extends even further into collective fears about the body. He did not write, direct, or produce the sequel, but the film is based upon characters he created, and the presence of social fears does not disappear. Both fans and critics joke about and evaluate the queer readings of the sequel, but in 1985 this movie could not have been more relevant to America's social climate. Homosexuality has never been an easy subject for the American public for many reasons, including religion, race, and politics. *A Nightmare on Elm Street 2* embodied national fears concerning the discovery of HIV/AIDS and the use of the "homosexual panic" defense in court cases. *Aliens*, which at the heart of its story has fear rooted in contaminated blood, is another that supports this notion. Even if a director or writer is not trying to provide an overt social message, s/he is influenced by the contemporary social consciousness, and that atmosphere becomes historicized in the film.

Along with all of the kitschy scenes of Jesse screaming, dancing provocatively, growing shy after a girl kisses him, and waking in night sweats after he has been stalked by a male figure in his dreams, there is also the pivotal murder where Jesse enters the dream state and finds his coach in what looks to be a bar filled with stereotyped leather daddies, butch lesbians, and other "alternative" lifestyle bar hoppers. Jesse's coach sports a leather outfit, punishes Jesse by making him run laps in the gym, and then tells him to hit the showers where he later appears. The coach is stripped of his clothes, tied to a shower faucet, whipped with towels, and then sliced with the infamous glove, which is revealed to be on Jesse's hand, and then, of course, Jesse screams.

This scene depicts classic stereotypes of master-slave relationships, bondage and S&M play, daddy-son relationships, and then the rejection of such by murdering the coach. In this one sequence America's fears of stereotypical homosexuality and behavior is both spotlighted and destroyed. Such repulsion was reflected in a 1980s court case in which "a defendant in a Louisiana murder trial ... claimed that when the victim touched his leg, it unleashed his 'excessive hostility toward and fear of homosexuals'" (Slovenko 313). Fear of bodily harm is common in slasher films, but Craven's creation of Freddy allowed the first sequel to highlight a social issue that still exists in the 21st century. More so than *Halloween* or *Friday the 13th*, *A Nightmare on Elm Street* reveals American society to itself, and fear presented on the screen invades the lives of the audience members; it is not easily shaken once the house lights come back up.

The film gave fear a new name, a new look, a new subtextual meaning, and also a new sound. One lasting image from the *Nightmare* series will always be little girls dressed in white dresses, jumping rope and singing a memorable tune. They sing, "One, Two, Freddy's coming for you. / Three, Four, better lock your door. / Five, Six, grab your crucifix. / Seven, Eight, gonna stay up late. / Nine, Ten, never sleep ... again." The sound of this nursery rhyme sung by children haunts the soundtrack and fills the viewer's ears with a melody that should be pleasant but eerily establishes the presence of the killer. Children are not inherently scary, but childhood can be, and most viewers will remember the things that scared them as a child compared to the fears they managed to overcome as an adult. The chant is a double play on childhood as a carefree time of freedom, growth and uncertainty, where everyone and everything seems more self-aware, larger, and threatening. Moreover, childhood is the one thing Freddy took from kids as a molester, rapist, and murderer. It is only fitting that the sweet, haunting sound of children at play guides the viewer through films that depict the loss of innocence; the chanted lyrics also serve as instructions for how to survive an encounter with Freddy. *A Nightmare on Elm Street*, like *Halloween* and *Friday the 13th*, lives on in classic slasher history with the fear it created for the American public. The film also scared up big box-office numbers and helped launch careers.

Wes Craven was already an established director by the time *A Nightmare on Elm Street* was produced, but the film put him in the spotlight as a horror movie director and showed that slasher films could be intelligent, have good narratives, and support strong performances from its actors. He went on to direct *The Hills Have Eyes II* (1985), *The Serpent and the Rainbow* (1988), and *New Nightmare* before large-scale success descended upon him with the production of *Scream* in 1996 and its two sequels in 1997 and 2000. It was a fresh start on a horror film with new characters, new kills, a new villain, and much more for audiences to digest. The *Scream* trilogy had a combined budget of almost $80 million dollars and earned over $290 million in profit at the domestic box office. Craven's career was secured and fully established by the *Scream* franchise, and he brought the franchise back to life after ten years with *Scream 4* (2011). Each of the films showcased rising and established young acting talent, including Neve Campbell, Courtney Cox, Drew Barrymore, Rose McGowan, David Arquette, Matthew Lillard, Skeet Ulrich, Liev Schreiber, Jada Pinkett Smith, Omar Epps, Heather Graham, Scott Foley, and independent film queen Parker Posey. *A Nightmare on Elm Street* and *A Nightmare on Elm Street 3: Dream Warriors*, however, introduced audiences to three young actors whose names would become just as recognized as those in the *Scream* films.

Heather Langenkamp appears in three *Nightmare* films as Nancy Thompson, one of two final girls it takes Freddy three times to successfully kill. Her career as an actress received a boost from the first film, and she went on to appear in the television hits *Just the Ten of Us* (ABC 1988–1990) and *Growing Pains* (1985–1992). Although she hasn't had an extended film or television career since *Nightmare*, her name is written in horror history as one of the genre's most memorable characters.

Nancy's boyfriend in the first film is Glen, who is portrayed by a young Johnny Depp in his feature film debut. The movie catapulted Depp into the public eye, and soon he appeared on the television vehicle that would make him an American heartthrob and a bankable product in Hollywood: *21 Jump Street* (FOX 1987–1991). Depp has starred in a host of films throughout his career, but before *21 Jump Street* came to a close he paired up with director Tim Burton in 1990 to star in *Edward Scissorhands* alongside Winona Ryder. That film solidified Depp and Burton as a collaborative film force as they continued to create critical favorites and box-office gems such as *Ed Wood* (1994), *Sleepy Hollow* (1999), *Charlie and the Chocolate Factory* (2005), and *Alice in Wonderland* (2010), all the while cranking out four films for the *Pirates of the Caribbean* franchise (2003–2011), with another on the way. Depp has always been known for his quirky film choices and character portrayals, and *A Nightmare on Elm Street* was the one movie that put him on the road to stardom and financial success beyond any other actor in the *Nightmare* series.

The other final girl Freddy desperately tries to kill is Kristen, first portrayed by Patricia Arquette in *A Nightmare on Elm Street 3: Dream Warriors*. Like Depp's, this *Nightmare* entry was Arquette's feature film debut; however, her success did not come as quickly afterward. Arquette worked steadily through the end of the 1980s and early 1990s until landing high-profile projects like *Ed Wood*, *Lost Highway* (1997), *Bringing Out the Dead* (1999), and *Holes* (2003). She returned to the world of the supernatural on television as Allison Dubois in 2005 to star in *Medium* (NBC 2005–2009, CBS 2009–2011), which wrapped its seventh and final season in 2011 after jumping networks, as many televised series seem to do lately. All of these actors became household names because they starred in an original horror film. Remakes, on the other hand, offer a different boost in star power (more exposure) because the actors are already well-known from television or other films.

Although Nancy, Glen, and Kristen die, one person can be seen in every *Nightmare* film: Robert Englund as Fred "Freddy" Krueger. Englund had been a working actor in television and film since the mid–1970s before he landed the role of Willie on the NBC cult miniseries-cum-television series *V* in 1983 (which became a remake production on ABC in 2009), but his role as Fred Krueger in 1984 turned him into a slasher icon. The role also made Englund into a horror genre household name and fan favorite, and even if he made cameos in low-budget or B-movie horror films, fans supported the movies just to see what he would do in his appearance. Unlike the actors and stuntmen who braved the horror waters as Michael Myers or Jason, audiences were able to see Robert Englund the actor beneath all the makeup; he was a slasher villain with personality, character, and a recognizable face. This gave the actor a bigger celebrity presence and star power than the other men whose followings have mostly been supported by horror and comic-book conventions. Other than the *Nightmare* films, Englund has never had a specific star vehicle to make him a mainstream name like Depp, but his work in horror has crowned him a living legend in the genre. His last portrayal of Freddy came in 2003 with *Freddy vs. Jason*, directed by Ronny Yu. Englund also appears in contemporary horror productions such as *Hatchet* (2006), *Jack Brooks: Monster Slayer* (2007), and *Zombie Strippers!* (2008), and maintains his pop-culture status with television appearances in shows like *Charmed* (WB 1998–2006) and *Bones* (FOX 2005).

The *Nightmare* franchise brought new life to slasher films, and it even helped revive its predecessors, *Friday the 13th* and *The Texas Chainsaw Massacre*, to do more sequels (*Going to Pieces*). It simultaneously signaled the end of the classic slasher film as the monstrous Freddy became comical and turned into a villain known for his catch-phrases instead of blood-curdling dialogue. Englund worked on the NBC television series *Nightmare Café* in 1992; and as he hosted episodes like the Crypt Keeper, the image of the slasher villain continued to decline. As stated before, Craven saved the slasher film with the production of *Scream*, but the *Nightmare* influence still lingered as films at the end of the '80s and '90s started to mix horror and the supernatural/dream state, sometimes with big talent: *Bad Dreams* (1988), *In Dreams* (1999) with Annette Bening and Robert Downey, Jr., and *The Cell* (2000) with Jennifer Lopez and Vince Vaughn.

To this day, the popularity of the *Nightmare* franchise continues, as viewers have seen imitations of Freddy show up on *The Simpsons* and a *Robot Chicken* episode that informs its audience that Freddy received his hat and red-and-green-striped sweater as bad Father's Day gifts. Some credit the box office disappointment of *April Fool's Day* (1986) as the beginning of the end for horror (slasher films specifically), as genre icons like Freddy started to become mass marketed to middle America. Studios wanted money, but audiences wanted innovation instead of narrative formula and their once-scary villains becoming camp (*Going to Pieces*). Only a year after *April Fool's Day* was released, the *Nightmare* series produced its second sequel, and at that time the gloved killer started using an abundance of one-liners before slaying his victims. In order to resurrect a most-beloved villain, filmmakers brought Freddy back in 2010.

Samuel Bayer's film separates itself from the *Halloween* and *Friday the 13th* remakes. Zombie is a clear fan of horror and worked to provide a cohesive story with visuals that matched elements of horror, and Nispel made a glam production that showed a connection to the original franchise in its mashup scenes and narrative. Bayer's production employs changes in character and story presentation vastly different from what the original franchise imparted to its audiences; however, his film still incorporates contemporary remake trends of using sleek visuals and casting young star talent—Rooney Mara from *Youth in Revolt* (2009) and Kyle Gallner from *Veronica Mars* (UPN 2004–2006, CW 2006–2007), *Big Love* (HBO 2006–2011), and *CSI: NY* (CBS 2004).

Freddy's physical nature onscreen in the remake is less menacing and sleazy than in the original production. The character (played by Jackie Earle Haley) is portrayed as more of a taunter (rubbing his finger-knives together like teenagers click tongue rings to teeth) and brute-force killing machine (punching his hand through a victim's back and slinging another victim to and fro across bedroom walls and ceiling) that evolved from someone who molested, raped, and killed children. In almost all of his speaking scenes—this Freddy does not talk much—the voice is dubbed and/or in voiceover, which is effective for theater sound or home entertainment systems. He seems to be all around at once. Being able to recognize this technical aspect of production also makes the experience of watching the film about viewers being savvy about film production. The atmosphere in the theater fills up with Freddy's voice, and that brings audience members closer to feeling as if Freddy has crossed over into their lives.

Freddy's back-story is also revisited in the film, which offers new considerations for the franchise. The original movies construe Freddy as a child rapist, killer, and son of 100 maniacs, but the remake tosses out a red herring that maybe he was unjustly burned alive. The last two victims, Nancy and Quentin, play Scooby Gang to uncover a school photo showing all the kids Freddy is murdering as teenagers, and along their journey they find more proof their parents may have killed an innocent man. The two are led to an underground room, hoping to find evidence that will clear Freddy of the crimes he allegedly committed, only to discover he wanted them to go there in order to remember all the bad things he did to them when they were children. In this manner the story reveals that the parents of the Elm Street kids all knew their children had been abused by Krueger and decided to kill him while simultaneously hiding evidence to keep their kids from remembering this part of their lives. It also puts the two teenagers in the awkward position of trying to clear the name of the man who abused them as children.

The original film does not suggest or even hint that Krueger abused Nancy, Glen, and the other teenagers when they were kids, and the audience is provided no evidence to direct the imagination to make such a connection. The original story simply tells the audience that parents burned Krueger for the crimes he committed against some (unnamed) children in the neighborhood. In the remake, the blame—for Freddy abusing the kids, the parents erasing the childhood of their sons and daughters, the teenagers working to exonerate their captor—is all around, and Freddy shares his status as antagonist in the film. The crimes he committed as a human and then again as a slasher monster are certainly evil, but the parents worked together to kill another human being and steal memories from their children. It is understandable that the parents do not want their kids to remember the abuse, but by removing photos, school enrollment information, and other documentation, they knowingly erase friendships and any other good life memories the children had when they were in school together. As long as child abuse continues to be a social problem it will remain relevant in film, and the *Nightmare* remake balances focus on the corrupt actions of the parents against the abuser and his victims.

Another issue to discuss is the idea of Fred Krueger as a child molester and pedophile. He is described this way in the original film, and the remake does the same, but one important change is made to the narrative. In the original movie he targets the teens of the parents who murdered him, but nothing is ever said about him specifically abusing their children. The remake makes it explicit that he abused all the children he now hunts as teenagers. The film further layers this idea by Freddy's sexual innuendos toward the victims before he kills them. He talks about having time to play while one victim's body bleeds out, and runs his finger-knife up Nancy's leg while saying, "Your mouth says no, but your body says yes." What is interesting about Freddy's interaction with his victims is that pedophiles are drawn to youth, to the untouched and pure life of children, but he continues to stalk these kids now that they are young adults. Typically, once a child reaches a certain age—usually puberty—a pedophile loses interest. Freddy's advances to his teenage victims only enhance his sinister profile as a child molester, and it is understandable that the victims would still fear Krueger as their abuser. His simultaneous desire and hatred for the kids is amplified because they managed to escape his grasp and grow up, although they are damaged from the childhood abuse. The filmmakers wanted to show how Fred Krueger, the child abuser, became Freddy, the slasher villain, and the result is a movie monster hazardous to the safety of all ages.

Re-envisioning a new *Nightmare* film was inevitable; it was called for mostly due to the success of other remakes before it, and it seems the character development and changes from the original were made to be the selling points. Alongside Freddy stands Nancy, the original final girl of the first film. In the remake Nancy works at a diner, is a loner, and has no boyfriend. Other than her name, which the film establishes in the opening sequences via her diner nametag and its prominent use by other characters, she is a completely different character from the original. She is extremely mousy and quiet, which could be a result of being abused by Krueger when she was a child. The new Nancy also refuses to take a shot of adrenaline to stay awake, while the original Nancy did whatever she could to keep from falling asleep. The original Nancy says, "I'm into survival," but the remade character is insecure and passive. Nancy's father is also missing from the story, and no explanation is given for his absence. Showing only Nancy and her mother makes it the responsibility of the audience to figure out if the father is on vacation, at work, deceased, or if her parents are separated or divorced, or if she is adopted and in a single-parent household. None of these situations are present in the film, and this missing narrative component lets the audience fill in the gaps.

Craven's original movie taps into the social atmosphere of the 1980s, and the remake adds a touch of the 21st century. The relevancy of social ills—alcoholism, strained parent-child relationships, teenage sexuality, strained parent relationships, bars on windows as representations of crime infiltrating suburbia and a notion to keep teens safe from the real world—are removed in the remake in order to focus on pedophilia, child abuse, and street justice. The film offers computer-generated special effects with a high-gloss production value. *A Nightmare on Elm Street* in 1984 contains an alcoholic mother, parents on the verge of divorce, teenage girls being pressured into sex by their boyfriends, the fear of growing old (Nancy's grey hair and her statement about looking twenty years old), teen suicide (Freddy kills Rod and makes it look like he hanged himself), and coping with death. In one scene Nancy's mother tells the story of how the parents killed Fred Kruger, and the audience learns she hid his glove in the basement as a keepsake. This scene illustrates a 1980s sensitivity to the threat of suburban home invasion. Freddy is never too far from Nancy because the symbol of his evil resides in her home. The remake does not incorporate this scene or provide Freddy any connection to the house, thereby making his proximity to Nancy restricted to the landscape of dreams.

In addition, the first film showcases the famous sleepover scene. Nancy sleeps in the guest bedroom, and her boyfriend Glen sleeps downstairs on the sofa while Tina and Rod have loud, raucous sex in her bedroom (we later see Rod roll from atop Tina's body to lie beside her, thereby indicating the sexual act is complete). Glen remarks, "Morality sucks" to the sounds of intercourse because he and Nancy are dating but have not taken their relationship to an intimate, physical level. When Freddy presses through the bedroom wall, a crucifix falls and awakens Nancy. She studies the Christ figure before returning it to its hook and going back to sleep. When Freddy attacks Tina in her sleep, Rod jumps from the bed, clad only in briefs, and begins to scream her name and reach for her, but he is helpless against the villain.

This one sleepover sequence is almost completely removed in the remake. Nancy is not at the house where her friend dies, and when Freddy moves within her bedroom wall there is no cross to knock down and wake her up. Nancy also has no boyfriend; Quentin (the new Glen) likes her, but they are not dating. The cameras never show any sexual acts between Chris (the new Tina) and Jesse (the new Rod), and the viewer only sees them sleeping next to each other. Also, when Chris is attacked, Jesse jumps out of bed wearing boxers and is unable to help his girlfriend. The differences between the two segments mark the films by the decades in which they were produced. The remake removes all aspects of religion or a tie-in to the "One, Two, Freddy's coming for you" chant by erasing the crucifix imagery as protection. It also eliminates the typical exploitation of teenage sexuality by removing allusions to sex between Chris and Jesse and not providing Nancy a boyfriend; the subject matter of sex in this film concerns abuse, not recreation. Moreover, when the depiction of male undergarments changes from briefs to boxers, the male body is less sexualized. Briefs show the male form and highlight sexuality by the impression of genitalia through the material. The '80s were much more representative of a body-conscious society, while "kids today" have baggier fashion tendencies. These changes allow the remake to stand on its own, separate from the original. Teenage sexuality and dating, religious concerns, and body obsession are all real issues for young adults and their parents, especially during the age of uncertainty in the '80s. The remake updates the story to showcase more dangerous social ills.

Original films, sequels/prequels, and remakes address these topics and more, and although they are all serious issues that do not fade away in American society, each film stamps its own time period on how the material is presented to audiences. The drugstore scene where Quentin tries to get more ADHD medication drops a hint about awareness to addiction or the idea that a 21st century teen population is being sedated. The burned visage of Freddy also easily alludes to burn victim survival—a human tragedy people face every day. Teenagers in the original films come together because of the shared nightmares they have about Freddy, and this delivers a poignant message about the collective fears American teenagers (and parents) have growing up; but the re-envisioned production shows how disconnected contemporary teens are from each other. The real-life situations audiences see reflected in film frighten them because they are windows into their lives. When these elements are highlighted, the fantasy of film gives way to reality, and the audience is no longer able to escape from real problems; this is tangible horror. Samuel Bayer's *A Nightmare on Elm Street* gives audiences something to think about with regard to their personal lives away from the theater experience.

6

Remake Central

Gus Van Sant's *Psycho*, Rob Zombie's *Halloween*, Marcus Nispel's *Friday the 13th*, and Samuel Bayer's *A Nightmare on Elm Street* represent the heart and soul of the American horror remake trend. *The Ring* and *The Grudge* (2004) definitely helped popularize remakes, but these two films stand for a movement of international cinema which is another full topic for a later discussion. There are a terrific number of other U.S. films that have been remade that deserve attention for their participation in this wave of cinema. These horror films have been plucked from the '30s to the '90s— and even the 21st century—and given the remake treatment to become bornagain trendsetters and genre representations for contemporary American horror.

John Carpenter's *The Thing* and David Cronenberg's *The Fly* (1986) are two powerful remakes that rank with the aforementioned titles, but they rarely receive the same amount of recognition. Although they are formidable remakes of the original films, they do not garner the same amount of attention as the more contemporary movies do because they fall outside of the generational influence of CW network actors and other popularized elements that have made this cinema phenomenon what it is today. There is a formula that constitutes the current horror remake trend, and by looking into key films throughout the years we start to see its development. The highest concentration of original horror films being remade currently resides in the '70s, but there are quite a few before that decade that deserve discussion, and even more in horror's '80s heyday that merit mention.

The 1930s brought us film adaptations of literary classics—*Dracula* (1931) and *Frankenstein* (1931)—along with the natural and scientific oddities found in *Island of Lost Souls* (1932), *King Kong* (1933), and *Bride of Frankenstein* (1935); the 1940s offered suspense and disbelief in *The Wolf Man* (1941), *Cat People* (1942), and *The Beast with Five Fingers* (1946); and the 1950s showcased aliens and monsters in *Invaders from Mars* (1953) and *Gojira* ([*Godzilla*] 1954), respectively. All of these films have been remade (some

77

with different titles), and at least half of them have been recreated more than once so far. Each of these movies exhibit the basics of horror storylines, which include fear of the unknown, body mutation, science gone awry, the undead, supernatural beings, and daunting atmospheres; however, they are not typically considered horror films. They are notable because they contain horrific elements and/or scary moments, but even their remake counterparts are better suited as suspense, thriller, literary adaptation, or hybrid sci-fi horror categorizations.

Before we take a look at the mainstays of horror that have been remade and those that have helped the remake trend develop into its current state, it is important to say a few words about some of the films that are not being included in the list. *Dracula, Frankenstein, King Kong,* and *The Wolf Man* are considered classics of earlier cinema, and each contains themes and motifs that contemporary horror films employ. The popularity of vampire films is currently in a frenzied state with *The Twilight Saga* (2008–2012) and the American remake *Let Me In* (2010). Vampires are immortal, or at least somewhat hard to kill, and their legacy in film has not dwindled since *Nosferatu* appeared in 1922. Over the years, cinema has provided audiences with unending vampire fare: *Dracula* (1979) with Frank Langella, *The Lost Boys* (1987) with the two Coreys, *Dracula* (1992) with Gary Oldman, *Interview with the Vampire* (1994) with Brad Pitt and Tom Cruise, the *Blade* series (1998–2004), and a host of other films. The idea of Dracula and the mystique surrounding vampires pervades all of these films and seems to always exist in a social consciousness for American audiences. Blood, mortality, and theories about what happens after death are constant concerns for all cultures, and this is why vampires continue to remain popular in horror cinema, especially in remakes of films about Dracula or the idea of vampirism the literary and historical associations hold. There is also the focus on romance and undying love that pulls patrons to the theaters.

Moviegoers also love a good freak-of-nature tale or a larger-than-life monster story. *Frankenstein*—as the undead—has seen its narrative mutated into the contemporary zombie film. Zombie features by George Romero, contagion/infection films such as *28 Days Later* (2002), and comedic enterprises like *Shaun of the Dead* (2004) and *Zombieland* (2009) all feature undead beings that are menacing creatures, cannibalistic hunters (some slow-paced and others that run), and some that are simply misunderstood (as was Frankenstein's undead monster). Most contemporary films are a far cry from *Frankenstein* in terms of story structure, but the undead basics are there; however, Romero's *Land of the Dead* (2005) depicts zombies as social outcasts like Frankenstein's monster, so the precedent carries throughout cinema history.

King Kong, on the other hand, epitomizes the creature feature that has dwindled in contemporary horror. This subgenre of horror and sci-fi represents cinematic novelties best known for revealing exotic and dangerous locations to American audiences in the early 20th century, showcasing the ills of science or nuclear fallout, and scaring people away from having household pets. There have been a few movies—the 1998 action-adventure comedy *Godzilla* remake and its upcoming 2004 remake, South Korea's *The Host* (2006), and *Cloverfield* (2008)—working to keep the creature feature alive, but this subgenre offers fewer and fewer productions as the years go by. Peter Jackson's *King Kong* (2005) tells the traditional "beauty and the beast" tale, and it is full of action, adventure, special effects, and old Hollywood filmmaking; however, it is not a horror film. Contemporary creature features are more recognizable in terms of mainstream comedic movies like the *Jurassic Park* series (1993–2001), *Lake Placid* movies (1999–2010), *Snakes on a Plane* (2006), *Slither* (2006), or *Primeval* (2007). But movies of the past—*Them!* (1954), *Frogs* (1972), *Ssssss* (1973), *Squirm* (1976), *Day of the Animals* (1977), *The Bees* (1978), *Cujo* (1983), *Slugs* (1988), *The Nest* (1988), *Strays* (1991)—are ripe for the remake treatment should someone deem any of them worthy to tackle. And some movies, such as *The Day of the Triffids* (1962), have been remade (into a two-part miniseries in 1981 and 2009) without anyone noticing.

Three creature-feature productions start our main discussion of over 20 original films—spanning almost 50 years—that have been remade into contemporary movies. The list hereby provided is organized chronologically by release date for the original film, but it is the contemporary release dates that illustrate the trend in directors, actors, narratives, and more that have formed the remake phenomenon. Original films and their remake counterpart(s) will be discussed to highlight changes in story; notable actors, directors, producers, and writers; social commentary where applicable; and why the remake is important for horror cinema. Box office results are located in the Remake Catalog, 1931–2013. Warning: There are hundreds of spoilers ahead...

First up is Erle C. Kenton's *Island of Lost Souls* (1932), which stems from H.G. Wells's *The Island of Dr. Moreau* (1896). In the novel, British gent Edward Prendrick is shipwrecked, picked up by a passing ship, and taken back to a strange island where the inhabitants—half-human, half-animal science experiments—are controlled by a mad scientist with a god complex by the name of Dr. Moreau. Prendrick learns the creatures have been vivisected to resemble humans and take on like characteristics, such as walking upright, working in a formed community, and rudimentary speech patterns. He makes an effort to adapt to the island way of living, but once the doctor and his assistant (Montgomery) are killed in conflicts with the creatures, Prendrick decides he should find a way to get off the island. However, with no means of travel, there are no viable options to leave. Eventually, luck finds Prendrick when a boat washes ashore. He vacates the island, gets picked up by a passing ship, and decides to remain silent about happenings on the island after the few people he's told his story to immediately deem him crazy. Prendrick makes his way back to English society and spends the rest of his life avoiding people as a result of his encounter with an island lifestyle that proved humans can be as vicious and cruel as wild animals.

Civilization, evolution, and the responsibility of scientific communities are themes at the heart of the narrative. At the time of the novel's publication, England (and locations beyond its borders) undoubtedly existed as a patriarchal society. The questioning of what makes a man so different from an animal was and continues to be a relevant question among various cultures. Moreau's experiments also highlighted real concerns over vivisection and the ability of science to interfere with nature. These concerns continue to be a focus for animal rights groups toward the study of science, product testing, and moviemaking in the 21st century.

The original film adaptation features Charles Laughton as the infamous Dr. Moreau and also Bela Lugosi—one of the most famous creature-feature actors of American cinema. The novel and film are not completely different from each other. Edward Prendrick becomes Edward Parker in the movie, but the biggest change occurs at the conclusion of the film when Parker's fiancée (Ruth) arrives on the island and helps him escape, with the assistance of Montgomery, before a huge fire consumes the land. For the 1930s, this ending restores the institution or idea of marriage, and it offers a happy ending to show that humankind (or "normalcy" in society) overcomes the sometimes overreaching manipulations of science.

Island was remade two times—as *The Island of Dr. Moreau* in 1977, with Don Taylor directing, Burt Lancaster as Dr. Paul Moreau, and Michael York as Andrew Braddock (the Prendrick character); and in 1996, with John Frankenheimer directing, Marlon Brando as Dr. Moreau, and David Thewlis as Edward Douglas (yet another altered name from the original Prendrick protagonist). Frankenheimer's version also starred noted actors Fairuza Balk, Ron Perlman, and Val Kilmer in the role of Montgomery.

Taylor's film strays from the original narrative the most. Braddock (engineering officer for the *Lady Vain*) and shipmate Charlie arrive on the island after enduring a shipwreck. Braddock goes off in search of water, and Charlie is captured and killed, but Montgomery later tells him his mate was buried after suffering from thirst and exposure. Our main character becomes part of the community and later begins to fall for Maria—a woman Moreau altered. When Braddock discovers the horrific truth behind Moreau's experiments, the mad doctor starts an experiment to turn Braddock into more of an animal. Moreau kills Montgomery and later dies at the hands (or paws and claws) of the creatures he created. Braddock and Maria escape from the island, attract the attention of a passing ship, and both begin to regain their humanity as the effects of Moreau's experimentation wears off. Unlike the novel, this version continues the concept of a happy ending, with man and woman restoring the chain of command in human nature.

Frankenheimer's production opens with Edward Douglas, a United Nations negotiator, summarizing in voiceover the events that led to him and two other men being abandoned at sea from a plane crash. The two unnamed survivors fight over a canteen of water, fall out of the small raft, and meet their demise in the mouth of a hungry shark. Douglas is picked up by a passing ship with Montgomery aboard, and the story continues in much the same vein as the other versions; however, this time Moreau has a daughter named Aissa (Balk). The good doctor is eventually killed by his creations, who wish to go back to their animal ways of living, and Montgomery assumes control of the island, which does not last long at all because he is addicted to drugs and incapable of maintaining order. Montgomery says, "I wanna go to dog heaven" to one of the creatures and is in turn shot and killed. We also discover that Aissa is another creation who begins to regress into catlike features and actions, and she is killed by the other creatures. Douglas sails off the island in a makeshift raft; he leaves behind the few Moreau creations that have enough human qualities to keep the island in order for a while. His final voiceover states, "I look about me at my fellow man and I'm reminded of some likeness to the beast people, and I feel as though the animal is surging up in them. And they're neither wholly animal, nor wholly man, but an unstable combination of both ... as unstable as anything Moreau created, and I go in fear." His final words are poignant, and they are delivered as images of news footage flash across the screen—depicting violent riots and fights—but the message was lost in the theaters and to critics.

The film was plagued by early casting changes during pre-production and did not fare well at the box office, but as the most updated version of the story, it showcased the talent of special creature effects workers to make realistic costuming for the human-animal characters. Frankenheimer's film is also important because it helped keep alive the spirit of the mad-scientist movie; such a subgenre of sci-fi horror has faded over the years. H.G. Wells's novel, the original film adaptation, and the proceeding remakes are not horror in the classic sense, but the influence exists in the story and characters. The popularity of the subject matter and narrative are also evident.

In the '70s there was a knockoff *Island* adaptation entitled *The Twilight People* (1973), with Pam Grier as Ayesa, the Panther Woman. In this telling, the protagonist is a diver who is abducted by Dr. Gordon on his island of misfit creations; he later tries to escape the evil scientist's clutches by enlisting the help of his daughter and some of the island's inhabitants. In the '80s, Stuart Gordon's *Re-Animator* (1985) showcased the cult hero Herbert West and his maddening plans to revive the dead, with gruesome results. And in a more contemporary film like Tom Six's *The Human Centipede (First Sequence)* (2009), we meet Dr. Heiter, whose plan is to link three humans together via the gastric system to create a human version of a centipede. These mad doctors and/or scientists remind us how the mind has no limits, but also how some imaginations can go too far. He—as the doctor or scientist is stereotypically male—is a character motif in sci-fi horror that does not pop up as much in 21st movies as he did in pre–90s cinema. This character toys with the boundaries of nature for personal pleasure and demonstrates a god complex to those who would oppose him. He is typically defeated in an effort to return or maintain order to established social and cultural ways of living; however, there is usually a successor to carry on. Wells's classic was published in 1896, but it also has to be noted that Robert Louis Stevenson's *Strange Case of Dr. Jekyll and Mr. Hyde* came out ten years earlier, in 1886. Over 125 years later the concept still rings true in movies. With *The Human Centipede II (Full Sequence)* released in 2011 and *The Human Centipede III (Final Sequence)* set for 2013, maybe this character still has some life left in him yet.

From mad scientist to Mother Nature and folklore creations comes a monster Dr. Moreau could have instrumented—the wolf man. The lore of the wolf man, or werewolf, reaches far back into ancient history; the tales of such a creature extend beyond writing into the oral tradition of storytelling. There are far too many unique origin tales (regional and cultural associations), causes for (curses, animal bites, devil pacts) and remedies to lycanthropy (talisman, exorcism, exercise, silver bullet) to discuss, but the modern and most accepted explanations in current literature, television, and film studies include being bitten by a wolf/werewolf, changing into the animal during full moon phases, and death by silver bullet or other silver instrument. A few exceptions include werewolf curses, genetic family legacies, and controlling the beast transformation by potion or will. Debates also focus on werewolf strength/power as simply strong or superhuman.

Much of this information was taken into consideration and presented in George Waggner's *The Wolf Man*, starring Lon Chaney, Jr., as the title character and, of course, featuring Bela Lugosi. The story is a simple one: Larry Talbot (Chaney) travels home to Wales for his brother's funeral. During his stay he visits a gypsy camp to have his fortune told, but the night ends with a woman being brutally attacked by a wolf—Lugosi as Bela, a fortune teller turned werewolf. Talbot kills Bela, but he is bitten before the fight concludes, and now he must face his own fate when the full moon rises.

When Talbot first arrives home he is immediately confronted by werewolf lore in a shop where he purchases a cane with a wolf's head and pentagram on the handle—and by his own father who recounts a superstitious saying. One of the ladies who accompany him to the camp talks about wolfsbane as they wander through the woods to the fortune teller. The signs are all around Talbot, but he is oblivious to the foreshadowing. After the biting incident, he returns to the camp only to learn from another gypsy that "a werewolf can be killed only with a silver bullet, or a silver knife, or a stick with a silver handle." She offers him a charm to wear over his heart to break the spell, and Talbot accepts it but remains somewhat in denial. He gives the charm to his love interest Gwen (Evelyn Ankers), and when the moon rises he is helpless against the transformation.

Maleva (Maria Ouspenskaya) kneels over the body of Larry Talbot in wolf form (Lon Chaney, Jr.) in *The Wolf Man* (1941). She sympathizes with Talbot, who was bitten by a werewolf, and tries to help him escape a search party led by hunting dogs.

Talbot transforms into the wolf a couple of times, deaths are involved, and in the end he is slain by his own cane at the hands of his father in the woods he roamed. In the end, the story is not much about romance or estranged family members or even the fear of things that go bump in the night. *The Wolf Man* explores lycanthropy to present ideas on the subject matter and let the audience decide if the content is believable or not. It also emphasizes the ways in which exotic cultures and communities exist and purport belief systems outside of mainstream society—American or international. The film, although terrifying for audiences of the '40s, is usually designated as a classic drama with some horrific elements. It explores the dark side of humankind but falls short of modern horror classification.

Werewolf films hold almost the same amount of popularity as vampire movies, and contemporary productions always find ways to bring the two together and double the pleasure at the movies—*Underworld* (2003), *The Twilight Saga*, *True Blood*, and *Vampire Diaries* are just a few film and television examples. *The Wolf Man* influenced a slew of movies, which include John Landis's *An American Werewolf in London* (1981) and Mike Nichols's *Wolf* (1994), with Jack Nicholson and Michelle Pfeiffer, which followed a similar story of wolf attack, transformation, and remedy. *The Wolf Man* was remade in 2010 by Joe Johnston, with Benicio Del Toro as Lawrence Talbot and Anthony Hopkins as his father, Sir John Talbot. The remake narrative is similar to the original film, with notable—but not overhauling—changes.

We learn that Talbot's father sent him to an asylum when he was younger because he witnessed his mother's death; he remained estranged from the family until his return years later to help locate his missing brother, whose dead body is found mangled. In this version, Gwen (Emily Blunt) was the fiancée of Talbot's brother, and it was she who contacted him to come home. Talbot goes to the gypsies to inquire about his brother, who left behind a charm he purchased at the camp. The community is attacked by a werewolf, and when Talbot tries to help a young boy, he is bitten by the creature. Like the original, Talbot finds out that most people know about werewolf lore and the town's history of lycanthropy; he also learns a dark secret—his father is a werewolf and killed his mother when he was younger. Talbot's father turns him over to the authorities; he is taken to the same asylum from his childhood. There Dr. Hoenneger (Anthony Sher) conducts experiments on him and brings him before a room full of others to observe his "mental illness"; and Talbot transforms, kills, and escapes into the night.

The film concludes with a fight between Talbot and his father—both in werewolf form—who falls victim to his son's strength and cunning. Unlike the original, the son outlives the father, but Gwen kills him with a silver bullet after he chases her in the woods and battles his own inner demons.

The original *Wolf Man* preserves patriarchy when the father kills the son, but its contemporary remake shows a more modern sensibility when Gwen outlives both men. In a sense, the remake is more romanticized because Gwen and Talbot fall for each other, and she struggles/hesitates to kill him. However, both versions secure a closed narrative by destroying the evil werewolf presence.

The wolf man (or werewolf), like the mad scientist, is a stock character for sci-fi horror films. Some productions focus more on the transformation itself, others concentrate on romance, and more rely on gore and the kill factor to attract audiences. Aside from the character's sporadic popularity in film—like its vampire counterpart—the werewolf influence can be seen in horror movies such as Joe Dante's *The Howling* (1981), *Silver Bullet* (1985), and *Ginger Snaps* (2000); "big bad wolf" dramas like *Freeway* (1996), with Reese Witherspoon and Kiefer Sutherland, *Hard Candy* (2005), with Ellen Page and Patrick Wilson, and *Red Riding Hood* (2011), with Amanda Seyfriend and Gary Oldman; and music videos like Michael Jackson's "Thriller" (1983). And the legacy lives on in MTV's *Teen Wolf* (2011), which serializes the 1985 Michael J. Fox film of the same name, and possibly revives memories of Michael Landon in *I Was a Teenage Werewolf* (1957). The werewolf character and its popularity are not fading anytime soon. It will remain in the cinema spotlight just as long or longer as its vampire complement. Even *Harry Potter and the Order of the Phoenix* (2007) has a werewolf, named Remus Lupin, who is coincidentally portrayed by David Thewlis from *The Island of Dr. Moreau*, which featured half-human/half-wolf creatures. The werewolf's bite lingers on in all genres of cinema and pop culture.

But sometimes the monster from these movies is not a vampire, werewolf, or mad-scientist creation; sometimes the thing we fear is just that—an unknown, alien thing, or *The Thing from Another World* (1951). Christian Nyby's film tells the story of the discovery of a plant-based alien being in Alaska with the power to consume all life on Earth. The humanoid being is found frozen in the snow by a team of military personnel and scientists who uncover (and inadvertently destroy) its space craft. It is accidentally thawed at base camp and beings to wreak havoc; it ingests blood from its victims for survival. Eventually, the creature is lured into a trap where it is electrocuted and reduced to embers. The film concludes with the survivors sending a message that humans should be on the lookout for what may come from outer space. Although it ends with an ominous warning, *The Thing from Another World* displays the power and intelligence of humankind to conquer an alien threat.

At the heart of the story are true-life societal fears concerning nuclear weapons and xenophobia from the fallout of World War II, but as a work of cinema the film remains a classic and surpassed its sci-fi complement (*The Day the Earth Stood Still*, which was remade in 2008 with Keanu Reeves, Jennifer Connelly, Kathy Bates, and Jaden Smith) at the box office the same year. As a competent film, box-office contender, and production with a good storyline, it was only natural it would be remade. Just over 30 years later John Carpenter released his revamp entitled *The Thing*.

Kurt Russell stars in the 1982 remake as R. J. MacReady, and the monster he gets to confront is nothing like the vegetable-being from the '50s classic. The storyline remains close to the original film, but stays even closer to the 1938 novella—"Who Goes There?" by John W. Campbell, Jr.—that inspired the '50s movie.

An Alaskan sled dog is hunted by a team of Norwegians in a helicopter, and the chase leads to an American research camp. The Norwegian team dies via explosion and gunfire as the Americans defend themselves from the odd encounter. And the dog is taken in as a stray. What the Americans do not know is that the stray dog is the alien being imitating a dog. The madness begins shortly after when the alien attempts to consume the other dogs it has been placed with in a kennel. As the team realizes there is an alien threat in camp—one that can assume the physicality of any living being it encounters—paranoia takes over and fear is heightened. Dr. Blair (Wilford Brimley) attempts to secure the threat by destroying all means of transportation and communication, but his actions only get him labeled as unstable and forcibly separated from the rest of the group. Everyone is convinced, however, that the creature must be destroyed and not allowed to spread beyond the camp. This proves difficult because the alien can transform itself into other fully-formed beings even after being split up into separate parts.

In an effort to recognize who is and who may not be human, the men devise a blood test to alleviate the atmosphere of suspicion. This is certainly one of the most memorable scenes in *The Thing*. The men are tired and scared, and trust is easily tossed aside if one person seems the tiniest bit out of sorts. After one character suffers a fatal heart attack (defibrillation never looked so painful) and another is shot by MacReady in self-defense, the men now face their greatest fear: the unknown. MacReady holds the men in mock-hostage in order to perform the blood test without everyone attacking him or each other. Each sample taken is introduced to a heated piece of wire to check for an adverse reaction that would prove alien contamination. As each sample is tested, the tension builds until the imitation-being is revealed and killed, with human loss as well.

One by one the men are picked off until MacReady faces the remaining beast alone ... and wins. The camp is completely destroyed, and MacReady seems to be the only survivor—until another team member, Childs (Keith

David), emerges from the destruction. Neither character is able to determine if the other is human or alien. There is no way to contact anyone outside the camp, and any means of transportation remains impossible. In the end, MacReady and Childs decide to have a drink among the ruins as the freezing weather will more than likely claim their lives. Unlike the 1951 film and its black-and-white all or nothing approach, Carpenter's remake concludes with uncertainty; the audience does not know if the creature has been completely destroyed, if the characters will live to tell their tales of horror, or if the alien will eventually come into contact with outside civilization and begin a reign of terror on Earth. Reflecting the '80s sensibility of horror films, we are left hopeless and helpless against the unknown.

Carpenter's film is considered a horror classic, and often a cult classic because of its worldwide recognition, although it did not do well at the box office. It is also extremely popular for its use of Rob Bottin's special creature effects that continue to stand the test of time among contemporary films with computer graphic enhancements. It is an important film in the remake annals of horror because it took an early sci-fi horror movie and made it pure horror. Unlike *The Island of Dr. Moreau* or *The Wolfman*, *The Thing* took a large step forward into horror with its use of blood, gore, and killings. *Moreau* and *Wolfman* have scary moments, but they are thrillers and dramas in comparison. *The Thing*, like *Psycho*, showed audiences that horror can have a recognizable face, and this is always a scary message to take away from the darkened theater and bring back into the comfort of the home.

The Thing from Another World represents one of only three films in this listing to be remade in the '80s—all other movies were recreated in the '90s (a few) or in the most-popular 21st century offerings. A prequel to *The Thing* was released in October 2011. It was helmed by first-time director Matthijs van Heijningen, Jr., and chronicles the events of a Norwegian science team encountering an alien life form. The movie serves as a true prequel to Carpenter's film, so we already know that the ending is the beginning of the 1982 production.

But focus now turns away from alien and human life to concentrate on another form of imitation found in Michael Curtiz's *Mystery of the Wax Museum* (1933). The film stars Fay Wray only months before her *King Kong* fame was established the same year. It is also a little-known movie in comparison to its remake—*House of Wax* (1953), which was directed by André de Toth and starred Vincent Price, with Charles Bronson.

Mystery tells the story of two business partners (Ivan Igor the sculptor and Joe Worth) who operate a wax museum. Worth attempts to burn down the building to collect insurance money when business bottoms out, but Igor refuses to go along with the plan. Worth and Igor get into a fight after the building is set ablaze, and Igor is left for dead among the flames. He survives and opens a new wax museum over a decade later. Igor remains badly burned and injured from the fire Worth constructed. In a maniacal twist of terror, Igor murders people and uses their dead bodies to create wax museum attractions. He makes a wax mask for himself and even avenges his own past by killing Worth. The women of the film—Charlotte (Wray) and Florence (Glenda Farrell)—uncover the truth that leads to Igor being shot and ironically consumed by his own wax. It was Worth's early actions that turned Igor into a corrupt man, but in the end they both meet their fate and all is made right in the world.

The 1953 version features the same plot; if anything, the remake attempts more fright than mystery, and one of the female characters dies. Vincent Price stars as Professor Henry Jarrod; he is the sculptor for the museum who turns into our madman killer and human body preservationist. In tribute to the 1933 film, Charles Bronson's character (Jarrod's assistant) is named Igor. Although this version is considered to be more horror than *Mystery*, the different perspectives of time periods play a major role. Audiences in the '30s found things to be frightening that audiences in the '50s found to be comical. And that is the way horror functions throughout history; there is always a need to heighten what was made previously to keep up with contemporary social mores and sentiments about cinema. The 1953 production is considered a thriller and a suspenseful movie in the 21st century, but its 2005 remake is clearly more of a horror film for our time.

Jaume Collet-Serra directed a youthful cast, which includes Elisha Cuthbert, Jared Padelecki, Chad Michael Murray, and Paris Hilton. Each of these young faces were previously known for being characters on the popular television dramas *24* (FOX 2001–2010), *Gilmore Girls*, *One Tree Hill*, and the reality show *The Simple Life* (FOX 2003–2007), respectively. Coincidentally, Murray also appeared on *Gilmore Girls* with Padalecki, and Hilton guest starred on *Supernatural* with Padalecki as well. Although this is not the first remake to sport a cast of up-and-coming stars from MTV, UPN, the WB, or the current CW networks, it is a perfect model. These actors carry a fan-base of television viewers that can be transported into the theaters for box-office revenue. Some of them have also worked together previously on television series, and fans become eager to see how the actors will take to their new roles in a feature film. The great remake trend's use of young actors did not start in 2005—Marcus Nispel's *The Texas Chainsaw Massacre* gave this part of the movement a kick in 2003—but this is the year the movement started to pick up steam by establishing such an element.

The actors worked with a script much different from the '30s and '50s versions. This rendition explores the relationship between two twin brothers—Bo and Vincent (both played by Brian Van Holt)—who are raised in a volatile household and grow up to rule over their small town, which they populate with human remains encased in wax bodies set up to look like the town is still a viable place to live. As with most teeny-bopper or young–Hollywood ensemble cast horror films, the group heads out on a roadtrip to a football game (there is usually a trip involved, to a concert or other major event). The trip is long, so the group takes a break to camp at night, and the next day one of the cars does not start. A local named Lester (Damon Herriman) offers to take Carly (Cuthbert) and her boyfriend Wade (Padalecki) into the small town of Ambrose to look for a car part while the others continue on the road to try to make it to the football game on time. And this is when the fun ends.

In true horror fashion, the entire group of friends is killed off throughout the film by Vincent and Bo—including a memorable death for Paris Hilton—minus Carly and her twin brother Nick (Murray). The brother-and-sister team survives to overcome the murderous brothers; the disfigured brother dies in a literal melting house of wax, akin to the sculptor character of the previous films dying within the materials used to create his house of horrors. The movie is completely different from its predecessors in narrative, and also character development for horror films in general.

Instead of a murder-mystery, this *House of Wax* is a horror film about family problems, production value, and breaking contemporary horror stereotypes. Bo and Vincent are disturbed brothers who murder people, and Carly and Nick do not have the best relationship, but both team up to work together in order to survive; however, good wins over bad in this scenario. The movie is shot extremely well, and part of the attention to detail in production value is what makes audiences want to see contemporary horror films. When the wax house begins to melt, it is a grand sight to see. Audiences want to be scared, but they also want to enjoy what they are seeing—even if it is Paris Hilton being spiked through the head with a metal rod. Moreover, *House* does not feature a final girl character. Carly and Nick break that stereotype to become a team that wards off the bad guys. And these two characters get roughed up in the process; Carly even has part of her finger cut off by one of the crazed brothers. Victor Salva's *Jeepers Creepers* (2001) showed horror audiences that brother-and-sister teams can be quite effective and a new model for horror survival when the final-girl motif has been used too many times. But the ending of *House of Wax* returns the audience to a horror mainstay when Carly sees Lester through the ambulance window. We learn that Lester is the third brother to the now-dead twins, and that means the horror behind the wax and the family legacy will continue long past the ending credits.

Carly (Elisha Cuthbert) barely escapes the clutches of Vincent (Brian Van Holt) as the *House of Wax* (2005) begins to melt from a raging fire.

This type of open ending in horror is not a new development, but for many of the remakes it makes for a stark comparison to the original films that typically functioned on a closed narrative to leave the audience feeling safe at the end of the movie. Many of the "safe" endings to classic sci-fi and emerging horror films were tacked on by the production studios that feared backlash from audiences, critics, and, of course, box-office earnings. The next film on the list—Don Siegel's *Invasion of the Body Snatchers* (1956)—is no different. Siegel's classic has been remade or reworked three times over the past 55 years, and there is plenty of time for more recreations to emerge.

Based on Jack Finney's "The Body Snatchers," the film follows Dr. Miles Binnell's journey into terror. His patients come to him with complaints that the people they love are no longer the same people; they look the same but are somehow cloned replicas of husbands, wives, and so forth. As the cases build, Binnell discovers people are being replaced by emotionless duplicates born out of large plant pods. He enlists the company of Becky Driscoll (Dana Wynter), and they both do their best to escape town and avoid being turned into pod people. But Driscoll tires from the continued running and lack of sleep. Binnell kisses her as she succumbs to slumber; when her eyes reopen, she is no longer the woman he formerly loved. Binnell takes to a

California highway, shouting the famous lines, "They're here already! You're next! You're next! You're next!" Many critics refer to this scene as an early cinematic technique for breaking the fourth wall—a direct address to the audience that shifts narrative from fiction to cinematic reality—but either way, Binnell's words echo for the story and as social commentary (to be discussed later). The film could have ended with Binnell on the highway; the passersby call him crazy and drunk as they continue down the road in their cars. The tidy ending of the movie, however, shows Binnell talking to the police, who do not believe his story. An official alert that plant pods have been discovered in a truck forces the police to take action, and the film ends with hope that the invading force can be stopped.

Alien invasion and hope are not often complementary words when it comes to films like this one, but before its remakes are discussed, it is important to note that the original *Invasion* is referenced quite a bit in television and film. *Big Business* (1988) is one example that used the film to get a laugh from its audience. Upon seeing her separated-from-birth twin for the first time, Sadie Ratliff (Bette Midler) screams, "It's pod people! I saw that movie!" Her twin, Sadie Shelton, responds, "I was at the premiere." And other post-classic sci-fi/horror films have had the same premise as *Invasion*—*Invaders from Mars* (1986), *The Puppet Masters* (1994), and *The Faculty* (1998) to name a few. The extension of the story into other films—especially those in other genres, like comedy—displays the popularity and staying power of the subject matter and the original movie.

There are few things in life we can control, but a vast majority of people appreciate the ability to control the body and mind. When these innate qualities are taken away from us, fear reaches a new horrifying level. Bodies under the control and manipulation of an outside force—alien (fictionalized) or government (reality)—represents one of our darkest thoughts, which we would rather not contemplate. This is another example of cinema being heavily influenced by the environment in which it was created. *Invasion* came about during continued national concern over residual emotions from the McCarthy era (1940s–1950s), in which government probes into personal lives was a very real situation. People were labeled communists, and the U.S. was a nation divided. These accusations distressed American citizens and made trust a rare commodity. *Invasion* presents our social climate of that time symbolically; alien vs. human is simply code for what the country was going through in those uncertain times. Binnell's words were a warning for Americans to keep an eye out for government interference into their personal lives, the act of being labeled a communist, and a need to distance themselves from others in such a strange political time.

The remakes do not carry the same social commentary because they were created during different decades of American history; however, the storylines typically frame the narrative around a character or two trying to convince others of the alien invasion before it is too late. In 1978, Philip Kaufman directed Donald Sutherland, Leonard Nimoy, Jeff Goldblum, Brooke Adams, and Veronica Cartwright in what many people consider to be a better film than the original, or at least a movie that stands on its own as a classic. Matthew Bennell (Sutherland) is now a San Francisco health inspector, and Elizabeth Driscoll (Adams) is his colleague—their names have changed slightly. The two discover the alien invasion plot but learn along the way that they can blend in among the pod people by simply not showing emotion. If they are discovered, the pod people identify humans by pointing and screaming at them. This tactic wears thin when Driscoll—in one of the film's memorable scenes—sees a dog with a human face and reacts to the strange creature.

The couple's fate is almost the same as the original characters, but with a twist. Driscoll falls asleep and becomes a pod person; Bennell escapes and wanders the streets alone. He runs into Nancy Bellicec (Cartwright), but before the two have time to talk, Bennell points at her and screams. Nancy's face fills with tears and she sobs hysterically. There is no hope in this ending; the humans lose. Once the protagonist of a story falls victim to the impending doom, the audience has nowhere safe to hide. And that sentiment could almost be the tagline for Abel Ferrara's *Body Snatchers* (1993), in which Carol Malone (Meg Tilly) whispers, "Where you gonna go? Where you gonna run? Where you gonna hide? Nowhere, 'cause there's no one like you left." Another notable featured actor is Forest Whitaker, who takes on the role of Major Collins.

Unlike the original film and first remake, *Body Snatchers* takes place at a military base in Alabama—far from the California coast line. The military angle is common for original sequels and remakes in sci-fi and horror. It typically offers more action on the screen and keeps the audience jumping, as seen in *Aliens*, *The Lost World: Jurassic Park* (1997), *The Hills Have Eyes 2* (2007), *28 Weeks Later* (2007), and *AVPR: Alien vs. Predator—Requiem* (2007). *Predator* (1987) worked in reverse by starting with the military and taking a turn toward a more localized narrative about one police officer in *Predator 2* (1990). The two characters we follow till the end of *Body* are Marti Malone (Gabrielle Anwar) and her stepbrother Andy Malone (Reilly Murphy). They face the growing threat of pod people, but only Marti survives via rescue by her love interest, Tim Young (Billy Wirth). The survivors destroy the military base and helicopter-bomb all trucks carrying pods to stop the invasion from spreading beyond the base. When they fly to another base, however, the movie ends with a military officer waving them in to land.

Cameras remain on the military man as Carol's earlier creepy questions are played in voiceover but slowed to sound inhuman and even more ominous. Although the previous military base and pods were destroyed, the audience cannot say for sure that the threat has been eliminated. This remake is not discussed much in sci-fi or horror circles, but it is almost always considered a competent presentation of the invasion story.

The '70s version depicted a defeated human race, the '90s version offered uncertainty, but the 21st century reissue revitalized the hope that the original film tried to impart to moviegoers. Oliver Hirschbiegel's *The Invasion* (2007) stars Nicole Kidman and Daniel Craig in the main roles as doctors Carol Bennell and Ben Driscoll, respectively. Leads and genders have been switched from the original film, as Kidman is the chief protagonist and Craig plays her complement. The meat of the film remains the same—Bennell and Driscoll discover the alien invasion and try to stop it; however, the opening action and closing message of the film are vastly different from the previous movies.

A space shuttle crashes with the alien plant life hitchhiking on its surface. Pieces of the shuttle are found and collected as keepsakes and moneymakers by random people; in turn, they become infected, emotionless remnants of their former selves. Tucker (Jeremy Northan), an infected worker for the CDC and Bennell's ex-husband, decides to use the organization as a way to spread the takeover by inoculating people for a fake flu virus when they are simply being turned into pod people instead. This version, however, does not contain any actual pods; victims fall asleep, we see their cells change via special effects during the REM stage of slumber, and they wake up to peel off some old skin before they embrace their new way of living. It is an interesting update for the story, because the 21st century is never without concern over vaccinations and new strains of viruses, like the H1N1/swine flu panic that spread across the nation in 2009. The shuttle crash also references the real-life tragedy of the *Columbia* disaster in 2003, in which the space shuttle broke apart upon atmospheric re-entry.

After the life forms begin to take over, Bennell and Driscoll formulate a way to survive the situation, with the help of a few others, including Dr. Stephen Galeano (Jeffrey Wright). Bennell also has a son named Oliver (Jackson Bond) she wants to rescue from Tucker before he is converted; however, we find out later that Oliver is immune to the change due to a medical condition from his childhood. After much subterfuge, running around the city, and narrow escapes (Bennell barely makes it out of a subway train while the aliens are spitting spores onto terrified humans), Bennell rescues her son, but Driscoll has already been converted. In the end, scientists/medical doctors are able to start manufacturing a cure that reverses the transformation and leaves the infected individual with hardly any memory of the incident.

We see Bennell and Driscoll a year or so later hanging out in the kitchen like nothing ever happened. Driscoll reads the newspaper, and his left hand sports a wedding band, which tells the viewer that he and Bennell developed a relationship that turned into marriage. Oliver appears ready for school; he is safe, too. Everything is as it should be, but Bennell is not completely happy. She thinks about the life the aliens wanted to offer—no emotion, no fighting, no killing, no wars ... no conflict—as a memory reminds her that an alien invasion was just one problem of many in the world.

At a dinner with friends early in the film, Bennell is introduced to Yorish, a Russian ambassador. His words offer poignancy to the movie and the previous productions. Yorish says, "I say that civilization is an illusion, a game of pretend. What is real is the fact that we are still animals, driven by primal instincts." Bennell counters, but Yorish continues, saying, "Perhaps being a Russian in this country is a kind of pathology.... Can you give me a pill? To make me see the world the way you Americans see the world. Can a pill help me understand Iraq, or Dafur, or even New Orleans?" His final argument is what Bennell thinks about at the end of the film. She hears Yorish say, "All I am saying is that civilization crumbles whenever we need it most. In the right situation, we are all capable of the most terrible crimes. To imagine a world where this was not so, where every crisis did not result in new atrocities, where every newspaper is not full of war and violence. Well, this is to imagine a world where human beings cease to be human." Bennell closes her eyes and the film ends.

The ambassador speaks about real concerns in contemporary America that offer insight into the human condition. His conversation with Bennell is the heart of the movie and the lasting impression that all the films in this set attempt to present to audiences. Dr. Galeano is also shown talking to the press at the end of the movie. When asked if the invasion was completely over, he simply states, "For better or worse, we're human again." The overall message is that we have a long way to go in our continued drive to embody the civilization we would like to consider ourselves as representing.

Our struggles do not end anytime soon, and neither do the remakes for the '80s. The last two films being discussed that were remade in the '80s were both originally created in 1958—*The Fly* and *The Blob*. Both movies are significant contributions to the ongoing split between sci-fi and horror films; however, their remakes pull away from the sci-fi category and make dedicated efforts to be recognized as true horror movies.

The Fly is an interesting critter because the protagonist—Andre Delambre (David Hedison)—is dead when the film begins. His body (arm and head) is discovered crushed by a hydraulic machine in his workroom. Helene (Patricia Owens), the wife, tells her story in flashback to Francois (Vincent

Price), Delambre's brother, in order to explain how situations led to his demise. We learn that Delambre was a scientist working on groundbreaking experiments to transport matter from one place to another—a teleportation device. Like any good or mad scientist in a '50s film, he tests the machine on himself, but a fly gets locked in the compartment with him, thereby fusing their genetic material. The accident results in him having the head and arm of a fly; the fly receives his human head and arm. If he is to survive, the fly must be captured to reverse the process. But Delambre's human mind starts to fade, and the fly instinct begins to take over. Before he loses all of his humanity, he destroys his research and has Helene help him get rid of his body as evidence by crushing him in the hydraulic press.

Helene is labeled a murderer and a madwoman, but before she is taken away from the house Francois and the police inspector discover a tiny fly with Delambre's head and arm trapped in a spider web. The aged creature cries out the famous words, "Help me! Help me!" in desperate repetition as a large spider advances, but the two onlookers simply stare in bewilderment. As the spider pounces, the inspector crushes the web and all its contents with a rock. The two men cannot believe what they have witnessed, and they are convinced no one else will believe them either, so they decide to keep the incident a secret. Helene is not taken in for murder or sent away for her mental health; everyone simply chooses to ignore what happened and move on with their lives.

The Fly is like *Island of Lost Souls* in its message about science and the boundaries that are sometimes crossed in the name of research and experimentation. Advances in medicine and science are always great, but many people often wonder at what price are the developments achieved. Delambre is not a mad scientist stereotype, but his experimentation falls into the category. The experiments continued in *Return of the Fly* (1959) and *Curse of the Fly* (1965), which focus on the Delambre family's need to conduct further experimentation—to the point of creating insane, disfigured people through scientific trial and error. Vincent Price reprises his role as Francois in *Return*, which could easily be called *Son of the Fly* because the story revolves around Philippe's desire to finish his father's work. *Curse* veers from the original and first sequel to become more of a mad scientist movie, with the main character simply having the last name Delambre. These sequels remain somewhat obscure in comparison to the original film, but the legacy and the idea of madness are explored further in the remake.

David Cronenberg recreated *The Fly* in 1986 with Jeff Goldblum as scientist Seth Brundle and Geena Davis as journalist Veronica Quaife. Brundle and Quaife initially meet to discuss his groundbreaking research and experiments with teleportation, but they form a romantic connection in the process. Brundle uses live baboons in his experiments, and his teleportation devices seem to work perfectly (after a gruesome early trial that turns one of the animals inside-out). Eventually, Brundle teleports himself in a test but is unaware that a fly found its way into the pod with him. The fly is absorbed, and their genetic material fuses together (unlike the separate creations in the original film). Brundle begins to exhibit fly-like habits; he is stronger, faster, and more virile, but the good side effects are soon joined by a need to vomit on food to liquefy it for digestion, the loss of body parts (hair, ear, teeth, fingernails), and deterioration of the flesh. He becomes addicted to the fascination of how his body is mutating or evolving.

Brundle's humanity starts to fade, which turns him into a volatile creature. He learns that Quaife is pregnant with his child and kidnaps her in an effort to prevent her getting an abortion. In his last moment of madness, Brundle decides to use his pods to fuse himself with Qauife and the unborn child so they can be transformed into a perfect, singular being. He traps her in one pod, climbs into another, and plans for the fusion to emerge from a third pod, but Quaife's ex-boyfriend foils the plan, which allows her to escape and causes Brundle to break through the pod while the process activates. His insect body becomes fused with parts of the pod, and in a move of desperation he crawls to Quaife so she can end his existence with a shotgun blast to the head. The mad scientist dies, but Quaife remains pregnant at the end of the film; the audience is left to wonder if the child will be born human, genetically altered, or if the interrupted abortion plan will be revisited. Again, it is an '80s ending of uncertainty, but for all practical purposes it would seem that the menacing presence has been destroyed. Goldblum was celebrated for his performance, and the film won awards for its special crea-

Seth Brundle (Jeff Goldblum) looks at his mutated form in the mirror in *The Fly* (1986). His transformation into a human-sized fly is almost complete after a teleportation experiment goes awry.

ture effects. It remains a modern horror classic and one of Cronenberg's most successful feature films; the director also made an onscreen cameo in the production as a gynecologist.

Many have said *The Fly* is about the HIV/AIDS epidemic, but *Aliens* is really the film that historicizes that moment in history, with its focus on how deadly blood can be and the fear of contamination, infection, or body invasion. Cronenberg's films always focus on the body—the wonder and fear of it. Although his productions typically feature lots of blood, *The Fly* concentrated on the body in motion via sexual activity, eating, digestion, ambulatory movement, alcohol, violence, and the sometimes scary process of aging and death. Most people experience all of these rather basic actions and functions during their lifetime, but Cronenberg uses film to examine the processes closer. He shows how scrutinizing something like digestion can simultaneously fascinate and completely gross us out. His film was released during the national recognition of HIV/AIDS as a serious health threat, but all of his movies have a story to tell about the body, and the good and bad influences upon it, including disease.

Chris Walas, who was awarded an Oscar for his makeup work on *The Fly*, directed a sequel to Cronenberg's movie three years later. *The Fly II* featured Eric Stoltz as Martin Brundle, the son of Seth Brundle and Quaife, who survives a birth that inadvertently kills his mother in the process. The story is somewhat of a retread of the romantic relationship that was formed in the 1986 movie; Brundle falls for Beth (Daphne Zuniga), and she discovers his monstrous genetic secret. It is also a movie that exploits the idea of an evil corporation trying to use Brundle for less-than-ethical scientific experiments, but the ending is akin to *Return of the Fly*, in which the son uses the telepods to rid himself of the mutated genes in order to live as a normal human. Brundle succeeds by absorbing genetic material from the man who holds him captive in the corporation's facilities, and the company carries on business as usual by conducting experiments on his previous captor, who is transformed into a genetic monster during the teleportation process. The sequel was a mild box-office success, but critics and fans have always favored the Cronenberg production in comparisons. In the current horror market, most horror fans are unaware the sequel was even made.

The hideous nature of man being combined with insect interested and scared moviegoers into seeing the original *Fly* and its remake. They were equally intrigued to see a movie about a threatening creature that was so vicious and seemingly unstoppable it could only be called *The Blob*. Irvin S. Yeaworth, Jr., directed this '50s creature feature. The amorphous being makes its way to Earth on a meteor that crashes in small-town Pennsylvania, where it latches onto a townie's arm after he pokes it with a stick out of curiosity.

Two local teens—Steve Andrews (Steve McQueen) and Jane Martin (Aneta Corsaut)—take the man to the hospital to receive medical attention, but the creature grows bigger by devouring the man, then consuming the doctor and his nurse for dessert. Andrews and Martin inform the police, who consider their story to be ludicrous, but before long the town comes to face the ever-growing creature with no solution in sight. Through trial, error, accident, and a memorable sequence of the blob attacking people in the local movie theater, the characters discover that the blob cannot tolerate cold temperatures. They freeze the blob with fire extinguishers, and the military comes in to ship it to the Arctic for safe keeping, since there seems no true way to destroy it for good. As the movie closes, "The End" flashes on the screen, but the title card turns into a question mark, which lets the audience know that what they just witnessed could happen again. And, 30 years later, it does.

Chuck Russell directed the remake in 1988, with Frank Darabont as screenwriter. The two local teenagers are played by Kevin Dillon (Brian) and Shawnee Smith (Meg) of the *Saw* franchise, and the narrative functions the same as in the original film, with a few changes. California is the chosen location for the story instead of Pennsylvania, and we learn that the creature is a tactical military experiment created to fight enemy forces that would threaten U.S. soil. As usual in cinematic situations like this, the military loses control over its own creation, and the consequences are deadly. The blob seems deadlier, quicker, and more violent in the remake, as it lashes out like a whip to smash and consume its victims; however, the townspeople take the lead and "destroy" the blob by freezing it with liquid nitrogen. Its remains are carried off to a large ice house in town. Unlike the ending of the original film, the remake makes it clear that the blob shall rise again. The last scene shows a countryside tent-revival hosted by the Reverend Meeker (Del Close), who was badly burned during the blob's reign of terror. He holds a glass container with a remnant of the blob inside like a captured pet, and that lasting image confirms that the creature will not be imprisoned forever.

Ghosts, on the other hand, like to break the rules of mortality and challenge the notion of living forever. Legendary director William Castle's *House on Haunted Hill* (1959) illustrates the destructive and terrifying force of the hereafter, and also the inhumanity of mankind. It is the last film of the '50s for our discussion, and the first that leaves behind science fiction for a strict classification of horror. Vincent Price makes his third and last appearance on the list as Frederick Loren; he is a millionaire married to his fourth wife, Annabelle (Carol Ohmart), and the two of them are throwing a theme party in which five guests have been invited to stay overnight at a notorious haunted

Scott (Ricky Paull Goldin) attempts to make a move on his date but is unpleasantly surprised when *The Blob* (1988) takes over her body.

house. Each guest who manages to live through the night will receive $10,000 the next morning as survival payment. All the invited guests are practically strangers to the husband-and-wife team—and each other—but they are all in dire need of the money for one reason or another.

The guests arrive at the house in funeral procession cars; they are also provided with guns to protect themselves during the night. But Wallace Pritchard (Elisha Cook)—the homeowner—reminds everyone that guns are useless against entities of the spirit world. The night is further complicated because Frederick and Annabelle despise each other; she and Dr. David Trent (Alan Marshal) conspire together to scare one of the other guests (Nora Manning, played by Carolyn Craig) into killing Frederick out of fear. Meanwhile, Pritchard tries his best to convince everyone that the house is truly haunted and that they have reason to fear for their lives. Half the cast of characters disappear into their rooms to protect themselves against any possible dangers, which turns the narrative into a more focused cat-and-mouse game of scares, faked deaths, and noises that go bump in the night. The $10,000 reward becomes a lost plot point. In the end, Frederick lives, while his wife and co-conspirator meet their ends in a vat of acid. Pritchard tells everyone that the house has claimed two more lives, converted them into trapped ghosts, and that they will certainly try to get him. He then turns to the audience and says, "And then they'll come for you." We hear a disembodied laugh and a chain rattling as the door closes to the house and the film ends.

House features quite a few chilling and startling moments. One of the most frightening occurs when Nora encounters the blind housekeeper, who appears out of nowhere and seems to float out of the room. But there are also moments of schlock or B-movie elements, such as the walking skeleton toward the end; it is not difficult to tell that the skeleton is plastic and being controlled by string pulleys. Castle was known for creating marketing gimmicks, and he utilized the skeleton scene to frighten audiences by having a glow-in-the-dark skeleton hover above the audience in some theaters during key moments. The gimmick ("Emergo"), like most, was not always effective, but it made the viewing experience unique. *House* is also innovative in its opening when the floating head of Pritchard comes onto the screen to introduce himself and prepare the audience for the terrors they are about to behold.

Annabelle (Carol Ohmart) screams at the sight of what she believes to be her husband's remains coming back to haunt her in *House on Haunted Hill* (1959). The movie questions what is real and what is fabricated to scare the invited houseguests.

Frederick's head appears next and offers members of the audience $10,000 if they spend 12 hours in the house and survive. Like the ending, these two characters break the fiction narrative to talk directly to the audience. This convention has the power to pull people deeper into the story or make them realize the fictitious setup even more. The ominous nature of Pritchard and Frederick's audience addresses, however, keep the mood daunting and eerie from the beginning to the end of the production.

William Castle's name lives on in the Dark Castle movie production company, and his film was updated in 1999 by William Malone. The remake features a cast of well-known actors, including Geoffrey Rush and Famke Janssen as Stephen and Evelyn Price—our married couple hosting the overnight stay worth $1 million per person who survives one whole night in the Vannacutt Psychiatric Institute for the Criminally Insane. The location represents a facility in which patients were tortured by medical procedures before eventually escaping, murdering the staff, and burning down the building. Jeffrey Combs plays Dr. Richard Vannacutt, the facility's lead doctor, in flashbacks throughout the film.

Stephen and Evelyn despise each other, as did the couple in the original film. Their invited guests include Watson Pritchett (Chris Kattan), Sara Wolfe (Ali Larter), Eddie Baker (Taye Diggs), Melissa Marr (Bridgette Wilson), and Dr. Donald Blackburn (Peter Gallagher); however, the guest list was altered by ghostly entities that wanted these specific people to come because they are all related to the now-dead staff that ran the facility back in the 1920s. In this respect, the remake does not hint at ghosts like the original; the presence manifests throughout the film as dark matter made up of the souls it has consumed over the years. The characters once again fall victim to cloak and dagger games of faked deaths, guns filled with blanks, and staged accidents by Stephen's assistant, but the ghosts eventually take matters into their own hands and the deaths become very real. Unlike the original, the cast of misfits do not disappear for a large portion of the action. All characters split up and come together in an effort to survive the harrowing night, but only Sara and Eddie make it out alive—coincidentally, with all the checks promised to the guests, valued at $5 million dollars. In the original, Pritchard thought the ghosts were coming for him, and this is proven true in the remake. His ghost, however, is the force that enables Sara and Eddie to escape the facility. Stephen and Evelyn are shown living out the rest of their time in the afterlife being tortured by the ghosts of the asylum.

There are clear differences in the narrative between the two movies: the remake features more payoff in the reward money, there are more deaths, and the audience is given proof that the ghosts exist. The use of skeletons on strings has also been thrown out and replaced by computer graphics to enhance the presence of ghosts and update the movie aesthetic for a 1999 audience. Also gone are the direct addresses to the camera; the remake keeps the story completely fictional, and allows the audience to distance itself or come closer to the action on the screen, however they may wish. The two films complement each other, as the '50s version is considered a B-movie, and the '90s version features a lot of horror camp. And oddly enough, the '50s version evokes more terror and fright with its subtle tactics than the update, which focuses more on star power and special effects. Although the remake does not feature a cast of up-and-comers from a network like the CW, it showcases the horror remake trend of securing big-name actors to bring audiences to the theater. Neither *House* movies were runaway box-office successes, but they have established themselves as memorable entries in classic and contemporary horror categories.

The '60s continue our discussion of classic horror and lead into the start of post-modern horror fare. *13 Ghosts* (1960), *The Haunting* (1963), and *Night of the Living Dead* represent a changing of the guards between what most critics consider traditional horror films (pre-dating the mid-1960s) and contemporary horror, which closes out the decade. These are also the last of the great black-and-white productions for the list, although color processing had been around (as it is always noted that Hitchcock decided to make *Psycho* in black-and-white). The films are just as effective as those made in color, and their longevity of appeal in horror proves it. This decade offers us ghosts, strange phenomena, more ghosts, and zombies.

William Castle returns with *13 Ghosts*. It is reminiscent of *House on Haunted Hill* because the story concentrates on an inherited house and the ghosts that come with it. Cyrus Zorba (Donald Woods) inherits the haunted house for his downtrodden family to move into, along with a buried treasure, a creepy housekeeper, and 12 ghosts previously collected by his strange uncle, Dr. Zorba. As a ghost collector, the uncle wrote about the ones he captured, but his diary has a space open for one more—the 13th ghost. The good doctor has also left behind special goggles that allow anyone using them to see the ghosts in the flesh, so to speak.

Minus the difference in narrative, *13 Ghosts* and *House* play upon some of the same fears in horror, including the afterlife and spiritual unrest. Castle's gimmick for the film, however, was interesting. He marketed the film with "Illusion-O," which was a way to protect faint-of-heart audience members from being too scared and simultaneously allowing brave souls to face their fears. Theaters provided patrons with special viewers that were tinted red to allow them to see the ghosts in the scenes or tinted blue to remove the ghastly apparitions from their sight. The process was not perfect; superimposing images of the ghosts onto the film, coupled with the use of the different glasses, did not largely enhance or remove the ghosts completely. Nonetheless, the gimmick provided audience participation in the film and made patrons consider their own levels of bravery in watching a horror movie. In the 21st century, moviegoers are offered the return of 3D screenings, but that is as far as audience participation goes currently, and it does not force moviegoers to judge their own courage boundaries while watching a film. Castle's gimmicks are considered a relic of horror's past, but with the remake trend, the tradition of his films are not allowed to fade from memory.

Steve Beck's remake, *Thir13en Ghosts* (2001), reflects the changing times in horror like the complementary remake of *House on Haunted Hill*. It boasts a cast of known names—Tony Shalhoub, Matthew Lillard, Shannon Elizabeth, and music MC Rah Digga—and is a special effects extravaganza. The gimmick in Castle's film plays out with CGI in this contemporary update. Characters use their special goggles to spot the ghosts as they travel through the maze of glass enclosures within the house, and along the way they battle vicious spirits with the intensity of an action movie.

The interesting part of Beck's film is the attention to detail given to the ghosts. Although the special effects created colorful characters that were visually pleasing to an early 21st century horror crowd, the back-story for the ghosts provided a stronger connection to the idea of the uncle being a collector of rare spiritual finds. The rest of the film does not match the emphasis on the ghosts, so the narrative unfolds a bit disconnectedly. *Thir13en* still pulled a respectable amount of money in from its box-office earnings, with a total of close to $70 million; however, its production budget—no doubt in correlation to the amount of special effects—was a little over $40 million. *House on Haunted Hill* did not fare any better by pulling in $40 million with a production budget of $37 million. These remakes let filmmakers know that horror films functioned differently from other cinema genres. Audiences for horror typically see a movie because of its story, gore, believability, characters (monsters), or the amount of fear it can induce in them. Big budgets and big-name movie stars were not the answer to revamping older productions for contemporary audiences; mainstream moviegoers were attracted by the star power but turned off by the film content.

The same can be said of John Carpenter's *Village of the Damned* (1995), which cost an estimated $22 million to produce and raked in less than $10 million at the box office. Since it was a 1960 British film, the original *Village of the Damned* does not fall into our American-horror discussion, but the remake's revenue is indicative of an early trend that had to be erased for remakes to start being financially successful. Jan de Bont's *The Haunting*, however, proves there can be exceptions. The original film's British-American production restricts it from this listing, but once again the American remake shows how star power (in director and actors—Liam Neeson, Catherine Zeta-Jones, Owen Wilson, and Lily Taylor), special effects, and a huge production budget can sometimes be a risk that pays off. *The Haunting* cost approximately $80 million to produce, but its domestic and foreign box-office numbers made the film quite successful, with almost $180 million in ticket sales. The film itself, like the *Village* redux, received poor reviews, but it caught moviegoers at a time when people heavily believed in the equation that movie stars plus special effects equal gold. Both are interesting remakes—for the high production values and affected acting performances alone—and the originals will never lose their places in the classic horror canon.

And then along came a man by the name of George A. Romero with a little film about zombies (and much more) entitled *Night of the Living Dead*. This is the moment for many critics and fans when horror left behind its classical ties and forged ahead into contemporary filmmaking. Although it is now recognized and lauded worldwide, *Night* began as a small independent film with an estimated production budget of $114,000. It has since earned approximately $30 million in box office sales via various theatrical releases over the years. How this indie horror flick became a universal phenomenon requires a bit of discussion.

Romero made his first feature-length zombie movie with a simple storyline. Barbra (Judith O'Dea) and Johnny (Russell Streiner) go to the cemetery to pay honor to their father's memory. They are attacked by what appears to be a drunken man, Johnny is killed, and Barbra flees to a nearby house where a man named Ben (Duane Jones) soon arrives and secures them both within the residence. There is a married couple and their child hiding out in the basement, along with a pair of teenagers, and soon all become aware of each other and the dire situation they are in; the bodies of the recently deceased are coming back from the dead with a need for human flesh. Through a series of arguments and failed attempts to escape and find better shelter, each member of the group dies by zombie or fatal accident. Ben, as the only survivor, hides in the cellar. He goes out the next morning to find a marauding group of rescuers arriving, but they mistake him for a zombie and shoot him in the head. Ben's remains are tossed onto a pile of dead bodies and burned. It is not the happiest ending to a zombie movie because the hero of the story is killed in the end, but the presence of a rescue group assures the viewer that humans will overcome the disastrous situation.

This was not the first zombie movie ever made; Frankenstein's monster was basically a body (multiple bodies) brought back from the dead. But the simple story of *Night of the Living Dead* did something far greater than any of its zombie brothers and sisters of its time and even today—it channeled the American social climate of the '60s into its narrative and made people take a hard look at themselves and the societies and cultures in which they were living. Aside from the noticeable correlation to the Vietnam War and the gruesome horrors of battle resulting from the conflict, the movie tackled issues of consumerism, racism, and mortality simultaneously in subtle and confrontational ways. In moments of zombie attacks, America was offered a vision of how the perceived greed of its citizens can become such a dangerous force that it resembles people eating other people. We consume information (via newspaper, television, radio, internet, word-of-mouth), food (home cooking, restaurants, fast food), business (hostile takeovers, mergers), vices (sex, smoking, drugs, alcohol), the environment (landfills, the ozone, exhaust emissions), and each other (emotionally, physically, spiritually) so much that eventually we will be the ones consumed, like the zombies eating people. It was a message to slow down and take a look at the damage we cause around us in our own lives, family members, friends, lovers, and even strangers.

The issue of mortality is the most basic and common among zombie films, because everyone at some point questions life and death and what happens to the body when the last breath is taken. *Night* made people face their fears about bodily decay six feet below the ground and gave rise to questions concerning the human soul. These are thoughts that never leave the social consciousness of any nation; however, racism was another matter.

It was 1968, and the civil rights movement was in full swing. The Civil Rights Act of 1964 had passed, the Civil Rights Act of 1968 had passed, and citizens found themselves in uncertain times of how to relate to one another. When Ben, an African American male, assumes the role of hero in *Night of the Living Dead*, one of the nation's greatest conflicts was put into the spotlight. Racial equality, stereotypes, ethnic panic, interracial relationships, and racism symbolically overshadowed the literal depiction of zombies killing characters in the film. Ben was scrutinized as not just another character in the film, but as a barometer reading for the social climate of the '60s. As the hero in the movie, he is not without his flaws, like all the other characters. Ben does not represent one ethnicity; he stands for social change to say that minorities were slowly receiving equal consideration for employment, housing, and other rights that all U.S. citizens were to hold as inhabitants of a free society.

Ben's death and burning, however, let audiences know that life in the States would not change overnight because of civil rights legislation. Police walk with attack dogs on leashes as the motion picture becomes a series of black-and-white stills; they resemble newspaper clippings showing historical accounts of race riots and the holocaust. The final images of Ben's body being carried out of the house and tossed atop a pile of other dead-again bodies fueled thoughts of lynchings, genocide, and the reality of the times. Some moviegoers and critics saw the ending as a slap in the face of national progression; others believed the conclusion to be a harsh visualization of the '60s; and more thought the film's finale was simply an ironic twist to the narrative. No matter how the ending was viewed, it offered more social commentary that any other zombie movie of its time and thereafter. But this was only part of the reason why the film has been so popular over the years and managed to bring in such a substantial amount at the box office.

When a movie garners critical praise and bashing, and audiences simultaneously applaud its effort and dismiss its content, it develops a small underground following that slowly builds into worldwide recognition. *Night* became a cult film that horror aficionados, film critics, and the unassuming moviegoer simply had to see to find out what all the commotion was about. Its growth does not mean that every person who watched it loved it, but word-of-mouth spread about the film, which caused others to want to see it for her or himself. Over forty years after its original theatrical release, *Night of the Living Dead* has spawned five sequels and two remakes, and influenced tons of other films and pop culture forms, including television series, comic books, and animated creations.

Originally, Romero created the "living dead" trilogy by directing *Night of the Living Dead*, *Dawn of the Dead* (1978), and *Day of the Dead* (1985)— one living-dead film for each new decade of horror films. The sequels, in short, continue to focus on consumerism and the search for individuality in American society. Characters in *Dawn* seek shelter from the undead invasion in a shopping mall, while soldiers and scientists hide out underground in *Day*. All of the movies were united by stories that illustrated how tense situations can become when a group is forced to face mortality in a single, enclosed location. Each film documented the human condition to show that we were worse than the zombies trying to kill us. Interestingly enough, each of the original trilogy movies have been remade, and most of them have remained true to Romero's vision. Here is a brief look at the remakes and sequels that have made Romero's living-dead movies, and zombie movies in general, a big part of contemporary horror.

Tom Savini sat in the director's chair for the first remake in 1990. Romero served as producer, worked on the original script, and brought in some of the original production team members to help make the film. It features Tony Todd as our protagonist, Ben, and Patricia Tallman as Barbara. The most notable difference is the remake is shot in color. Although the original film had previously been re-released colorized in the '80s, and other colorizations would follow into the 21st century, Savini's vision was shot in full-color as an update for the times. In a way, it makes the film more visceral and real-to-life; however, black-and-white movies can instill just as much fear and fright in moviegoers as their color counterparts.

The screenplay was altered for a few scenes that enhanced Romero's social messages. One small change occurs at the beginning, in which we see Barbara and Johnny visiting the grave of their mother instead of father. It is also a nice touch that when Ben arrives at the house, our first glimpse of the character shows him carrying a crowbar like a hook—reminiscent of the *Candyman* (1992) role Todd would take two years later. Toward the end, Barbara escapes the house and comes back the next day with the group of law officials, hunters, and other random men with guns. Ben has turned into a zombie, and one of the men kill him with a gunshot. Barbara finds Harry—the cowardly husband character from the original—alive, but shoots him square between the eyes for the inhumanity he displayed during all the chaos. When others come to her side after hearing the gunshot, she simply tells them Harry's body is another zombie for the pyre. Barbara looks around at the mayhem outside, which features what most would call a redneck aesthetic of shotguns, hangings, flannel shirts, baseball caps, and camouflage jackets, and says, "They're us. We're them and they're us." Her words exhibit the original film's message about what it means to be human and a consumer in

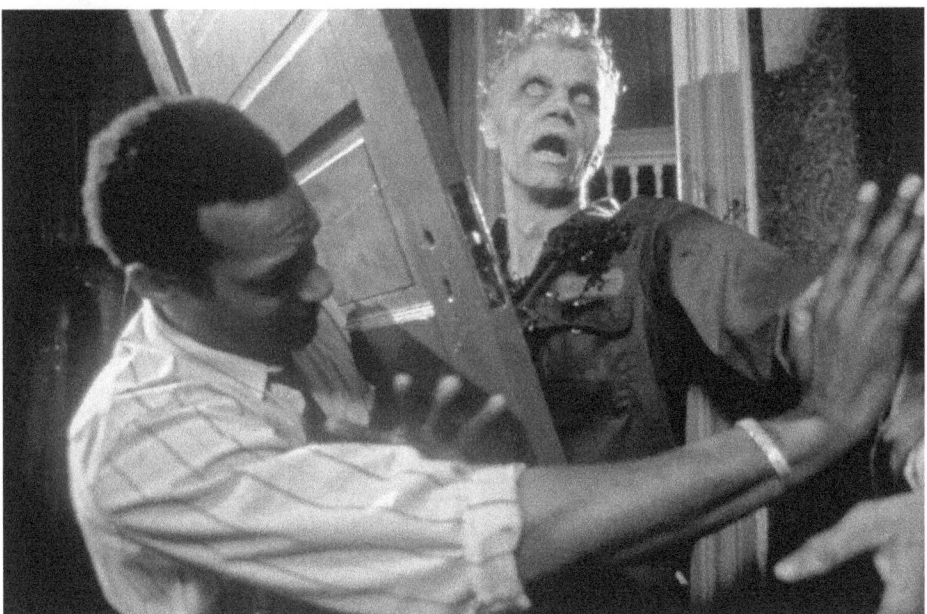

Ben (Tony Todd) fends off a zombie attack as he tries to secure a safe house in *Night of the Living Dead* (1990).

American society; the two elements have not changed much from the 20th to the 21st century.

Jeff Broadstreet's 2006 update—*Night of the Living Dead 3D*—removed much of the original narrative, minus a few key moments that astute viewers would recall from the first remake or the '60s production. This version is more of a reinvention than a complete remake, and the story illustrates the difference. Barb and Johnny head to the cemetery to attend their aunt's funeral, but they are attacked by zombies; Johnny flees the scene and leaves Barb to fend for herself. She eventually gets out of the cemetery and encounters a host of unique characters, including mortician Gerald Tovar, Jr. (Sid Haig), who runs her away from his facility. Barb meets Ben, they travel to a weed-growing farmhouse with even more colorful characters, and zombie antics ensue. It is revealed that Haig's character started the zombie attack and keeps his own father alive by feeding him blood. All the characters are killed in the end by the horde of zombies, and the closing credits begin to roll.

Broadstreet's version removes any notion of social commentary about consumerism, race relations, or human morality. Ben is no longer an African American male, and there are no roaming groups of hunters and law officials to destroy the zombies and "save" America. Two of the more interesting tidbits added include the opening scene, which seems like a black-and-white establishing shot until the camera slowly pulls back to reveal the original film playing on a television in a gas station. The road on the screen is a mirror of the road we see the real characters of the movie traveling upon as they pass the gas station. Also, after Barb and Johnny are separated, she later receives a text message from him that reads, "COMING 4 U BARB." These two instances pay homage to the original and get the viewer in the mood for a sociocultural zombie movie, but the subtext is removed to showcase a newer and somewhat raunchier presentation of the material. If a viewer recognizes the name Sid Haig before watching the movie, s/he will understand the production will be somewhat over-the-top. It is reminiscent of the way *The Texas Chainsaw Massacre: The Next Generation* (1994) was shot, with Renee Zellweger and Matthew McConaughey; the sensibility and nostalgia of the original film is present, but many liberties are taken to keep the productions from being comparable to each other.

The five sequels to the original *Night of the Living Dead* continue the story from the first film to illustrate the struggles that humanity and zombie culture go through to fight against each other in a battle of wit, strength, and mass numbers, and in some sense their opposing forces clash in order to coexist.

In the original *Dawn of the Dead*, a group of misfit characters (television studio employees and SWAT team members)—like most in the living-dead series—find themselves in a shopping mall attempting to secure themselves away from the growing number of zombies sweeping across the nation. The mall is a haven for them in their time of need, and functions somewhat the same in society without a zombie attack; however, their security is violated when bikers break in and inadvertently let a number of zombies follow behind them. Peter and pregnant Francine are the only two people able to escape the chaos inside the mall. The characters journey to the roof, jump into a helicopter, and fly away. They do not have enough fuel for a long trip, which makes their destination and future unknown.

Romero's sequel solidified the significant breakdown in social codes as evident by humans locking zombies in basements, fighting against each other when the goal of survival is common, and taking solace in the one place that represents a zombification of humanity—a mall. The open-ended story reflects the loss of individuality in the American citizen, which is a common thread that binds the living-dead movies and correlates to social trends of national ideals. It is a message that was not lost in the remake.

Zack Snyder updated the movie in 2004 with an all-star cast, including Sarah Polley, Ving Rhames, and Mekhi Phifer. Consumerism and morality remained at the heart of the story, but the movie contained different scenes that embodied the feel of the original. The misfit group of characters still finds its way to the mall, but this time they include a nurse, a police officer, an ex-con and his pregnant girlfriend, and the mall security they encounter after breaking into the facility. Other characters make their way to the mall by escaping different zombie attacks, and the entire group start to develop a fond feeling of safety as they allow the mall to become their new home. But the sanctity of the mall is ruined when zombies finally creep in and overrun its majestic halls of department stores and coffee shops. Luckily the group previously transformed two shuttle buses into reinforced zombie-protection machines, and they use them to escape and head to a marina, with hopes of taking a boat to an island free of zombies. The plan, as in almost every horror film, does not work perfectly, and many of the characters are killed in sequences involving a chainsaw accident, zombie attack, and suicide. But for the characters who do survive and sail away, everything seems hopeful until they come to an island, only to discover that the zombies are everywhere. We do not see the final characters die, but by the sounds of screams it is understood that no one survives.

Snyder's production is sleek and crisp; it fits the contemporary style of original and remake horror, which does its best to prove that horror films can be simultaneously visually pretty and still scare the heck out of audiences. The colors are bright and saturated, and the special effects are extremely detailed for realism. His remake takes into account the generational divide between audiences for the original film and new crowds for his production. Johnny Cash's "The Man Comes Around" plays during the opening credits, which provides the moody tone for the rest of the film, and other key songs and musical interludes help highlight the movie's scenes of intense attacks, pleasant moments, and even comedy. Richard Cheese sings a cover of Disturbed's "Down with the Sickness" during a montage that shows the characters getting comfortable with their new life in the mall, and an instrumental version of Bobby McFerrin's "Don't Worry, Be Happy" plays in the elevator when the group escapes the chasing zombies. The quality of acting is certainly heightened by the presence of seasoned veterans as well, but one part of the update has zombie fans split.

The first zombie attack is made by Ana's (Sarah Polley) neighbor. She is a little girl, who viciously attacks Ana's husband. When Ana rips the girl away and throws her down the hallway, the little zombie quickly charges back for another attack. "Quickly" is the key word. Snyder's zombies are track runners and make escape nearly impossible. In a way, fear is intensified because it is more difficult to escape the zombies compared to their '60s, '70s, and '80s brothers and sisters, who moved like they were being filmed in slow motion. The change from slow to fast zombies, however, made other audience members think the film belonged more to the contagion-infection subgenre of horror instead of zombie cinema. People made arguments about living-dead bodies experiencing the effects of rigor mortis and how such a process of death should keep them moving slowly once reanimated. And this one aspect of the film has continued to keep fans of all zombie films divided because most contemporary portrayals depict faster-running zombies and consider the slower undead a part of zombie history.

Snyder's debut feature film—debated or not—took in a huge haul at the box office, much like the original. His career skyrocketed after *Dawn* and led to critical and financial success with *300* (2006), *Watchmen* (2009), and *Legend of the Guardians: The Owls of Ga'Hoole* (2010). Unlike the *Night* remakes, *Dawn* was much more of a commercial success and paved the way for the last film in the original living-dead trilogy to be remade, as well.

Romero's *Day of the Dead* pushed human characters seeking refuge to one of the last great (and safe) hiding places—an underground military bunker. Scientists and military officers live in the bunker, charged with the assignment to find out how to stop the zombies once and for all, specifically regarding the zombification process. The lead doctor works with a zombie named Bub, who retains and displays remnants of his former human existence by recognizing and comprehending the operation of domestic objects; he's a teddy bear version of a zombie ... almost. Things seem to be going well, if at an extremely slow pace, for the operation, but it all eventually cracks in the microcosm that starts to surface. Claustrophobic spaces, paltry food supplies, imbalanced personal and romantic relationships, and disagreements concerning authority positions push the group to the edge of sanity. The doctor (Dr. Logan) and lead military officer (Captain Rhodes) begin to lose their minds, and before long zombies invade the bunker. Bub finds the doctor's remains and goes on a rampage; he successfully operates a handgun to shoot the military officer, which leaves the man as wounded prey for the flesh-hungry zombies. Bub even salutes and proves zombies can be taught to be civilized members of society, although that society is completely turned upside down by the presence of zombies coupled with humankind's own personal struggles.

Three characters manage to reach a helicopter but are attacked by zombies once inside; however, this is simply a dream sequence experienced by one of the characters. When she awakens, we see the three on a beach, with their helicopter safe and sound. Overall, the initial group of bunker characters easily represent a discord in American society; it shows the ease in which community and nation-at-large can break down and turn into complete turmoil. The somewhat happy ending shows that peace can come from chaos even when chaos continues to loom all around, but most moviegoers and critics felt the film was too depressing at the end. Romero's message was received, but many liked the presentation in the first two films better. *Day* was still a success for the filmmaker at the box office, and it has made the trilogy of movies respected enough to be revered in horror and mainstream cinema through the 21st century.

Savini worked with Romero a second time in creating special makeup effects for the zombies; his first time was on the set of *Dawn*, and he would have worked with the director on *Night* had he not been called to duty in Vietnam. Makeup effects, however, could not contribute to a positive reception for the *Day of the Dead* remake in 2008.

Steve Miner directed Mena Suvari and Nick Cannon in a straight-to-video update, and although the story does not bear much resemblance to the original, there are enough elements strategically placed to allow the movie to be called a remake. Suvari and Cannon—Sarah Cross and Salazar—play military officers under the command of Captain Rhodes, as portrayed by Ving Rhames in his second appearance in a living-dead series remake. The military is working to contain an outbreak (of zombie infection) in a small town when all heck breaks loose and the zombie epidemic begins. Another solider named Bud (Stark Sands) likes Cross, but he is bitten by an infected Rhodes; however, Bud does not exhibit the same killer instinct as the other zombies because he was a vegetarian before becoming infected. Cross,

Salazar, and a couple of teens, with Bud along for the ride, take shelter in an underground bunker where they learn about the government's involvement with the outbreak. In true zombie-movie fashion, nothing seems to go right, which leaves Cross and the two teens to flee the town, with the zombies destroyed in a fire they leave behind. As the three survivors drive away, a zombie suddenly appears in front of the camera and the movie ends.

Miner had previous success in the horror genre by directing the first two *Friday the 13th* sequels in the '80s and the "true" sequel to *Halloween II*—*Halloween H20: Twenty Years Later*. His experience in the genre did not pay off, according to fans and critics who responded negatively to the *Day* remake. The film was initially set for theatrical release but found its way directly to video as a result of issues during and post-production. Although a large number of viewers considered the movie to be a less-than-faithful representation of the original, it did offer an interesting story angle regarding Bud's vegetarianism being the reason why he did not attack and eat flesh like other zombies. The situation adds a bit of comedy to the story, but it was an element not previously explored in other zombie movies.

Night of the Living Dead, *Dawn of the Dead*, and *Day of the Dead* are certainly George Romero's legacy to horror, and the remakes for each of the films—though not universally accepted as great productions—offer proof that his living-dead series touched on something collectively human for fans and critics to admire, debate, and remember for years to come. Romero's last three entries are currently stand-alone films that have not been touched by the remake machine. Each movie takes the living-dead narrative a step further to show the degradation of human society, the rise of zombie society, and the uncertain future both face in an effort to share Earth or dominate the land.

When Romero announced *Land of the Dead* would premiere in 2005, fans were ecstatic that the series would resume 20 years after the release of *Day of the Dead*. Box-office returns for the film were equally matched by fan appreciation and enthusiasm that the zombie master filmmaker had returned to the world that started his feature-film career. *Land* features a post-apocalyptic, zombie-torn America that somewhat resembles *Mad Max Beyond Thunderdome* (1985), only a little less of a complete wasteland. Paul Kaufman (Dennis Hopper) runs the town, much like Tina Turner did in *Thunderdome*. He keeps the rich people rich within the safety of a luxury building and the poor people poor outside its walls. Basically the "true" citizens of the land—the poor and the zombified—overthrow Kaufman's government to bring everything back to a level playing field for rich and disenfranchised. John Lequizamo, Simon Baker, and cult horror icon Asia Argento also star in the film.

The movie showcased much of Romero's dark sense of humor, charismatic horror, and social commentary. It characterized the American ideal of a government working for the people and by the people that could easily be destroyed by the people if society is not being run in the best manner possible. Although we see rich and poor people divided in the movie, the zombies function as the homeless and those individuals of American history whose livelihood was forcibly taken away from them; now they roam the earth in search of a place to settle down and rebuild their community. Romero also furthered his exploration of zombie intelligence previously shown in *Day* by presenting zombies that could learn to break their repetitive action patterns, work as a team to complete minor tasks, and even follow a leader to take them to a place of better undead living. They do not speak, unlike in some other zombie movies, but their moans and grunts function as communicative speech patterns they can recognize between each other. At the end of the film the zombies leave the decrepit city in search of a new land, and the surviving humans do the same in opposite directions. There is no attempt to stop the zombies because it is understood that they too need a home; however, Romero's next dead film seemed to remove the social consciousness of zombies in order to focus more on the 21st century obsession with technology.

Diary of the Dead came out in 2007 and featured a host of newcomers and working actors, but the casting of big-name stars was gone; box-office figures reflected the change in formula, as the movie made more than it cost to be produced, but not by very much. The story involves a group of teenagers making a horror film, but the production is interrupted by news of what later becomes understood as a zombie outbreak. We watch the characters try to understand the situation as they attempt to locate relatives and find places to safeguard themselves, and we see it all through the lens of their own video camera chronicling the events as they happen. Three characters live to the end of the movie, but being locked in a panic room does not ensure the best means of survival. They briefly contemplate human life and morality when we are allowed to see hunters using bodies as gun-range targets, but all other social messages have been removed from the usual mood of the series. Romero acknowledges the 21st century and its teenage craze over recording everything, watching playback on YouTube, communicating via text messages and Facebook, and so forth, but it is more of a highlight of technological progress than a focus on our dependence on the various technologies and applications. And in another about-face move, Romero's most current entry in the living-dead series of films breaks away from technology to explore the primal dispute over land ownership.

Survival of the Dead—much like *Diary*—was produced with new talent and working actors, but there was no Hollywood elite to be found playing roles. Unlike *Diary*, the film did not break even at the box office in its limited release and remains the least financially successful movie in the entire franchise. The story gets a bit complicated in its attempt to connect families and feudal arguments, but at its core it is a story of two warring Irish families—the Muldoons and the O'Flynns—that reside on an island with two very different ideas about zombie control. The Muldoons believe in keeping zombified family members "alive" until a cure can be found, but the O'Flynns favor the more direct action of killing zombies because the risk is too great to keep the flesh-eating undead around the living. There is a final standoff in the film, which results in the captured zombies being released and family members on both sides being killed. Again, three characters escape the island to seek a better life; but back home the zombified leaders of the Muldoons and O'Flynns attempt an Old West showdown, but their guns are no longer loaded.

Zombies in *Survival* exhibit traces of their former human lives, which was previously exploited in *Land* and *Day*. The newest contribution to zombie lore made in this movie, however, is the fact that in one pivotal scene the zombies feast upon a horse. In no other previous Romero film (including remakes of his works) has a zombie fed upon an animal. This point mirrors the vegetarian zombie idea presented in the *Day* remake. It is an interesting turn of events because people have long questioned why zombies did not eat animals, as they have living flesh just like humans. Other than the zombies being trained to figure out that they could eat animals, the film makes no other commentary about the event. It remains an anomaly in the living-dead series, but has since been repeated in the AMC series *The Walking Dead* (2010). So far there has been no word on a new living-dead film, but Romero has been linked to a rumored remake of Dario Argento's Italian giallo classic *Deep Red* (1975); he also served as executive producer for a new horror documentary entitled *Into the Dark: Exploring the Horror Film* (2012). His legacy is ever-present in films such as *Resident Evil* (2002), *28 Days Later*, *Shaun of the Dead*, and *The Zombie Diaries* (2006).

Night of the Living Dead closed out the '60s to make way for rape-revenge movies of the '70s. Rape-revenge movies have a place all to themselves in the world of horror, and *The Last House on the Left*, from 1972, is one of the top two in the category (the number one film in the subgenre came six years later and eight movies further down our discussion). This early example of rape-revenge horror was directed by Wes Craven, with Sean S. Cunningham serving as producer. It was an early collaboration between the two who later went on to create horror's legendary Freddy Kruger and Jason Voorhees characters. The production budget was quite limited, but Craven managed to create a film that continues to be simultaneously heralded for its stark depiction of the inhumanity of humankind and rejected as a movie with no cinematic value whatsoever.

The story for *Last House* is actually centuries old. It comes from a 13th century Swedish ballad that was later transformed into Ingmar Bergman's *The Virgin Spring*, which is a must-see for horror fans if they would like to see how much it influenced Craven's production. *Last House* tells the story of two teenage girls—Mari and Phyllis—who venture to a rock concert, then go in search of marijuana only to encounter four of society's most relentless undesirables (Krug, Sadie, Fred, and Junior), who thrive on rape, murder, and sadism with smiles on their faces. Junior is Krug's son and a reluctant member of the gang; his participation in the proceedings is very limited. The two girls are brutally raped, ridiculed, and eventually killed by the gruesome foursome ... only a short distance from Mari's home, which is the last house on the left.

The villains need a place to stay because their car initially broke down near Mari's house where they tortured the girls, so they make themselves look presentable and head to Mari's home, where they are allowed to stay for the night. Mari's mother, Estelle, recognizes her daughter's necklace

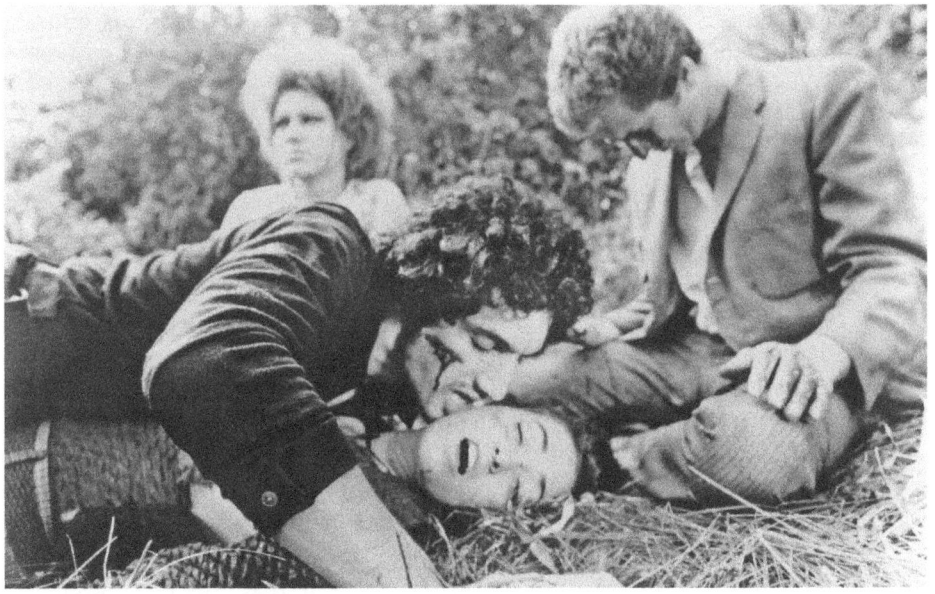

Mari (Sandra Peabody/Cassell) closes her eyes in an attempt to mentally escape the humiliating and brutal attack by Krug (David A. Hess), as Sadie (Jeramie Rain) and Fred (Fred J. Lincoln) sit in the background, in *The Last House on the Left* (1972). Each of the deranged characters takes a turn terrorizing Mari.

around Junior's neck, and eventually the parents discover that this group of traveling salespeople are not who they claim. Estelle later learns that the group tortured her daughter; she heads into the woods with her husband to discover Mari's body, which leads the two to form a plan of revenge for their daughter's death. Through a series of violent encounters, the parents kill off all four criminals, and the police arrive at the end too late to stop the mayhem or take matters into official hands.

On paper the story sounds simple: parents seek revenge upon criminals who killed their daughter. On the screen, however, the movie played out in ways moviegoers and critics had never seen before. The realism of the violence and sadistic acts caused many to claim the film heralded a dark time for cinema. People had witnessed violence before in movies, but the intensity of violence in *Last House* caused them to think about possible moral codes that filmmakers should follow in making horror movies. Between Mari and Phyllis, the two girls are raped, stabbed, made to urinate in public, forced to have sex with each other, disemboweled, amputated, and shot. But the violence enacted upon the girls is equally matched by the parents, who slice open Sadie's throat, bite off Fred's penis, allow Krug to convince Junior to commit suicide, and chainsaw Krug to finish off the group. These actions throughout the film have made it one of horror's most notorious films, although some still do not consider it a part of the horror genre; in a way, rape-revenge films are a genre completely separate from others, but for general purposes, *Last House* has a home in horror.

The one lasting impression most viewers come away with is the repeated play of the song lyric "and the road leads to nowhere," which epitomizes the seemingly lost generational connection between parents and their children— Mari and her parents discuss bras, drugs, and rock concerts early in the film—and the immoral gang of criminals. *Last House* left its own impression on cinema, as it was banned and censored in various countries; it was also listed as a "video nasty" in the '80s, which was a significant mark against its production via being labeled a film of extreme violent content. Even with so much negativity being thrown at the movie, it was able to rake in millions of dollars at the box office, which was a hefty feat for a feature that cost just under $1 million to produce. The controversy that has surrounded the film since its release was easily a contributing factor in the consideration of it being remade.

It is difficult to recapture the gritty aesthetic that '70s rape-revenge movies had, and most critics (and a lot of fans) question why anyone would ever want to re-release or remake these films, but they are culturally significant even though they continue to remain an eyesore in cinema. Contemporary movie reviewers label films like *Saw* and *Hostel* (2005) as torture porn, but these newer productions are entirely too sleek in design to recreate the awkward moments and boundary-pushing ethical treatment of actors onscreen. Torture-porn movies of today are quite tame in comparison to '70s presentations, and this road leads to us to Dennis Iliadis's *The Last House on the Left* (2009).

His feature updated the '70s atmosphere to a more contemporary production; clothing was modern, technology was brought into the 21st century, and there was no longer a parental-advisory relationship between the parents and their daughter. The rock concert plot point is gone, but the two girls—Mari and Paige—still manage to run into trouble when they meet Justin (the former Junior character), who invites them to smoke some marijuana back at his hotel room. It is here that the girls, meet the rest of the group that will forever ruin their lives. The crew kidnaps the girls and Mari convinces them to drive toward her parents' house so she can attempt to escape; however, the car crashes (instead of breaking down, like it does in the original) not too far from her home, and the gang proceeds to rape and kill the girls in the nearby woods. Unlike the original, there is less grit presented in the assaults, and when Mari is shot in the lake, her body drifts away, but she does not die.

The gang members go to Mari's house for shelter from a storm, and when Justin realizes the people inside are Mari's parents, he purposely puts Mari's necklace in plain view for it to be discovered as a tip that something has happened to her. Emma and John, Mari's parents, find their daughter on the front porch, clinging to life. The couple decides to take her to the hospital—but not before they exact revenge on the lowlifes who tortured their child. Instead of killing all four gang members, Emma and John are joined by Justin to rid the world of the criminals and get Mari to the hospital as soon as possible. Although John paralyzes Krug and sentences him to death by placing his head in a microwave, the film ends with a happier ending because Mari lives and Justin does not follow his father's footsteps into a life of crime.

Reaction to the remake was split down the middle. Some liked the modern update and thought the film was a strong reminder about the ills of society that continue to exist. Others seemed to only like the remake's ability to make people remember the original film and see it as a groundbreaking contribution to horror. Either way, Illiadis's movie got people talking about horror and rape-revenge movies in general. It opened a door many people thought had been closed since the end of the '70s. And it exhibited a trend of past and future filmmakers collaborating on remakes, as Craven's own film studio produced the remake. *Last House*—original or remake—highlighted a violent American landscape that never truly seems to go away. Whether these are believed to be quality films or not cannot overshadow their importance in pointing out some of life's unfortunate happenings.

Social messages in horror cinema boomed in the '70s, and one of the great fears the films explored was the threat of contamination. George Romero was previously discussed in terms of his zombie productions, but he also gave us *The Crazies* in 1973. A military plane carrying a bioenvironmental weapon crashes in a small town in Pennsylvania and contaminates the water supply, which causes people of the town to start exhibiting odd behavior and become "crazy." The military is sent in to contain the infected area; they are allowed to shoot anyone on sight that may be affected by the contaminant. Government officials also authorize bombing the town if necessary to alleviate any chances that the contagion will spread. A small group of civilians, unaffected by the contagion, try their best to avoid the infected crazies and military, who could easily shoot them without much probable cause. One doctor makes it his goal to find a cure and save the town, but just as he achieves his goal he is ordered into quarantine by military officials who suspect he may be infected. The doctor is corralled with a group of crazies; they knock him down a flight of stairs, and his test tubes containing the cure are destroyed. In the end, the entire town remains in complete chaos, and the leader of the military operation is called away to investigate another town battling the contagion. It seems no one will escape the military's accidental contamination.

The Crazies tapped into an ever-present national fear of water contamination and what people would do should natural resources become unreliable. Although sociopolitical concerns about the environment reached peaks during the '80s and '90s, the message was clear in Romero's movie. The film never received a wide release or much attention, and to this day most horror fans do not know about the production unless they are diehard viewers of the genre. Its remake came almost 40 years later and is more memorable in the contemporary horror market.

Breck Eisner's 2010 remake of *The Crazies* represents more of a contagion/infection film than any kind of zombie movie, although many moviegoers will classify it as such. The original focused on how easily the environment can become a deadly place if a bad element is introduced into it, and the remake updated the story with more focus on horror entertainment (special effects and scary moments), but the production is solid and the acting is strong. Its cast is recognizable, with Timothy Olyphant taking the lead role as David, the town sheriff, and Radha Mitchell playing Judy, his pregnant wife and the town's doctor. We follow David and Judy, with a few other characters, through the initial infection cases, the overrun of the town, and the final battle between crazies and military officers. Throughout much of the same mayhem and madness the original film showcased, David and Judy are the sole survivors of the situation; they barely escape the town being airbombed. But as the two characters walk toward hope in a neighboring city, the viewer is alerted that contamination has already started where they are heading.

As a whole, the remake was quite successful at the box office, and with critics and fans. Its updated take on the original provided audiences with higher production values, eerie makeup effects, modernized story elements (like allowing the viewer to see that the town is being monitored via space satellite), and narrative tension equal to the original film. It is also much more fast-paced than Romero's production; the sheriff is forced to shoot one of the first infected townspeople at a baseball game in the opening scene. In many horror circles, *The Crazies* remake ranks well atop other horror recreations and sits in good company with the likes of Snyder's *Dawn of the Dead*.

Any character that survives an outbreak of crazies deserves a holiday vacation, but for the sorority sisters in Bob Clark's *Black Christmas* (1974), seasons greetings come bearing killer gifts. It is Christmas time, and while the holiday spirit is in the air, a deranged killer stalks, harasses, and murders girls in their sorority house. What starts innocently as a few obscene phone calls the sorority sisters ignore turns into a bloodbath that leaves almost no one alive. The killer murders the sisters one by one in violent fashion, including suffocation by plastic bag, hook hanging, and fatal stabbing by unicorn ornament. No one knows who the killer is, but one of the sisters mistakenly suspects her own boyfriend toward the end of the film and kills him with a fireplace poker. He, along with a police officer stationed outside the sorority house, are the only two men to die in the film. And as police officers try to make sense of why the murders happened, the final girl of the story (Jess) is left to sleep off the tragedy while the killer continues to hang out in the attic with his first two kills that everyone suspects are still simply missing persons; the police never checked the attic. We hear the killer whisper, "Agnes, it's me, Billy," as the camera pans out to reveal the sorority house looking peaceful in the winter snow while a police officer stands guard outside the front door and the first victim's face—wrapped in plastic—stares blankly at the attic window, unnoticed. The phone rings continuously as the credits roll. We can only assume that the holiday nightmare is not over yet.

The film helped start a great tradition of holiday horror movies, such as *New Year's Evil* (1980), *Silent Night, Deadly Night* (1984), and even the mock-trailer for Eli Roth's *Thanksgiving* (2007). It combined a traditional celebration for family and friends with a psychotic murderer to turn the film into what many label "one of those mean holiday horror movies." The two opposing forces work well by bringing extreme joy and intense fear and sus-

Clare (Lynne Griffin) stares out of the attic window as her lifeless body remains undiscovered while the killing rampage continues in *Black Christmas* (1974). Viewers are left to stare back at her suffocated image through the attic window as the movie concludes.

pense together on the screen. And although it is a Canadian film by origin, it is included in our discussion for the large influence it had on later U.S. productions, like those previously mentioned and the mainstay horrors *Friday the 13th* and *Halloween*.

Black Christmas offered some slight social commentary because Jess, the protagonist, informs her boyfriend that she is pregnant with his child and wants an abortion, which he refuses to accept. Ironically, Jess kills her boyfriend at the end of the film because she suspects he is the killer. In a way, there is a feminist reading for the situation that informs the viewer a woman's body is her own, and no man or other woman has the right to tell her what to do with it. But other than this one situation, the film remains clear of social messages and sticks to suspense and horrific moments.

Its cast is a showroom of actors whom we have come to see in other horror films over the years. John Saxon (Lt. Fuller) later appeared as Nancy's father in *A Nightmare on Elm Street*; Margot Kidder (Barb) found success in the *Superman* series (1978–1987), *The Amityville Horror* (1979), and *Hal-*

loween II (2009); Olivia Hussey went on to star in *It* (1990); and Andrea Martin's career covers television, film, and voiceover work, with the added bonus of being the only person from the original film to return to *Black Christmas* in the 2006 remake (as the sorority housemother).

Glen Morgan's remake production is filled with color and mood to match the Christmas season of the narrative. The violence in the film is heightened to extremes—eyes are eaten, Martin's character is killed by a falling icicle, one of the girls is beheaded—and the most notable change is a monumental backstory given to Billy the killer. We find out about his troubled childhood, which includes being born with a yellow skin pigment condition and having an unhealthy sexual relationship with his own mother. Billy also has a sister named Agnes who assists in the killings, but in the end both are killed and there is no room left for sequel consideration (unlike the original film's open ending). It is an extremely graphic horror film, but it pushes so far to the extreme of violence that much of what is shown becomes somewhat campy to horror fans and less scary. The gore did not stop the movie from making a decent haul at the box office, and a cast of young actors, including Michelle Trachtenberg, certainly helped bring moviegoers to the theater.

From infected crazies to a psychotic killer, we now come to a cannibalistic, murderous, depraved family. *Black Christmas* was loosely based on real-life murders that occurred in Canada around the holiday season, and Tobe Hooper's *The Texas Chain Saw Massacre* (1974) was inspired by real-life serial killer Ed Gein. Gein was certainly no mass murderer, but his actions—killing women and using dead bodies for making crafts—made him a figure worthy of tribute in horror films. He was first transformed into Norman Bates by Hitchcock in *Psycho*, but his actions and history were also inspiring for *Chain Saw, Halloween, Friday the 13th, A Nightmare on Elm Street, The Silence of the Lambs*, and feature films about Gein himself. Although *Chain Saw* is linked to *Psycho* and Gein, the story it tells is not true; however, the legacy of its "true story" lasts when new viewers come to see the movie for the first time and believe the events really did take place in American history. A little word of mouth has gone a long way for this film over the years.

Comparable to its '70s brother and sister films, *Chain Saw* was a violent film for its time. It was banned in numerous countries upon release, which only made people want to see it even more. For its small production budget, the movie was a box-office smash, and much of the success is owed to its spirit of cinema vérité and terrifying performances by a cast of new faces that were not jaded from working on a lot of previous films.

In a nutshell, five teens go to visit the gravesite of one of their grandfather's to make sure it has not been vandalized or the body exhumed and corrupted; they had previously heard reports of such happenings in the area. On their way to visit a house from the family's holdings, they pick up a cagey hitchhiker that they have to kick out when he brandishes a straight razor and cuts himself and one of the teens. After they arrive at the house, the teens also discover another residence and think it best to ask the inhabitants for gas so they can get back home safely; however, they stumble upon an insane, cannibalistic family, and one by one they are tortured and killed until the final girl character escapes into the back of a passing truck. There she screams and laughs until out of sight, while the scariest family member—Leatherface—twists and turns his chainsaw in the air in a fit of aggravation at the girl's escape.

The story sounds simple enough for a horror film, but audiences were mortified by the terrors inflicted upon the teens and the existence of such a crazed family—even if they were only movie characters. Teens are locked in large freezers on meat hooks, killed with a chainsaw, and beaten over the head with a hammer, while the family members fashion furniture out of bones and Leatherface dresses in drag because there is no mother figure in the house. Events in the film made audiences think twice before stopping on the side of the road to ask people for directions or seek assistance during emergencies. We never really know what is going on in houses that lie outside the boundaries of urban and rural "civilization," but *Chain Saw* gave us one possibility.

The film embodied a sense of the lost American landscape as the Vietnam War was coming to a close. On the other hand, some critics claimed it depicted entirely too much violence against women, like *Last House*; filmmaking was still a predominately male-oriented field, and *Chain Saw* made people question its system of patriarchy and misogyny. The exploitative nature of the movie gave rise to anti-feminist arguments that continue today when the movie is discussed, but other scholars felt the film was simply a reflection of the moral degradation of the American society in times of economic struggle. No matter what viewpoint a critic or moviegoer took, the movie sparked debate from all sides and became one of the most important horror films of all time.

Its popularity helped spawn three sequels to ingrain the mythology of Leatherface into our memories—*The Texas Chainsaw Massacre 2* (1986), with Dennis Hopper, which also faced censorship; *Leatherface: The Texas Chainsaw Massacre III* (1990), with Viggo Mortensen; and *The Texas Chainsaw Massacre: The Next Generation*, with Zellweger and McConaughey—but none of them were ever as popular with fans or at the box office as the original. During production of the sequels throughout the years, the spirit of the original lived on in other horror films that featured masked killers with tools like

Leatherface (Gunnar Hansen) totes his chainsaw as he runs after the escaping final girl in *The Texas Chain Saw Massacre* (1974).

nail-guns, hammers, drills, electric knives, and a host of other automated or hand-held weaponry. The crazy family theme was also recurrent in many movies, such as *Motel Hell* (1980), *House of 1000 Corpses*, and the recent French *Frontier(s)* (2007), which shows that horror's narrative connections have no national boundaries.

The power of an independent film like *Chain Saw* to spark debate, receive censorship and national bans, produce sequels, make money at the box office, and influence film internationally demonstrates that the horror genre is a credible cinematic category against much criticism that the genre has nothing to offer serious filmmaking. It also seemed to make it clear that a remake would be a natural progression in the franchise's development. Marcus Nispel's direction of the 2003 *The Texas Chainsaw Massacre*, coupled with Michael Bay as producer and Tobe Hooper serving as co-producer with Kim Henkel (co-writer of the original), gave the remake movement its first big formulaic success. *Chainsaw* was Nispel's first feature film; he had previously worked on music videos, so he knew how to construct a movie that would be visually pleasing and highlight the best looks for the actors, even in moments of extreme duress in a horror film. Until this movie, Bay's producing credits belonged to *Armageddon* (1998) and *Pearl Harbor* (2001), which were both filled with gigantic action sequences, and both movies scored big money at the theaters. The combination of visual style and a sensibility for big-budget action produced a film that was scary, filled with suspense, and beautiful to watch, with its attention to detail showcasing a '70s atmosphere to a 21st century audience. And with Hooper and Henkel backing the project, it was bound to be a successful endeavor.

The icing on top was the movie's cast, which featured Jessica Biel and Eric Balfour. Biel was already a household name and face from her work on *7th Heaven*, and Balfour had his own television following from his appearances on *Buffy the Vampire Slayer* and *Six Feet Under*. The other young actors rounding out the group were newer faces, but even they had had some exposure from early work in television and film. Costuming for the young cast gave them a '70s look with an updated feel; moviegoers who shop at big-name chain stores, and those who find their own style at thrift stores, could relate to the outfitting and surface look of the actors, and the overall makeup of the film. The production team made sure to show that horror films can be visually appealing, from the camera shots to the landscape to the costuming. Most of these surface elements could be seen during the opening scenes of the movie, but people sat in the audience wondering if the story would grab them. It did.

There are changes from the original narrative, but none that seriously alter the mood of the film; more plot points are added to increase tension and conflict. Two of the protagonists in the original are siblings, but that connection is removed; the brother character was in a wheelchair, but that aspect was taken away, too. The hitchhiker from the original becomes a female character who commits suicide in the van instead of lashing out with a razor blade and being kicked out of the vehicle. This element sends the characters in search of police to handle the situation, which puts them into contact with the family unit that will claim their lives. Characters are cut in half, amputated, and hung on hooks in some of the same fashion as the original. Biel's character (Erin), however, does not suffer the same fate as the Sally character of the original. Instead of being subjected to a "family dinner" and escaping in the back of a passing truck, Erin plays hide-and-seek with Leatherface when she flees the house and eventually rescues a baby the family has kidnapped. Erin drives away in a truck with the rescued baby while Leatherface takes to the road as he did in the original movie. Most would agree that Erin's character is a much more positive portrayal of women in horror, because she takes control of the situation and finds her own way out instead of luckily coming across a passing truck in which she can hitch a ride. Erin takes the driver seat (pun intended) in the remake.

The last sequence the audience sees is black-and-white archive footage of the police investigating the basement of the home. As the police are going over parts of the room, Leatherface jumps out of nowhere and attacks them. The camera freezes on a blurred image of his face, and a voiceover (by John Larroquette) tells us that this is the only image ever captured of Leatherface, who is also known as Thomas Hewitt. We are left to consider the scary thought that Leatherface is still alive and waiting for new victims to stumble upon his homestead.

Nispel and Bay gave the movie more of a horror-action sensibility as the most noticeable update, but the blend of genre components simply brought in more people to see the film. It was a formula that the remake movement embraced and still toys around with in current productions. One visual director plus one action-oriented producer plus support from original production team members (and possibly actors) plus a cast of young and popular actors plus recognizable bands for musical accompaniment equals remake gold. Jonathan Liebesman directed a prequel in 2006 entitled *The Texas Chainsaw Massacre: The Beginning*, with Jordana Brewster leading a young cast, and although it was successful at the box office, the movie took in only half the revenue that Nispel's production made, and fans and critics were not as enthused with the final product they saw in the theater. The series tradition will continue when John Luessenhop's *Texas Chainsaw 3D* is released in 2013.

The '70s gave us horror that illustrated the nuclear family gone bad; it often forced us to see the many ways in which adults and authority figures could not always be trusted. But the children, too, were not always reliable. Richard Donner's *The Omen* (1976) presented us with a little boy by the name of Damien. This is one film where it is difficult to say the narrative is simple, because it is quite an involved story. Robert Thorn and his wife Kathy (Gregory Peck and Lee Remick) give birth to a child in Rome, but due to complications the child dies. Without Kathy knowing, Robert agrees to substitute another newborn for their recently deceased child that a priest convinces him to take. The family moves to England, and odd things begin to happen as Damien grows into a young boy. Their nanny kills herself at Damien's birthday party; a new nanny arrives and tries to take over motherly duties; the nanny allows a strange black dog to protect Damien; and Damien reacts viciously to the idea of visiting church. Robert is informed that the child was born from a jackal, and that he must be destroyed. Through a series of events—a priest's death, Kathy becoming pregnant and then miscarrying, Kathy jumping to her death, the revelation that Damien's mother was a jackal, and the discovery that the original Thorn baby was killed in order for Damien to be substituted—Robert is convinced he must kill his son with special daggers. Robert takes Damien to a church to kill him, but as he raises a dagger to stab the child he is shot and killed by the police. The film ends with Damien attending Robert and Kathy's funeral as the heir to Robert's business and holdings. He is now under the guardianship of the president (of America), who happens to have been Robert's college roommate.

The story is an involved narrative, but this is necessary when dealing with plots that involve politics, religion, abortion, murder, and satanic rites. Reaction to the film was positive in terms of the acting performances, the musical score, and even its horror aspects. Jerry Goldsmith won the Best Original Score Academy Award for his contributions to the film, which involved music that starkly contrasted the evil presence of Damien and the good intentions of the Thorn family. Horror finds many of its awards in the technical aspects of filmmaking, and an Oscar certainly gave the film a legitimacy that other horror films are typically not awarded. Its box-office revenue was massive, and the film became a commercial hit for the horror genre. Over the years *The Omen* has paved the way for other evil-child and satanic movies, such as *The Good Son* (1993), *Stigmata* (1999), and *Orphan* (2009), but it was influenced itself by previous films like *The Bad Seed* (1956) and *The Exorcist*. It generated two theatrical sequels and one released to television—*Damien: Omen II* (1978), *Omen III: The Final Conflict* (1981), and *Omen IV: The Awakening* (1991). And as much as the original film contained taboo subjects, it was never truly attacked for its material; *The Exorcist* had received enough backlashes for proceeding horror movies that contained religious material and demon possession.

Probably the most interesting and lucky marketing tool the 2006 remake utilized was releasing the film on June 6, which gave the impression that the film had a real connection to the Mark of the Beast—666. It was directed by John Moore, who had previously worked in the action genre on *Behind Enemy Lines* (2001) and *Flight of the Phoenix* (2004). Liev Schreiber and Julia Stiles took on the roles of Robert and Katherine Thorn, with David Thewlis as the photographer Keith Jennings, Mia Farrow as the nanny Mrs. Baylock, and Pete Postlethwaite as Father Brennan. Minus Seamus Davey-Fitzpatrick as Damien, the cast was filled with seasoned actors. Harvey Stephens, who portrayed the original Damien in the '70s, made a cameo appearance in the remake as a reporter.

Moore's update plays true to the original, down to the memorable scene of Damien riding his bike in the house and knocking Kathy over the second-floor railing. The major difference between the two films involves Kathy's death, which is the result of Mrs. Baylock killing her in the remake when she visits her in the hospital. As an updated version, *The Omen* is probably the only contemporary remake to keep the story and events so parallel to its original. There were no awards for this version of the film, however, and the biggest criticism it received was the casting, which some felt was too hodgepodge or too young for the roles of the parents. These slightly negative responses did not stop the film from being a successful movie. Also similar to the original film, the remake was a runaway hit at the box office, taking in almost $120 million on a fairly meager Hollywood production budget of $25 million.

Starting with Nispel's *The Texas Chainsaw Massacre* in 2003 and continuing on with remade films made thereafter, this is the time when the remake movement put a lot of emphasis on production value, acting, star power, action scenes, and special effects. We notice that a lot of social commentary from the original films have been removed and replaced with a concentration on horror entertainment. In many cases the narratives are the same, but the stories do not and cannot socially, politically, culturally, or economically connect to contemporary America. Issues we faced in the '50s, '60s, '70s, '80s, and even '90s are always present in some form in the 21st century, but they are typically not as urgent, widespread, or new to the public. The remaining remakes in this discussion demonstrate the value placed on star power, visual aesthetics, depictions of violence, and directorial recognition (career advancement), which all function together as a unified model to attract patrons to the theater to help the films become financial successes; and when the movies make money, everyone involved benefits via revenue or name recognition.

In 1977, Wes Craven directed *The Hills Have Eyes*. In the film, nuclear radiation has caused mutations in people living in a hill region, which in turn results in their insanity and aggressive behavior toward each other and "normal" humans who stumble into their region. The mutants rape, impregnate, kill, and eat non-mutants in this dark (literally) movie. *Hills* falls into the category of vacation-horror films, although most of the movies usually involve a few friends taking a trip overseas. Craven's film showed audiences that danger easily resides here in the States. The original story depicts the Carter family—Bob and Ethel, and their children Brenda, Bobby, and Lynne, with her husband Doug, their daughter Katy, and the family dogs Beauty and Beast—traveling for vacation. But their happy trip comes to a grinding halt when the car goes off the road because of a trap set by the mutant beings who live in the region. The mutant family is comprised of gas-station attendant Fred, his son Papa Jupiter, and Jupiter's kids, Mars, Pluto, Mercury, and Ruby. As the Carter family members split up and seek help, no luck befalls them. Later, Bob is burned alive, Brenda is raped twice, Lynne and Ethel are fatally shot, Katy is kidnapped, and Beauty is killed. Only Doug, Brenda, Bobby, and Beast survive the first round of mutant attack to rescue

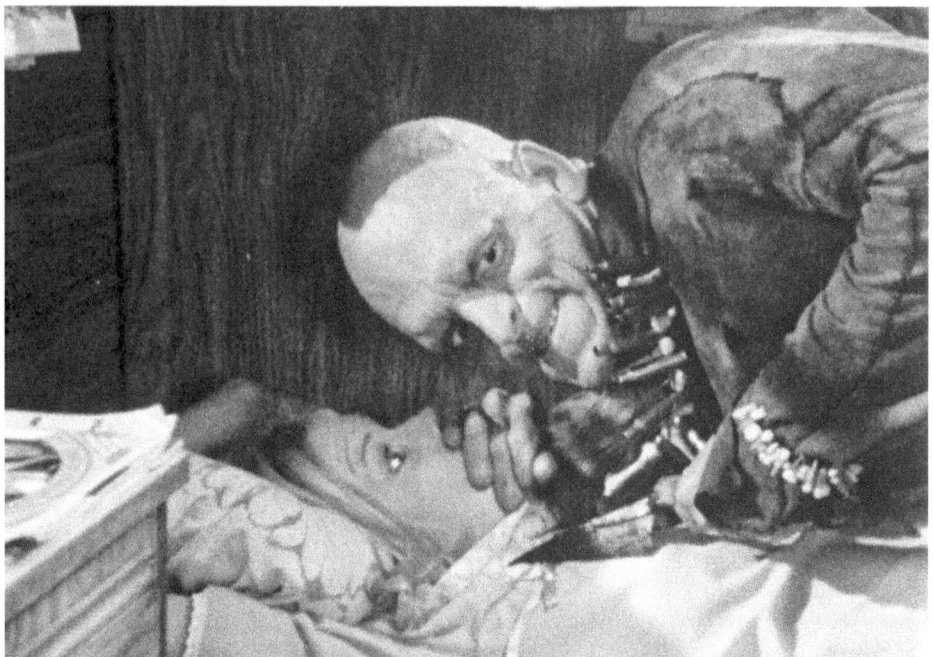

Brenda (Suze Lanier-Bramlett/Susan Lanier) struggles to keep from crying out as Pluto (Michael Berryman) holds his hand over her mouth and a makeshift knife to her throat in *The Hills Have Eyes* (1977). Brenda is raped by Pluto and another mutant cannibal while her family is distracted outside their trailer.

Katy and kill off the mutants to avenge the deaths of the other family members. Ruby is the lone member of the mutant family that survives, because she kept Katy safe during all the turmoil. The final scene shows Doug repeatedly stabbing Mars while Ruby cries over the situation.

It is a dark movie in mood and actual lighting, especially for many of the outdoor scenes filmed at night. The rape and murders are brutal and not to be dismissed, but U.S. audiences had seen such violence before. *Hills* is reminiscent of *Chain Saw* and the unstable people we may encounter who live on the edge of civilization. Both families carried past histories of incest, cannibalism, and mental health imbalances; however, the family in *Hills* is more predatory because they purposely set traps for people passing through the area instead of luckily stumbling upon victims like the family in *Chain Saw*. *Hills* was a film that showcased the vast loneliness and emptiness of the Western landscape in the '70s, even as America was touted as the greatest nation in the world. All nations have dark underbellies that can be revealed if someone travels to the right (or wrong) place.

The *Hills Have Eyes* remake devoted its focus to production formula to ensure a successful film. Alexandre Aja directed the remake in 2006; he had previously helmed the internationally-acclaimed French horror film *Haute tension* (*High Tension*) in 2003. Aja was no stranger to horror, but *Hills* would be his feature debut in America. The original movie history in cinema, its financial strength (production budget of under $250 thousand and revenue of approximately $25 million), the growing movement of remakes being produced, and a developing recognition of French horror directors as innovative filmmakers for the market guaranteed that Aja would become a recognized director in contemporary American horror. Aja's *Hills* was not the dark film that Craven created in the '70s. Aja's remake was bright and harsh in the light of day; it hid nothing from the cameras in an effort to bring the audience closer to the violence. There was much more blood, more action, and more mutants to fight and learn about during the course of the film.

The revealing visuals were further used to highlight special makeup effects seen in the movie, such as the wheelchair-bound mutant named Big Brain whose head seemed almost the same size as his body; it was too big for him to lift, so his days were lived out in a wheelchair. Brain is also the character who informs the viewer how the mutants came to be in their homeland. Aja made the film an overt horror experience as opposed to Craven's violent but more subtle exploration of the monsters and madness. Fans of the new wave of horror remakes found the updated version to be visceral, fast-paced, frightening, and extremely well-made. Kathleen Quinlan, whose acting career covers television and film since 1972, and Ted Levine (Buffalo Bill from *The Silence of the Lambs*), who has been in the business since 1983, added a solid foundation to the remake, with a younger cast of fresh faces to play the other family members. Horror maven Dee Wallace played the role of Lynne. The movie did not require the element of recognizable teen actors because the focus was geared toward production quality for the visuals, makeup effects, and violence.

Although the original *Hills* and its remake both produced sequels, the two are not related. Craven directed *The Hills Have Eyes Part II* in 1985. The movie revisits the origin story and returns with characters from the original, including Beast, who has psychedelic flashbacks to the terror he encountered with the mutants. Michael Berryman is celebrated by horror fans as Pluto from the original film, and he returns as the same mutant character in the sequel. Fans of the films remember that Berryman required no makeup for the movie because the actor was born with over 20 birth defects that provide him with a recognizable appearance no matter what role he assumes. The 2007 *Hills* sequel focuses on a military reconnaissance operation that gets ambushed by mutants in the hills. It was Martin Weisz's feature-film debut on a national scale, but the director has yet to make another movie.

Like its predecessor, Aja's *Hills* made a lot of money from ticket sales. Its DVD sales were also quite impressive—in the double-digit millions. Unlike a lot of other remakes, *Hills* was released in the theater as an R-rated movie, but it was still made to seem new for its DVD release by allowing consumers to purchase it in an unrated version. The marketing of remakes is never just about the theatrical releases; studios are business-savvy enough to consider releasing various formats of the movie on DVD so that different consumers can purchase appropriate copies, or curious buyers can pick up the separate copies to compare them. Money is made in the theater and on home viewing more so today than any other time in cinema history; remakes benefit from this rich market because fans can watch the movie in the theater; buy it on DVD in different formats; rent, purchase, or download it from Redbox, Amazon, or Blockbuster; or acquire it through pay-per-view screenings.

The widespread exposure that Aja received from making *Hills* opened doors for him to become a household name in contemporary American horror—and subsequently direct a remake for the next film on our list. When Steven Spielberg's *Jaws* came out in 1975, the water became a new space that horror filled. When Joe Dante's *Piranha* came out in 1978, the water overflowed with tiny fish, thousands of teeth, and a mix of screams and laughs from the audience. In *Piranha*, an unlikely pair of people (Maggie and Paul) accidentally drains a pond containing mutant piranha, allowing the fish to enter into local swimming waters, a camp, and a resort. The fish were a holdover from a government project intended to use the mutated creatures as a military weapon during the Vietnam War. We follow Maggie and Paul throughout the rest of the film as they try to warn the locals and avoid a threatening military presence that intends to poison the waters in an attempt to kill the fish. After various attacks and deaths, it is Maggie and Paul who save the day by releasing a toxic waste into the water that destroys the piranha. But as the movie concludes, we hear the thematic sound of piranha "purring," combined with visuals of a beach. It is obvious to the audience that not all the piranha were killed; they have reached open water.

Piranha was in no way a commercial success, and critics and moviegoers considered the film to be schlock; however, it has always been influential to other creature features, both in water and on land. The production team behind the scenes was also a major group responsible for making some of the most memorable (good and bad) films over the years after *Piranha* was released. Dante went on to direct *The Howling*, *Gremlins* (1984), *The 'Burbs* (1989) and a host of other films. John Sayles made his screenwriting debut with *Piranha*, and his career blossomed into later writing *The Howling*, *Passion Fish* (1992), *Lone Star* (1996), *Sunshine State* (2002), and many other celebrated independent features. Rounding out the group was Roger Corman, who is definitely one of Hollywood's most prolific producers since 1954; he directed *The Little Shop of Horrors* (1960) and is still going strong today. All these men continue to direct, write, and produce contemporary work, and in many ways *Piranha* was a springboard for Sayles's and Dante's careers.

Aja continued his career of remaking horror in 2008 with *Mirrors*, and in 2010 with *Piranha 3D*. His rendition took in much more than movie insiders could have predicted and was clearly a successful remake financially. The movie remained mostly true to the idea of the original, with a few scenes paralleled, but there were certainly updates added into the mix. Over-the-top characters were featured, like Derrick Jones (Jerry O'Connell)—a filmmaker of cheesy Spring Break porn. O'Connell was joined by the elite acting forces of Elisabeth Shue (Sheriff Julie Forester), Ving Rhames (Deputy Fallon), Christopher Lloyd (Carl Goodman), and an opening scene cameo by Richard Dreyfuss (Matthew Boyd). Aja and the actors made *Piranha 3D* a hyper-representational horror film; the kills were larger-than-life, the nudity was gratuitous, the situations were unbelievable, and the onscreen actions involving the fish made audience members jump and laugh out loud. It is a remake focused on entertainment value meant to bring in big bucks at the box office, and it succeeded. Aja's new film *Horns* (2013) stars Daniel Radcliffe, but with the path he is taking it would not be wrong to assume another remake might be on the horizon. *Piranha 3DD*, the sequel to the remake, was released in 2012 with little box-office success. The movie is being directed by John Gulagar, who brought us the *Feast* trilogy (2005–2009); it stars Gary Busey, David Hasselhoff, and Danielle Panabaker, and features returning appearances by Christopher Lloyd and Ving Rhames.

It should be noted that Aja's remake is actually the second remake of the original film. Scott Levy directed a television version in 1995, with Roger Corman as producer. The movie featured Soleil Moon Frye of *Punky Brewster* (NBC 1984–1988) fame, and a young Mila Kunis of *That '70s Show* (FOX 1998–2006) and other popular television and film projects in a role from her first year as an actor. Even more interesting is the original sequel to *Piranha*—*Piranha Part Two: The Spawning* (1981); this time the mutant fish are able to fly. The movie served as the directorial debut for none other than James Cameron, and it featured Lance Henriksen, who would later go on to star in Cameron's *Aliens*. Cameron's directing career started with a water movie; he continued using the element in *The Abyss* (1989) and *Titanic*, and rumor has it that one or both of the planned sequels to *Avatar* (2009) will be filmed entirely underwater. Not many people could have predicted that the director of *Piranha Part Two* would go on to make *Avatar*—the highest grossing movie of all time, with over $2 billion dollars in sales worldwide. Horror definitely has a rich past.

The fun of *Piranha* gives way, however, when we turn to the rape-revenge subgenre. Meir Zarchi's *I Spit on Your Grave* (1978) is the most controversial movie to appear on the list, as the original was banned in 13 countries upon its release for its graphic violence, nudity, and cinematic immorality. *Spit* was originally billed as *Day of the Woman*, but when it was picked up for distribution in 1980 it was thereafter titled *I Spit on Your Grave*—this is the title by which most people have come to know the production. The film's DVD cover art describes the story by saying, "This woman has just chopped and mutilated four men beyond recognition ... but no jury in America would ever convict her!" Like *Last House*, *Spit* was labeled a video nasty and considered by most critics to be misogynistic, cruel, and of poor taste (and production quality). Others found the film to carry a strong message about the strength and resilience of women to overcome harrowing situations and regain control over their lives. It remains a hotbed of debate over 30 years later, and in some cases the movie has only just been made available in the 21st century due to censorship and previous bans.

The controversy surrounding the movie has much to do with its narrative, but even more to do with how the scenes are acted out and filmed. Jennifer Hills (Camille Keaton) is a fiction writer from New York who decides to take up residence in a country cabin for the summer in order to get away from the city and write a novel. Jennifer catches the attention of a few locals—Johnny, Andy, Stanley, and Matthew—who eventually make their way to her cabin, brutally and repeatedly rape her, and leave her for dead. They also destroy the novel she had been working on. Johnny orders Matthew to go back into the cabin and kill Jennifer to keep their identities safe, but he simply puts some of her blood on a knife and returns to lie to Johnny about killing her. Jennifer regains her strength and mental faculties over the next few days, and she later visits a church to ask for forgiveness because she is about to take revenge on the men who assaulted her. She lures the men back to her cabin one by one and kills each of them in graphic ways. After killing the last man, Jennifer sails off in a motorboat and the film ends.

Characters had been raped previously in films like *Last House* and *Hills*, but the assault on Jennifer by multiple men was filmed so realistically that many people questioned whether what was happening was acting or a real gang-rape caught on camera. The clumsiness and awkwardness of the sequence made it seem un-choreographed and unscripted, which added to its visual realism. Gratuitous nudity (for both the victim and assailants) also added to the shock value of the rape sequence. It also seemed that the violence would never end, as Jennifer is repeatedly raped trying to escape the men in the forest; her cabin provides no safe haven, as they enter the residence and continue the assault. But the violence did not end with the rape sequence; Jennifer's retaliation caused even more of a reaction from viewers. She hangs Matthew; invites Johnny to take a bath with her, then slices off his genitals and lets him bleed to death; axes Andy in the back; and eviscerates Stanley in the lake with the blades from the motorboat she uses to leave the cabin and bad memories behind.

It is one of American cinema's grittiest depictions of rape (for a male or female victim) and a sinister presentation of revenge. Unlike either versions of *Last House on the Left*, *Spit* grants the battered party a voice to speak out against her attackers and the physicality to avenge the crime. Keaton was rewarded for her performance at the Catalonian International Film Festival, where she received Best Actress recognition; however, this was the production's only acknowledgment by any organized institute of cinematic accolade. When it was announced that Steven Monroe would direct a remake for 2010, cult horror fans and critics were abuzz at the news.

Monroe started his directing career in 1996, so this would not be his first feature film; however, the surprising decision to remake *Spit* provided him worldwide attention during production of the movie. He chose working actors whose previous work included big parts in television shows and feature films, but there were no superstar names attached to the film. Monroe's production is about paying homage to the controversial original film and testing the limits of visual violence for a 21st century audience. The narrative situation remains the same, with a few details altered, but the kills are different; they are more drawn out, sadistic, and shocking. Jennifer strings a noose around Matthew; covers Stanley's face in fish guts for crows to come and pluck out his eyes; burns Andy's face with lye; pulls out Johnny's teeth, makes him perform oral sex on a gun, and chops off his penis; and anally rapes the sheriff (who had allowed her to be assaulted) with a shotgun. Jennifer also records her actions using one of the assailant's cameras; the addition of technology is certainly a nod to the contemporary viewing audience.

Both films keep the debate alive about crime and punishment. People question whether the men would have been appropriately punished had Jennifer reported the crime to law officials. Others admit that vigilante justice is simply sometimes a better answer for a legal system that often seems to side against the victim. Moral judgments exist in the remake, but are not as fresh as they were when the original was released. The remake gets viewers to remember the original and its controversy while simultaneously acknowledging the updated version as a piece of cinema meant to be seen as a production instead of a representation of feminism or justice in America.

The final film rounding out the '70s contains hardly any controversy or moralistic outrage in comparison to *Spit*; however, it is often considered the best babysitter–horror film ever made, and its production has influenced tons of other films in the genre and beyond. Fred Walton's *When a Stranger Calls*

(1979) is not known for its intricate plot, gory kill scenes, cinematography, or other technical aspects of filmmaking. It is best known for its opening sequence of approximately 20 minutes that features Jill Johnson (Carol Kane) babysitting. Most people cannot recall what happens after the opening scenes because the intensity of suspense seems to climax so early in the narrative.

Jill starts to receive phone calls from a stranger who asks, "Have you checked the children?" To her knowledge, the kids are upstairs and asleep in their beds, so she considers the calls to be someone's creepy prank. The calls continue and the voice becomes more menacing, which causes Jill to phone the police to alert them to the situation; in turn, the police tell Jill they will trace the call if she gets another one from the man and can keep him on the phone long enough to pinpoint the location. After one last threatening call, Jill hangs up and the police immediately call her back. They tell her the call has been traced and is coming from upstairs, inside the house. At this moment a light turns on upstairs. Jill is able to see the caller's shadow at the top of the stairs, and she runs to the front door to escape and get help.

Although this situation could have been a cat-and-mouse game of pranks suitable to fill an entire movie, the mini-story takes place at the beginning of the film. We learn that the police—led by John Clifford, played by Charles Durning—arrived in time to catch the man, but the children had been murdered in their beds when Jill thought they were still alive. Jill is safe, and the killer is sent away to a mental hospital ... until he escapes seven years later, only to attempt the same murderous scenario on Jill's kids while she is out to dinner with her husband. Jill receives a call at the restaurant that asks, "Have you checked the children?" which prompts her to call the babysitter and alert the police. The children are fine, but later that night Jill goes downstairs to get a drink, and when she gets back into bed the killer has replaced her husband lying next to her. She is saved by Clifford, who shoots the killer, and her husband is found unconscious in the closet.

Stranger has all the makings of a stereotypical horror film in which an insane asylum patient breaks out to seek revenge on a family member or other person who previously did her/him wrong; however, the realization that the calls were coming from inside the house was such a huge focal point of the movie that it still remains the most memorable aspect of the film. This same action happened five years earlier in *Black Christmas*, but it was not highlighted enough to draw attention to it as an important modus operandi of the killer.

The repeated phone question—"Have you checked the children?"—is influential for other catchy phrases we have heard, such as "In seven days..." from *The Ring* and "What's your favorite scary movie?" from the *Scream* series. It even lends a connection to Jigsaw's "I wanna play a game" recordings from the *Saw* series. All of the taunting by the killers can be traced back to the call in *When a Stranger Calls*. The phone call sequence is also extremely memorable because it represents an important element of horror that is now long gone—the land line. We are accustomed to seeing people use a home phone (or maybe a pay phone on the street) to call the police in horror films from the '80s and before. Often times the killer would cut the lines, or the phones would be dead, but the telephone was always a staple of horror. When the cell phone (not specifically the cordless or car phone) came into mass production, horror changed. Killers could no longer cut phone lines or call from inside the house on the same line; cell phones gave victims the freedom to notify friends or police if they were in trouble. But nothing is ever too easy in horror. Killers are typically prevented from easy capture because the victim's phone cannot receive service in a certain area or the battery dies. Times change and the horror genre adapts to new technology. This is what happened in Simon West's *When a Stranger Calls* production in 2006.

The original is updated but made to keep some of its '70s vibe by having Jill babysit in a house with a land line; her cell phone and car have been taken away from her for a month as punishment for going over the allotted minutes allowed on her phone plan. This probably would not happen in real life, but we are dealing with movies, and movies need plot devices and conflict to drive a story. Other updates include making the house enormous (so that the killer can stalk his prey), allowing the children to live, and showcasing other deaths (a babysitter and her charges are murdered across town at the beginning of the film, Jill's friend is murdered at the house, and the family's maid is killed, as well). At the end, after the bad guy has been captured, Jill wanders the hospital she has been taken to in a dream sequence. The killer attacks her in her room, and she wakes up to doctors and nurses trying to keep her calm and reassure her that she is safe. It is an ending reminiscent of *Carrie*, *Friday the 13th*, and other horror gems that depict the final girl traumatized after surviving a tormenting night of hellish events. Although West's film did not break any box-office records for a horror production, it managed to scare up a little over $50 million in ticket sales, which is standard fare for successful contemporary remakes in theatrical release.

The babysitter movie has been a staple of horror for many years, and the original *When a Stranger Calls* ranks at the top. Its telephone sequence opening was not completely original, but the concentration applied to the scenes has made it memorable enough to influence other films and spawn a remake of its own. Ti West's *The House of the Devil* (2009) offers a more contemporary babysitter horror film, with the added bonus of it being filmed to represent the late '70s and early '80s. An innovative movie such as *House* lets us see the influence of *Stranger* and the many ways horror films continue to connect with each other throughout the decades of cinema. Walton went on to direct *When a Stranger Calls Back* in 1993—a televised sequel to his original film, with Kane and Durning reprising their roles as Jill and John from the original. The movie focuses on the killer's ability to camouflage his body with paint, but he is no match for Jill and John, who take him down in the end. All in all, the '70s introduced graphic violence, disturbing images, and heated debates about subject matter in the films of its decade; the time period ended with the same amount of aggression, cruelty, and bloodshed that started its history in cinema.

Horror remakes often are created from films that were not originally classified as horror. Some remakes continue social commentary from original films, but many of them cannot due to changes in the social climate; they become simply horror entertainment, with no message for viewers to take away with them when the screen goes black. The '30s, '40s, and '50s were about science and creatures; the '60s focused on the dead; the '70s put crazed killers into the spotlight; the '80s were a mixed bag about the unseen killer with a few supernatural events thrown into the mix and leftover crazed families from the '70s; and the '90s were considered a time of limbo for horror in which the rise of the American independent film benefited.

The 20 films previously discussed represent some of horror's most influential and representational movies that have given birth to and maintained a phenomenon of remakes, but the list is not complete and probably never will be, given the amount of remake productions currently in development, being written, or rumored to be produced. In order to understand how expansive the movement has become, it is necessary to take a brief look at the '80s, followed by a small overview of films that did not make the list but deserve mention for the particular original and remake filmic qualities they possess. During the '80s the horror genre created its golden age or heyday of slasher films. It was also an era of holiday horror, high school horror, supernatural horror, and road horror. This is the decade the remake movement is currently pulling productions from for its theatrical releases.

The biggest remakes taken from original '80s horror genre are certainly *Friday the 13th* and *A Nightmare on Elm Street*, but let us not forget some of the movies that the 21st century generation may not know had the originals not been remade. *The Fog* is one of John Carpenter's classics about a fishing town plagued by a fog that contains corporeal ghosts avenging their wrongful deaths from almost 100 years before. The fog plays its own character in the movie as it slowly drifts in to let the audience know the ghosts are not too far behind and someone is probably about to die. It added mystery and suspense to a scary ghost story, and the atmosphere of the fog is what makes the movie memorable; it fills the imagination of the viewer and holds her/him in constant tension regarding what will happen next.

Three actors in the film equally match the power of the fog. The casting of Adrienne Barbeau and the mother-daughter team of Janet Leigh and Jamie Lee Curtis brought together three of horror's favorite scream queens. Barbeau plays a plucky radio DJ, Leigh is one of the town's most respected women, and Curtis makes her way into the story as a hitchhiker. It is one of those rare occasions when horror icons get to share the screen, although their characters do not interact throughout the movie. And Carpenter complemented the elements of fog and iconic actors by once again composing original (and always moody) music for the film.

The Fog was remade in 2005 by Rupert Wainwright, who had previously worked on music videos and music documentaries for talent such as MC Hammer and N.W.A. The remake cast featured Tom Welling from *Smallville*, Maggie Grace from *Lost* (ABC 2004–2010), and Selma Blair from *Hellboy* (2004) in lead roles. The plot changes a bit to introduce the characters and their connection to the town, but the horror part of the story still involves the ghosts coming back to avenge their deaths. What viewers will notice the most between the original and the remake is the fog. The remake utilizes contemporary special effects to create fog with computer graphics. Although the technique is effective, most fans and critics look back fondly upon the original for its lo-tech accomplishment in maintaining its eerie atmosphere. However, both versions posted good numbers at the box office.

A movie that did not do well financially (original or remake) is *Mother's Day* (1980). Charles Kaufman directed this Troma film (the company responsible for indie/cult horror titles like *The Toxic Avenger* [1984] and *Tromeo and Juliet* [1996]) about a mother and her two deranged sons who live in backwoods America and like to torture people that stumble upon their land. It is an exploitation film in the same vein as *Last House on the Left* and *I Spit on Your Grave*, but Kaufman's aesthetic with Troma films keeps the movie from becoming as disturbing to viewers as the other productions. The most interesting aspect about *Mother's Day* is that it represents the same style of film that the remake movement pushed for with Iliadis's *Last House* and Monroe's *Spit*, but its remake was not given anywhere near the same amount of publicity as these other films; many people do not even know a remake was produced. Darren Lynn Bousman directed the remake in 2010, with Rebecca De Mornay in the role of the unstable mother. De Mornay—as fans may remember—came to fame with her role as another unstable mother figure in the suspense-thriller *The Hand That Rocks the Cradle* (1992). Although the remake's production value is high, the acting solid, and the elements of violence and horror are powerful, it has yet to receive a wide release. To date, the film has only been shown on limited screens in the Netherlands, and with a production budget of over ten million dollars it is highly unlikely it will be able to recoup its expenses.

But for every financial disappointment there is always a success to balance out the releases. *My Bloody Valentine* is one of many holiday horror feature films released in the '80s. Like its holiday horror partners, *Valentine* takes a day meant to be celebrated with love and turns it into a horrific event that characters and movie viewers will come to remember as dark and tragic. George Mihalka directed the film, which is actually a Canadian release; it is being included here because most people accept it as part of American horror, and its remake is a strong representative for contemporary American horror.

The story involves a coal mining explosion that claims the lives of a group of coal miners because their supervisors left them to attend a Valentine's Day dance. A sole survivor later kills the supervisors for their ineptitude and warns the town to never have another dance; however, years later a dance is planned and then cancelled after the police receive a human heart and a warning. Young locals decide to ignore the police and hold a party in the coal mines themselves. And soon, people are being killed off in graphic ways.

Valentine is notable for its kill factor and obvious influence from *Halloween* and *Friday the 13th*. It created a character out of a gas mask, miner helmet, work jumpsuit, and pickaxe in the same fashion that Michael Myers came to be represented by a William Shatner mask and knife; Jason Vorhees by a hockey mask; and Freddy Krueger by finger-knives, a striped sweater, and a dirty hat. The movie is often lumped together with the other holiday-horror features, but it stands on its own merit. Patrick Lussier—better known for sequel productions such as *The Prophecy 3: The Ascent* (2000), the *Dracula 2000* series (2000–2005), and *White Noise 2: The Light* (2007)— directed the remake in 2009, with Jensen Ackles in the lead role. Ackles shared the horror remake trend with his *Supernatural* co-star (Padalecki) whose *House of Wax* movie came out in 2005.

The updated *Valentine* has a more intricate story that involves the sole survivor of a collapsed mine accident killing the other trapped men in order to keep oxygen levels high for his personal safety. He is rescued after falling into a coma, wakes up on Valentine's Day, goes on a killing spree (including teenagers having a party in the mines), and is believed to have been killed by local law enforcement. One of the teenagers who survived the attack in the mines comes back to town after an absence of ten years only to discover that the killer has returned on Valentine's Day to finish the job he started previously. The twists and turns in the story are common in contemporary horror films to keep the audience guessing whether or not the killer has returned, or if it is someone else carrying on the legend. And with the addition of 3D special effects, the remake was able to scare up over $100 million at the box office—an extremely impressive number that beats out the remakes for *Halloween*, *Friday the 13th*, and many others. The formula for mixing a recognizable television heartthrob and other young actors with special effects and a visual director for horror elements paid off well. Lussier continues his track record of making remakes and sequels; he is currently working on developing *Halloween III* for a future release.

Turning from the mines, we head to a place horror rarely seems to go anymore—the road. In 1986, Robert Harmon directed what is now considered a cult classic by the name of *The Hitcher*. Rutger Hauer, C. Thomas Howell, and Jennifer Jason Leigh bring the story to life. Jim Halsey (Howell) is transporting a car across state lines and picks up a hitchhiker (Hauer) that makes his life a living hell. Hauer plays John Ryder, a serial killer on the run. Halsey gives Ryder a lift, and, through a series of events manipulated by Ryder, becomes the top suspect for Ryder's crimes because the police do not know the identity of the killer. Halsey befriends truck-stop waitress Nash (Leigh) and enlists her help in the dangerous situation. The movie dips into several genres, with its mix of violence, car chases, and a memorable scene of one of the characters being somewhat "quartered" (or simply torn in half) by a Mack truck and its trailer hitch. All of the elements of the film come together to make a unique horror movie that has been celebrated for its acting and genre-bending for years.

Music video director Dave Meyers made *The Hitcher* (2007) remake, his second and only other feature film to date. Sean Bean, Zachary Knighton, and Sophia Bush starred in the principle roles as John Ryder, Jim Halsey, and Grace Andrews. The story is altered by Halsey and Andrews being a couple who pick up Ryder; and it is Andrews who becomes the protagonist and object of Ryder's malicious affection instead of the boyfriend. Other than the gender switch in character placement, the movie plays out much like the original but with a higher production budget. However, the story seems a bit dated in the 21st century because too many people know the dangers of hitchhiking and picking up hitchhikers. If anything, we are a society of overly-cautious people, but some of that reality has to be suspended in order for the film to work as a horror movie. Its release did not bring in the big bucks, but it managed to catch the attention of enough moviegoers to take in several millions.

The final '80s film in the group was released a year before *The Hitcher*, but it is at the end of the list because its remake is the most current release of all the films being discussed. We return to the subject of vampires in Tom Holland's *Fright Night* (1985). Charley Brewster (William Ragsdale) knows his neighbor Jerry Dandrige (Chris Sarandon) is a vampire, but no one believes him. When his girlfriend Amy (Amanda Bearse) and best friend Evil Ed (Stephen Geoffreys) fail to take him seriously, he turns to Peter

Vincent (Roddy McDowall)—television's fictional "fearless vampire killer"—for help in discovering the truth. Of course Charley is correct, and the bunch find themselves fighting a powerful vampire who wants Amy for a companion, turns Evil Ed into a vampire, and is set on killing our protagonist.

There is a homespun element to *Fright Night* that makes the movie a standout from the '80s; it works in the same way that *Silver Bullet* presented its werewolf story. It is also the only film in this small group of '80s horror that spawned a sequel—*Fright Night 2* (1988), which reunited Ragsdale and McDowall in their original character roles. *Fright Night* is a working combination of quality acting (especially with the accomplished McDowall), solid '80s special effects, and a classic story of the vampire seeking companionship but mortal love winning in the end. The original film fared quite well at the box office, and its staying power certainly helped prompt its 2011 remake.

Craig Gillespie—previously known for *Lars and the Real Girl* (2007) and *Mr. Woodcock* (2007)—returned to feature films with a new *Fright Night*. His version stars Colin Farrell as Dandrige, David Tennant as Vincent, Anton Yelchin as Charley, Christopher Mintz-Plasse as Evil Ed, Imogen

"Fearless vampire killer" Peter Vincent (Roddy McDowall) unknowingly holds the vampiric Jerry Dandrige (Chris Sarandon) at bay with a cross in *Fright Night* (1985).

Poots as Amy, and Toni Collette as Charley's mom. The remake hit theaters August 19, 2011, and before its release the trailer showed lots of special effects and a storyline that looked similar to the original. Farrell gave the people over at DreadCentral.com his own take on what the remake offers moviegoers:

> I mean, I loved the original, and I hope the film is—on its own—entertaining and works. Because I really did love the original, so much so that—as I've said—I was hoping I wouldn't like the remake when I read it, because I didn't want to have to answer questions about remakes and lack of originality and all that shit. I didn't want to think of myself in those terms either, so I was hoping that I didn't like it. But [I] read it and I'm an actor and I loved it and I went, "OK, let's go to work." I mean, it's close enough in structure and story [to the original], but there are some things that have been changed. Peter Vincent's a lot younger, and what he does has kind of been put into a very contemporary setting. There are some changes.

The changes in story involve a different location (Las Vegas), Charley as the non-believer who has to be convinced his neighbor is a vampire, Ed and Charley as estranged friends because Charley wants to fit in with his girlfriend and the cool kids in school, and Peter Vincent as a Criss Angel character who performs gothic, pyrotechnic vampire shows at casinos in Vegas—fully equipped with wig, fake facial hair, and leather pants that give him a rash.

The Charley we see in the remake does not follow the career of Vincent as the character does in the original. It is Ed who believes strongly in the existence of vampires and tracks disappearances of kids from school in connection to a theory about Jerry. He is hunted and turned by Jerry, which makes Charley start to believe in vampires when he cannot locate his longtime friend. Charley's ultimate proof comes when he breaks into Jerry's house and discovers a girl held captive and being drained for her blood; he witnesses Jerry bite and drink from her before he later attempts to rescue her.

After a creepy encounter with Jerry—they discuss Charley's mom and his girlfriend with only an open doorway separating them because Jerry has not been invited into the home—Charley's mission becomes one of survival; he must do everything in his power to protect the women he loves. He tries to secure help from Vincent but is turned away by the performer. Jerry uses his sinister smarts to get Charley, his mom, and Amy out of the house and the confrontation takes them from a car chase to a fight in Vincent's high-rise penthouse and to the final battle at Jerry's house, in which Vincent joins to help. Charley's mom is injured during the first leg of the battle and is hospitalized, but, much like the original, the good guys win in the end.

The characters are altered more than the overall story from the original (Jerry is a wild hunter from a rare breed of vampire instead of a civilized creature of the night looking for love); however, the remake makes use of memorable original dialogue, such as Ed saying, "Oh, you're so *cool*, Brewster," and Jerry saying, "Welcome to 'Fright Night' ... for real." And most of the film is updated to match 21st century items like Google and eBay, which is where Peter Vincent acquires some of his vampire-killing tools and artifacts. The film production was also updated; audiences could opt to see the film in 2D or 3D theatrical presentations, and there are many action sequences filled with special effects (vampires being killed, Jerry tossing a revved motorcycle onto the back of a moving car, Ed jumping to the ceiling as a newly-made vampire, etc.).

It is a film with high production values—a staple of the horror remake wave—but the final box-office returns showed that more people prefer *Twilight* vampires. The budget was estimated at $30 million; it debuted in fifth place with $8.3 million, and only grossed a little over $18 million domestically while in theaters. The film did not hit a home run on the big screen, but it is sure to earn more with DVD sales, which will offer more revenue now that it is available for rent and purchase in various formats.

The starpower comes from recognizable seasoned veterans Farrell and Collette, and young faces Yelchin and Mintz-Plasse. Farrel is known for his bad-boy characters in action, suspense, and thriller movies, and recently worked on Len Wiseman's *Total Recall* remake in the Doug Quaid/Hauser role previously played by Arnold Schwarzenegger; it was released in August 2012 and made good revenue due to the foreign market. Collette's film career spans over 20 years, and she was most recently praised for her work as the title character in Showtime's *United States of Tara* (2009–2011). Yelchin has been working in film and television for years but made a big splash in the role of Chekov in the 2009 *Star Trek* reboot by J.J. Abrams. Mintz-Plasse—last, but certainly not least—became a household name in *Superbad* (2007), in which he played the iconic McLovin character. But the biggest character of all is the concept of a vampire movie.

The vampire craze in television and film is still at a fever pitch. The original *Fright Night* and the other films from this brief '80s recap established horror as a genre that might utilize formulaic narrative patterns and stock characters, but also as a field that is full of influential cinema.

Honorable mention to those movies from the '80s that have been remade goes to: *The Shining* (1980 / 1997), *Prom Night* (1980 / 2008), *Children of the Corn* (1984 / 2009), *The Stepfather* (1987 / 2009), and *Night of the Demons* (1988 / 2010). Each of these films has either been remade for television, video, or theatrical release, with minimal to above average success in terms of monetary returns. The original movies, however, helped contribute to the field by offering horror fans creepy locations (cornfields, funeral homes, mansion-like hotels), scary creatures (children, demons, spirits, relatives), memorable lines ("Here's Johnny!"), and lots of blood and mayhem for future films to reference in the genre.

There are a slew of other films from the '30s through the '70s that also merit honorable mention for their original contributions to the field, their influence on other productions, and their remakes. They include Tod Browning's *Dracula* (1931), which is a novel adaptation loosely remade in 1958 as *Horror of Dracula* by Terence Fisher, again in 1979 as *Dracula* by John Badham, and once more in 1992 as *Bram Stoker's Dracula* by Francis Ford Coppola; James Whale's *Frakenstein* (1931), which is another novel adaptation loosely remade as *Flesh for Frankenstein* in 1973 by Paul Morrissey and Antonio Margheriti, and again as *Frankenstein* in 1994 by Kenneth Branagh; Merian Cooper and Ernest Schoedsack's *King Kong* (1933), which was remade in 1976 by John Guillermin and in 2005 by Peter Jackson; James Whale's *Bride of Frankenstein* (1935), redone as *The Bride* by Franc Roddam in 1985; Jacques Tourneur's *Cat People* (1942), remade in 1982 by Paul Schrader; Robert Florey's *The Beast with Five Fingers* (1946), inspiring Oliver Stone's *The Hand* (1981); William Cameron Menzies's *Invaders from Mars* (1953), which led to Tobe Hooper's film of the same title in 1986; Ishirô Honda's *Gojira* (1954), which was remade by Honda and Terry O. Morse in 1956 as *Godzilla*, and in 1998 by Roland Emmerich; Herschell Gordon Lewis's *Two Thousand Maniacs!* (1964), leading to Tim Sullivan's 2001 *Maniacs* (2005); Herschell Gordon Lewis's *The Wizard of Gore* (1970), which resulted in Jeremy Kasten's 2007 similarly-titled remake; Larry Cohen's *It's Alive* (1974), remade in 2008 by Josef Rusnak; Bryan Forbes's *The Stepford Wives* (1975), which Frank Oz remade in 2004; Brian De Palma's *Carrie* (1976), leading to David Carson's television remake in 2002 and Kimberly Peirce's 2013 production; Dennis Donnelly's *The Toolbox Murders* (1978), resulting in Tobe Hooper's *Toolbox Murders* redo in 2004; and Stuart Rosenberg's *The Amityville Horror* (1979), which was remade in 2005 by Andrew Douglas.

Each of these films holds a special place in horror for content (vampires, wondrous creatures, ghosts, aliens, killers, supernatural powers, possession, and fantasy), but they are also notable for the directors who helmed the productions and the actors we watch on the screen. *Frankenstein* and *Dracula* films are just two movies that inspired tons of reinventions and remakes on the big and small screen; the popular roles within the films have given us Dracula played by Bela Lugosi, Frank Langella, Gary Oldman, and even Udo Kier (*Blood for Dracula* [1974]), Leslie Nielsen (*Dracula: Dead and Loving It* [1995]), and Gerard Butler (*Dracula 2000* [2000]). We have also seen Frankenstein played by Kenneth Branagh, Udo Kier, and Sting; with Boris Karlof and Robert De Niro as the monster; and his monster's bride creation played by Jennifer Beals. The recognizable names and popular actors in horror films are endless. The honorable mention list of remade films alone offers up big names such as Keanu Reeves, Winona Ryder, Michael Caine, Naomi Watts, Nicole Kidman, and Ryan Reynolds.

Their stories continue to entertain us and sometimes—though typically not as with much as the original productions—inform us about the current social atmosphere. The original *It's Alive* shows the dangers of fertility drugs and how science should never mess around with Mother Nature. These were and still are real concerns in our contemporary American society; if we think about the "octomom," the film resonates with clarity—not that a woman will give birth to monster babies, but that pregnancies can turn into interesting situations, such as birthing octuplets. The remake, however, was only screened in the Philippines, so it was unable to reach audiences in the States to deliver its message; interested viewers have to catch the release on DVD.

These are the American horror remakes, but there are many international film productions that have been remade in America that fall into a separate discussion large enough to fill another book. The number of these films does not dwindle, and they pull in big names for their remakes: *The Wicker Man* (2006) features Nicolas Cage, Ellen Burstyn, and Leelee Sobieski; *The Eye* (2008) has Jessica Alba and Parker Posey; and *Don't Be Afraid of the Dark* (2010) stars Katie Holmes and Guy Pearce. Sarah Michelle Gellar and Naomi Watts made part of this trend possible when they were cast in *The Ring* and *The Grudge*, respectively. Other foreign titles that have been turned into American productions include Jee-woon Kim's *A Tale of Two Sisters* (2003), which was remade by Charles and Thomas Guard as *The Uninvited* (2009); Sung-ho Kim's *Into the Mirror* (2003), remade by Alexandre Aja as *Mirrors* (2008); Jaume Balagueró and Paco Plaza's 2007 *[Rec]*, which became John Erick Dowdle's *Quarantine* in 2008; Tomas Afredson's *Låt den rätte komma in* (2008), which we know as *Let Me In* by Matt Reeves; and

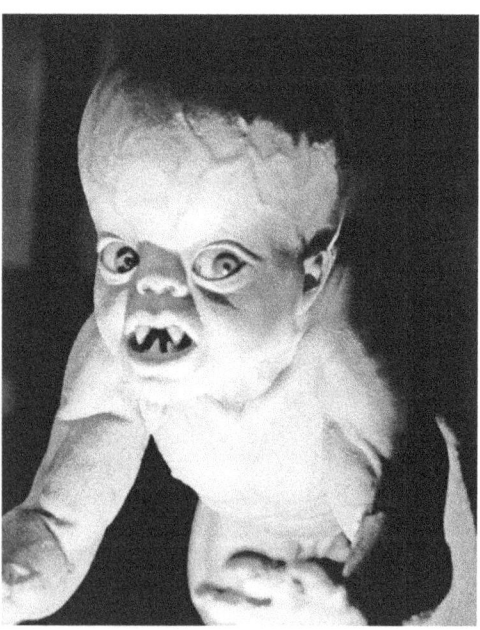

The Davis baby—also known as the *It's Alive* (1974) monster baby—sits in shadows and awaits its next victim.

Gustavo Hernández's *La casa muda* (2010), which Chris Kentis and Laura Lau turned into *Silent House* in 2011. It is remarkable how fast the turnover for these remakes is becoming; barely a year separates the original from the remake production in contemporary features.

The international appeal for remakes, as well as Stateside productions, will continue to rise as long as fan interest supports the trend formula of mixing television stars, high production values, popular music, and notable or first-time directors. Another reason the trend will continue is due to the way many of the original films were produced. Countless filmmakers sold copyrights to studios to get their films made, and others did not copyright their films properly. This allowed many of the original films to fall into public domain, which allows anyone to take the material and reuse it as they see fit. And some of the original production studios are having remakes made of their own films, with or without the involvement of anyone from the original movies. We continue to see many original horror films from the '30s through the '80s receive the remake treatment as a result of these actions. And the current rumor mill is filled with talk of remakes for these '70s and '80s gems: *Kingdom of the Spiders* (1977), *Happy Birthday to Me* (1981), *Hell Night* (1981), *The Entity* (1982), *Maximum Overdrive* (1986), *The Fly* (a remake of the remake), and *Hellraiser* (1987).

7

The Interviews
Industry Professionals Riff About the State of Horror

Critics, movie reviewers, and fans all have something to say about horror—about the technical aspects of the filmmaking, the quality of writing and acting, the cinematography, the film's endings, the levels of gore, sex scenes, favorite lines, and even the goofs and bloopers. Industry professionals, however, work on the development of films and often offer critical insight about the state of horror filmmaking that no critic, movie reviewer, or fan is able to provide. These are the people responsible for creating the films audiences clamor to see or avoid altogether. It is only fitting that a few industry professionals speak about the current state of horror and its proliferation of remakes, reboots, and re-envisioned productions.

Six insiders—Jef Delman, Robert Englund, Tony Timpone, Matt Riddlehoover, Kane Hodder, and Bruce Campbell—agreed to give their perspectives on the current state of American horror, the invasion of remakes, and what the future holds for the genre. With diverse backgrounds in writing (screenplay and journalistic reporting), acting (Englund, Hodder, and Campbell are easily classified as horror icons), and directing, each offers a unique point of view; they, too, are also fans of the genre who have become a part of its professional cadre. All interviewees were asked identical or similar questions to keep the interview process formal and balanced. Opinionated commentary from the interviewer was avoided in order to leave bias on the cutting room floor. At most, the interviewees were provided the title of this project and asked if they would participate in a Q&A session about contemporary American horror films. All interviews are presented complete and unedited.

Interview Conducted May 12, 2010 / Interviewee: Jef Delman

Jef Delman is a director whose first job in the horror market was working as a production assistant on the set of *Friday the 13th Part 2* in 1981. He has worn many filmmaking hats: director, actor, writer, and production crewmember. His horror directing debut came in 1986 with the film *Deadtime Stories*, which appeared at a time when most were saying the slasher film and horror in general was on the decline. But Delman's film is not a slasher; it is a take on childhood bedtime stories with an adult-horror twist. The film features three segments that focus on a witch, a Little Red Riding Hood character, and the framework for *Goldilocks and the Three Bears*. This sets Delman apart from many contemporary horror film directors because his film focuses on storytelling. There can be no element of fear without a good story to hold a movie together, and *Deadtime Stories* works well because its storytelling highlights one of the scariest times in life: childhood.

Horror films and children's literature have always had close ties to the storytelling perspective of fright. Everything about childhood is grounded in fear: physical size in relation to others, the dark, open spaces and confinement, the closet, the crawlspace under the bed—all the terrifying unknowns that children have to confront in order to recognize fear and defeat it. Children are also made to address very real, direct concerns of fear through childhood teasing from others, abuse, abandonment, and other overtly cruel or situational circumstances. They cannot rely on parents to protect them from fear, as adults are quite often the fear inducers (who, for instance, randomly instill in babies and children how much they want to "eat them up"). Childhood is simply a phase of life when fear comes from all sides and even relates to all senses— what is seen and unseen, what is heard and silent, what can be touched or touches back, what can be smelled or sniffs back, and what can be tasted or possibly tastes and consumes in return. It is these elements of fear that lie at the root of much of children's literature and the narratives of horror.

Delman's concern with storytelling in *Deadtime Stories* makes him an industry professional worthy to comment on the growing field of horror remakes that use the narratives from original films; even if the remake changes the dialogue, action, opening/ending sequences, and actors, the framework of the original story remains. The remake is given new direction and its impact on the genre is often evaluated by audience response at the box office.

Q: What are your thoughts on contemporary American horror cinema?

A: I am troubled by two things: the plethora of remakes, and lack of originality they demonstrate. I also have concerns about so-called torture porn films. Horror, at its best, should project the identifiable, inner fears and anxieties of well defined characters in a grotesque way on the surrounding world. Films that are merely about pain may strike visceral cords, but ignore the deeper core of what horror has to offer.

Q: What is creative and original about contemporary American horror cinema?

A: The new freedom that technology offers, from low-tech indie films to well utilized CGI effects. But story is still critical, and too many filmmakers let spectacle get in the way of plot, character, and (especially in horror) theme.

Q: Horror remakes are currently in full force. What do contemporary horror remakes accomplish?

A: Remakes accomplish little more than generating income for creatively vapid studios. One rationale might be industry concerns that the original movies being remade seem dated to modern sensibilities. While this is a valid point (and the charm of nostalgic cheesiness is at best debatable), the rush to remake perpetrates creative laziness.

Q: What designates success for a horror remake? Which horror remake would you classify as the most successful and why?

A: I've seen bits of a few, but not enough to comment. If pressed, I'd have to say Philip Kaufman's 1978 remake of *Invasion of the Body Snatchers*. At least until the last few minutes, when it completely falls apart.

Q: Have you seen Gus Van Sant's *Psycho* remake? What makes films such as *Psycho* too classic/sacred to remake?

A: I recall as Van Sant's *Psycho* was released, the public rationale for it was that the modern audience won't watch black-and-white films, and so a color remake is necessary so kids today can see this classic. (Sort of like saying Shakespeare is too hard to understand, so here is *Hamlet* in Classic Comics form.) Aside from the fairly moronic rationale (never mind the question: Why is it so critical everyone see *Psycho* in the first place?), the remake did not do what it was supposed to do. It was supposed to be a shot-by-shot remake, but even though each shot was similar to each corresponding shot in the original, critical details were ignored. For instance, take the scene where Norman meets Marion Crane. In the Hitchcock version, there is a mirror in the shot, so we see two Normans. Hitchcock uses the motif of visually doubling to shadow Norman's secret. The shot in the Van Sant version is flat, and no such mirror is in frame. This is just one example of the attention to detail that makes Hitchcock Hitchcock. In a Hitchcock film, every frame was saturated with multi-leveled meaning. His films were great not because they were lurid potboilers, but because they were lurid potboilers that attained high art, that commented on the human condition using cinema-as-poetry.

Q: What responsibility do the people (directors, actors, studios, etc.) who produce horror remakes have to the original productions?

A: Filmmakers need to take just the germ of what works in the original's premise and re-shape it to fit a new point of view, as opposed to simply re-shooting an old premise whole cloth.

Q: Horror films of the 1970s and 1980s carried strong social, cultural, and moral messages of their eras. What messages do horror remakes convey to contemporary audiences?

A: Each film reflects the tastes, aesthetics, and peculiarities of the creative team making it. In this way, a remake is not necessarily different from an original film, unless the filmmakers are simply coloring by numbers off the sensibilities of the earlier version.

Q: What film would you like to see get the remake treatment and why?

A: I haven't been giving this question much thought. Generally, I'd say I would not remake hit films, but films that for one reason or other screwed up a really good premise or hook.

Q: What sets horror apart from all other genres? Is there one film that best represents American horror cinema in your opinion?

A: Hmmm. One film. That's kind of like asking, what's the best rock 'n' roll song. Are we talking 1950s, 1960s, 1970s? Horror at its best works to expose our frailties, secret fetishes, and fears. Any film that taps into these often cringe-worthy emotions is a great horror film. It is tapping into the inner recesses of our minds, hearts, and souls that makes horror such a timeless genre. That answers both questions, by the way.

Q: Where do you see the horror genre venturing in the next decade?

A: That depends where the pop culture goes. Even though in each wave of horror, one film will set a trend; that film taps into the prevailing zeitgeist. The zeitgeist is now in a transition, so it is hard to say.

Delman's commentary demonstrates his awareness of the importance of story in any film genre, but certainly horror, which sometimes can be overwhelmed by special effects and shock value. He laments the manner in which story value seems to disappear in horror as more remakes are made. Although the growing number of remakes is a clear phenomenon, Delman focuses on an element of filmmaking missing from many movies in general: meaning. The original *Psycho* fills each scene with layered meaning and symbols, but its remake seeks to accomplish a different goal by switching to color in order to hold the interest of contemporary movie audiences and separate itself from the original. Hitchcock chose to shoot his film in black-and-white, and Van Sant opted for color. Delman purports that the future of horror is anyone's guess, but its direction will certainly follow popular culture to offer commentary upon the times. His overall discussion demonstrates concern over the amount of remakes in production but offers hope that no matter what kind of horror film is created—remake or original—as long as the film makes a connection to the audience (emotional or physical) there can still be worthy additions to the genre forthcoming.

Interview Conducted May 31, 2010 / Interviewee: Robert Englund

Story is also a major concern for Robert Englund, who is best known as the iconic star of the *A Nightmare on Elm Street* franchise, playing its villain, Freddy Krueger. As discussed earlier, his importance to the horror genre is unquestioned. His expressed views on horror and the remake trend are vital, especially with the remake of his career-launching film released in 2011.

> Q: What are your thoughts on contemporary American horror cinema?
> A: I think horror films have gained popularity in recent decades because they have adapted classic ingredients to contemporary expectations. However, it is disappointing that when technology permits immense creativity, so many of the stories are recycled or unoriginal.
> Q: What is creative and original about contemporary American horror cinema?
> A: Movies like *District 9*, *28 Days Later*, and the Swedish original *Let the Right One In* have invigorated contemporary cinema with their fresh interpretation of classic stories.
> Q: Horror remakes are currently in full force. What do contemporary horror remakes accomplish?
> A: Remakes do provide an opportunity to unleash the newest technology on classic stories. Sadly they often rely only on

visual whizbang instead of adding anything new and interesting to the story.

Q: What designates success for a horror remake? Which horror remake would you classify as the most successful and why?

A: A remake that re-imagines or improves upon the original is a success. John Carpenter's *The Thing* qualifies as a success.

Q: Have you seen Gus Van Sant's *Psycho* remake? What makes films such as *Psycho* too classic/sacred to remake?

A: Some films are products of their time and represent a perfect moment in cinema history. *Psycho*, *Wizard of Oz*—these are not improved by remaking them. However, there will always be the drive to remake because there is a built in audience, a brand name recognition factor, and there are only so many stories to tell.

Q: What responsibility do the people (directors, actors, studios, etc.) who produce horror remakes have to the original productions?

A: Sadly, none. Obviously, if you can't improve it, why remake it? The responsibility should be to preserve the core integrity of the original storytelling.

Q: Horror films of the 1970s and 1980s carried strong social, cultural, and moral messages of their eras. What messages do horror remakes convey to contemporary audiences?

A: Very little. It is mostly nostalgia for some viewers and an introduction to others.

Q: What film would you like to see get the remake treatment and why?

A: *Forbidden Planet*, because as wonderful as the original is, it is also a prisoner of its '50s production design. It is such a great story: a sci-fi/horror reworking of Shakespeare's *The Tempest*.

Q: What sets horror apart from all other genres? Is there one film that best represents American horror cinema in your opinion?

A: Horror makes you confront your own mortality more than any other genre. *Rosemary's Baby* because it confronts the American preoccupations of greed and consumerism.

Q: Where do you see the horror genre venturing in the next decade?

A: I would like to see the new technology used to enhance period horror.

Englund's responses are quick and to the point, but they offer a wealth of insight into the current state of horror from a key figure who helped the genre achieve popularity and sociocultural relevance for more than twenty-five years. He credits advances in technology for hindering story value; however, it is his hope that new technological discoveries can be used in the future to highlight specialized horror. This is an approach that shows recognition of the field and the direction it is heading, but with a caveat that its current path does not have to be as limiting to the genre as many people predict. Englund identifies characteristics of the remake movement—audience participation, star power, and reverence for a time long gone; he also states there are a finite number of stories to tell, with rare American and international productions like *District 9* and *Let the Right One In* proving to be exceptions. Horror films certainly exhibit common themes, motifs, storylines, characters, settings, music, camera techniques, and scare tactics, but there is definitely space for filmmakers to present original narratives and concepts on the big screen. The production of remakes suggests to the American public that horror creations—old and new—never die. Englund reiterates the notion that horror films are significant because they touch upon human existence like no other genre, and it can only be hoped that this single point of distinction keeps the field pertinent, especially in the growth of the remake movement.

Interview Conducted May 12, 2010 / Interviewee: Tony Timpone

One man who has been integral in keeping an eye on these up-and-coming films, with a vast knowledge of all that has come before, is Tony Timpone, longtime editor of *Fangoria* magazine (May 1987–February 2010). Under Timpone's direction, *Fangoria* helped genre fans stay current with all horror happenings, from films in production to new creature creations. He has held the position of magazine editor longer than any other since its inception in 1979, and these twenty-plus years have allowed him to see the face of horror change from the heyday of the 1980s to the remake explosion in the 21st century. Timpone's career extends beyond the magazine into cameos in horror films like *House of the Dead* (2003), producing the television mini-series *The 100 Scariest Movie Moments* (2004), and helping establish the popular Weekend of Horrors conventions where fans and industry names like George A. Romero, Clive Barker, and Bruce Campbell can mix and mingle to explore the world of horror together. His knowledge of the genre and its trending films is unmatched in horror entertainment publications.

Q: What are your thoughts on contemporary American horror cinema?

A: It's in pretty sad shape if you look at the major studios. Everything is either a remake or a sequel, just about. The most daring and interesting work is being done in the independent field, as usual.

Q: What is creative and original about contemporary American horror cinema?

A: That it continues to break taboos. Good example is the U.S.–Canadian-French co-production *Splice*, which explores the ethics of gene splicing but also deals with some intriguing sexual themes.

Q: Horror remakes are currently in full force. What do contemporary horror remakes accomplish?

A: They are usually more popular than the films that inspired them. *The Crazies*, for example, probably made more at the box office in its first day than the original did during its entire run. Plus they have the benefit of (hopefully) introducing modern audiences to the original works. They also have today's incredible FX technology as a tool in their creative arsenals.

Q: What designates success for a horror remake? Which horror remake would you classify as the most successful and why?

A: A successful horror remake should be able to stand on its own. *The Crazies*, again, is a good example. Though not a perfect film, it is actually better than its inspiration, which fell short due to lack of budget. The new version is legitimately scary and suspenseful all on its own.

Q: Have you seen Gus Van Sant's *Psycho* remake? What makes films such as *Psycho* too classic/sacred to remake?

A: I have nothing against remakes if they go in a new, fresh direction. Van Sant made the mistake of trying to make an exact copy of the Hitchcock original, but fell short because he did not have the great cast and skills (and talent!) that Hitchcock had at his disposal. The new *A Nightmare on Elm Street* also failed because it stuck too close to the previous version. Remakes are better when they go off in totally different directions, like the *Dawn of the Dead* and *Texas Chainsaw Massacre* reduxes did.

Q: What responsibility do the people (directors, actors, studios, etc.) who produce horror remakes have to the original productions?

A: They should respect the creators of the original films and their fans by not disparaging their work to build up their own.

Q: Horror films of the 1970s and 1980s carried strong social, cultural, and moral messages of their eras. What messages do horror remakes convey to contemporary audiences?

A: *Texas Chainsaw Massacre, Night of the Living Dead, Dawn of the*

Dead, The Hills Have Eyes, to name a few, spoke to the eras in which they were made, the turbulent 1960s and 1970s. The potential messages of the remakes are lost in the search for box-office revenue or diluted by mainstream and commerce sensibilities.

Q: What film would you like to see get the remake treatment and why?

A: The 1958 sci-fi horror film *Fiend Without a Face* would be a good remake. As would *Squirm, Prophecy, Horror Hotel*. Films that were made poorly the first time, like *The Keep*, are better fodder for remakes than films regarded as classics.

Q: What sets horror apart from all other genres? Is there one film that best represents American horror cinema in your opinion?

A: Horror films, more than any other genre, are a more visceral and immersive experience. You go into one for a specific emotion: to be scared.

Q: Where do you see the horror genre venturing in the next decade?

A: More 3D and immersive experiences (IMAX) will become the norm rather than the exception. More low-tech, DIY horror too, in the vein of *Paranormal Activity*, as Hollywood tries to capture lightning in a bottle.

Timpone identifies major studio/mainstream, big-budget filmmaking as a force that is driving horror away from creativity, while independent films struggle to see the light of day to bring something new to the field. On the other hand, having a sizable production budget can help a film achieve its goals; he notes the original version of *The Crazies* suffered while its remake performed better financially and as a film overall. Money is always an issue with remakes and lush mainstream horror productions, especially with the ease that film companies have discovered in developing "cheap" ($10–15 million) projects whose return will be great enough to spawn sequels, prequels, and other related enterprises. Advanced technology in special effects does not hurt either.

The longtime editor makes a point to say that directors are not the only people responsible for remake misfires; films are cohesive projects involving directors, producers, actors, writing, and much more. His comments about *Psycho* reveal that the contemporary star power of Janet Leigh and Anthony Perkins, coupled with the direction of Hitchcock, was unable to be matched by Anne Heche, Vince Vaughn, and Gus Van Sant. Remakes are going to be made, but they have to take a different path from the original to adjust to the era in which they are being produced; without this attention to detail, the films become mere cinematic vessels trying to make money at the box office.

Interview Conducted: May 17, 2010 / Interviewee: Matt Riddlehoover

Money, however, is never the concern for the independent filmmaker—at least not in profit. As a writer, director, and actor in independent films, Matt Riddlehoover represents the unrepresented in filmmaking. His third directing effort, *To a Tee* (2006), garnered the MySpace Film User's Choice Award and put his name on the map as a new independent filmmaker to watch. From the independent side of the filmmaking spectrum, Riddlehoover understands the difficulty of creating original content in a sea of retold stories. He is currently in post-production for his next feature film—*Scenes from a Gay Marriage* (2012)—and has been in talks about making his first foray into horror. He is currently in post-production marketing.

> Q: What are your thoughts on contemporary American horror cinema?
> A: Let's unleash some new ideas! Surely Kevin Williamson isn't the only person with an imagination. What are studios so afraid of? Now there's a horror movie!
> Q: What is creative and original about contemporary American horror cinema?
> A: Nothing.
> Q: Horror remakes are currently in full force. What do contemporary horror remakes accomplish?
> A: Big numbers at the box office, that's what they accomplish.
> Q: What designates success for a horror remake? Which horror remake would you classify as the most successful and why?
> A: I enjoyed *Dawn of the Dead* (2004). Is it the most successful remake? That I cannot say; I tend to stay away from the remakes. (I've yet to see the *Friday the 13th* and *Last House on the Left* remakes, and a number of others.) I also tend to dislike them greatly. I recently saw *A Nightmare on Elm Street* (2010), and, in all honesty, I'm not mad at it. It's a well-written, well-directed, wonderfully-executed production. However, it unfortunately lacks the simplistic authenticity of Craven's 1984 classic. But what can you do? Kids these days need backstory, right? What's so wrong with allowing the monster to just be a monster?

Q: Have you seen Gus Van Sant's *Psycho* remake? What makes films such as *Psycho* too classic/sacred to remake?

A: I saw it twice in the theater as a way of convincing myself, "Yep, it really was as every bit of awful as you thought." First of all, a closed-framed shot-by-shot remake is a ridiculous thing for anyone to do. (Unless, of course, you're Michael Haneke and you're reintroducing your film *Funny Games* to U.S. audiences. But even as authentic and well-executed as the remake of *Funny Games* was, that shot-by-shot formula left a trite, posed kind of aftertaste.) Secondly, and most importantly, *Psycho* is Hitchcock. You don't touch Hitchcock, Mr. Van Sant. I'm sorry, but no. I can understand wanting to introduce the story to a new generation, but let's face it, the masses don't have patience for stories like *Psycho* anymore. Besides, who doesn't know who Norman Bates is? Who can't reference that infamous shower scene, even if they've never seen the original? I mean, really? Van Sant, your film lacks a major ingredient: the element of surprise. Not to mention bad casting. Vince Vaughn? Seriously? Joaquin Phoenix would've been a better choice, and I'm not even giving it much thought. Anne Heche? You didn't want us to care when she died, did you? I certainly didn't. The most exciting part of the movie was Marion's non sequitur parasol.

Q: What responsibility do the people (directors, actors, studios, etc.) who produce horror remakes have to the original productions?

A: They make money and take the blame.

Q: Horror films of the 1970s and 1980s carried strong social, cultural, and moral messages of their eras. What messages do horror remakes convey to contemporary audiences?

A: Basically: evil does not exist. Something made that person evil. So, shame on whatever that something was. Are we teaching kids to be injustice collectors? My life isn't working out so well and I do bad things because this happened and that happened? If the monsters were really monsters, void of bad childhoods or wrongful accusations, we'd see responsibility being taken for something. Freddy is a prick because he enjoys being a prick—not because someone made him that way.

Q: What film would you like to see get the remake treatment and why?

A: I don't even know. If *Rosemary's Baby* happens, I'll be first in line—but only because I'd want to see how ineffective it was.

Q: What sets horror apart from all other genres? Is there one film that best represents American horror cinema in your opinion?

A: I absolutely love the original *Black Christmas*. It's a masterpiece of subtlety. No motive, no backstory—just pure evil lurking in your home at Christmas.

Q: Where do you see the horror genre venturing in the next decade?

A: Hopefully we see it venturing in another direction—an original one where new monsters exist.

Riddlehoover's words offer support to previous interview commentary; contemporary American horror has seemingly lost some perspective of originality in trade for financial gain. He also proposes that, if competent directing, acting, and intent are featured elements, some remakes can be successful artistically as well as financially. But the strongest opinion in Riddlehoover's remarks concerns horror villains. The problem with remakes is they try to explain too much and spoon-feed audiences entirely too much information to explain the horrific killing sprees of iconic (and new) monsters. Zombie's *Halloween*, for example, gives viewers a killer born of his environment: his mother a stripper, a father figure absent, bullied, kept in a mental health facility away from his mother and baby sister, driven deeper into depression and maniacal thoughts. Nispel's *Friday the 13th* shows the viewer a young boy who witnesses his mother's decapitation by a camp counselor, which sends him on a murderous rampage (although the mother talks about her son being a drowning victim, so the storyline is off-kilter). And Bayer's *A Nightmare on Elm Street* depicts a despicable human being, but one who should have been turned over to the police in order to be legally prosecuted for his crimes instead of being burned in a ring of vigilante justice. Where there is no longer a monster, fear no longer exists. Riddlehoover's independent filmmaking experience allows him a voice to speak out against contemporary horror films that tell instead of show, thereby leaving a story open enough to let audience members use their imaginations to fill in the natural narrative gaps. Sometimes monsters can just be monsters without overwrought explanations, and maybe the horror genre will revisit this idea in the future.

Interview Conducted February 15, 2012 / Interviewee: Kane Hodder

One such famous monster is the well-known Jason Voorhees, a figure whose body count dominates the slasher subgenre, which is only rivaled by the various ways he is revived in sequels to kill again. The masked villain has been portrayed by several actors and stunt professionals over the years, but no one has taken on the role more than Kane Hodder, who has brought Jason to life onscreen in four of the sequels from the original franchise. He is also widely known for playing Victor Crowley in the *Hatchet* franchise (*Hatchet III* is set for a 2013 release) and is noted for quirky contributions like his role as Freddy Krueger's arm in *Jason Goes to Hell*. Hodder's commentary on the horror genre provides an insider perspective, but also a reasonable account of happenings in horror as someone who is celebrated for his work onscreen, appearances at conventions, and behind-the-scenes work. This is a man who knows horror from all sides.

> Q: What are your thoughts on contemporary American horror cinema?
> A: Horror in general is constantly changing. Whenever a filmmaker comes up with an original topic for a horror film and it becomes successful, then suddenly there is a glut of similar type movies on the same subject or filmmaking style. Good examples of this are *Blair Witch Project* and *Paranormal Activity*. Horror has always gone through trends and will always continue to do so.
> Q: What sets horror apart from all other genres?
> A: Not every moviegoer wants to be scared, but there are plenty who do. Horror audiences are definitely a breed unto themselves. Particularly the hardcore fans. I consider myself a member of the latter group.
> Q: What film(s) would you consider to be the best representation(s) of horror?
> A: The one movie that had the greatest success of terrifying and horrifying the public by the way it was made and particularly with its subject matter was *The Exorcist*. I don't think that any other horror movie has had the impact on people like that one had. It remains my all-time favorite horror movie.
> Q: Horror remakes are currently in full force. What do these remakes accomplish or offer?
> A: I would much rather see a horror movie based on an original idea because I think the impact is greater. However, I do have to admit seeing certain remakes in which I enjoyed the original version.
> Q: What are your thoughts on the growing use of special effects (CGI, 3-D) in horror?
> A: I have never been a big fan of 3D in general, and I would much rather see practical Special Effects and Make-up Effects. I know how much work goes into creating practical effects, and I enjoy when they are well done.
> Q: What designates success for a horror remake? Which horror remake would you classify as the most successful and why?
> A: I enjoyed Rob Zombie's *Halloween* remakes.

Q: As someone who has played the iconic role of Jason Voorhees more than any other actor and created a huge following for Victor Crowley with the *Hatchet* films, how do you feel about *Friday the 13th* and other horror films being remade?

A: I would rather have seen Jason's story continue instead of remaking it, but I understand the reasoning behind it.

Q: What are your thoughts on other actor portrayals of Jason Voorhees compared to your performances of the masked killer? Have you seen the *Friday the 13th* remake, and if so what is your response to the film and its new Jason?

A: I didn't see the remake, but I did enjoy Ted White and CJ Graham in the role.

Q: What responsibility do the people (directors, actors, studios, etc.) who produce horror remakes have to the original productions?

A: I would hope that a filmmaker would try to maintain some of the feeling from the original film while making a new version of an old movie. At the same time I would like to see some original ideas added to give the film somewhat of a more current feeling.

Q: Horror films of the '70s and '80s carried strong social, cultural, and moral messages of their eras. Do horror remakes convey any messages to contemporary audiences?

A: Not as much as in the past. It's hard to come up with any untouched opinions or ideas anymore. So many films in the past had tackled unexplored subject matter.

Q: A lot of scholars and critics acknowledge *Scream* for changing the face of horror in 1996. Have you seen *Scream 4*, and if so, what are your thoughts on the film?

A: I didn't see that film.

Q: The above statement has been made about Hitchcock's *Psycho* in 1960, as well. What are your thoughts on the Gus Van Sant remake in the '90s?

A: To be honest, I don't remember having an opinion on that film, but I have enjoyed much of Van Sant's work in the past.

Q: What film would you like to see get the remake treatment and why?

A: It's hard to even think of a successful horror movie that hasn't been remade.

Q: Are there any remakes on the horizon that you are anticipating?

A: *Hatchet*. In 20 years.

Q: Where do you see the horror genre venturing in the next decade, and what part would you like to play in its continued development?

A: As long as I can, I would love to continue killing every human being that ventures into my vicinity. In movies ... mostly...

Hodder honors and identifies original genre productions, but offers responses that illustrate there is room for remakes as well. There is a sense of new fear created when an original idea or completed film comes into the horror genre. Hodder celebrates those who work in special effects and makeup effects—two areas that have been crucial to horror films over the years—but he also recognizes how successful films pave the way for trends in cinema. One successful remake that utilizes 3D or other such special effects and film-making techniques, like "found footage," easily starts an avalanche of productions that seek to attain the same visual, commercial, and sometimes critical success. Horror, like most genres, is trendy; a big development, new idea, or successful financial enterprise is going to alert others to follow suit, and the trend of remakes is exemplary of this for contemporary American horror.

Interview Conducted March 1, 2012 / Interviewee: Bruce Campbell

Freddy vs. Jason is one of the big ideas that developed in the 21st century. Its success as a hybrid film certainly aided in the development of *AVP: Alien vs. Predator* in 2004 and its sequel in 2007; however, a feature-film sequel to *Freddy vs. Jason* has eluded fans for years only to become the stuff of horror-mill rumor. One development pitted Freddy and Jason against another iconic figure—Ash from *The Evil Dead*. Although the trio never made it to the big screen together, a new *Evil Dead* is set to return to theaters in remake form in 2013. Bruce Campbell originated the Ashley "Ash" J. Williams character in 1983, but this time around the popular *Burn Notice* actor finds himself in the producer chair for the new production. His interview contribution sheds light on the horror industry from the vantage point of someone who helped create one of horror's most memorable heroes in the '80s and continues to participate in the genre's development and growth by working on projects for the next generation.

> Q: What are your thoughts on contemporary American horror cinema?
> A: Get rid of torture porn—it's bad filmmaking, lazy filmmaking. Get back to being scary, build suspense, make people jump. Horror comes in many hues.
> Q: What sets horror apart from all other genres?
> A: The visceral response that horror elicits. Only the comedy genre comes close.
> Q: What film(s) would you consider to be the best representation(s) of horror?

A: *The Tenant* because it's all in your head (Polanski). It was very risky horror. I doubt today's filmmakers and execs would try it.

Q: Horror remakes are currently in full force. What do these remakes accomplish or offer?

A: I'm not a fan if they get cranked out like action flicks. With the *Evil Dead* remake, we're trying to keep it a handmade film.

Q: What are your thoughts on the growing use of special effects (CGI, 3-D) in horror?

A: It's no different than other genres using it. I'm fine if it helps tell a tough story, as long as the effects are not *the* story.

Q: What designates success for a horror remake? Which horror remake would you classify as the most successful and why?

A: I can't say because I really don't track them in my head.

Q: You created and are known as Ash from *The Evil Dead*, *Evil Dead II*, and *Army of Darkness*. How do you feel about the original being remade?

A: I feel fine because the original three partners are all very involved. I hope cranky fans will take a chill pill—we have no intention of screwing it up or selling out the franchise.

Q: What would you say the original *Evil Dead* films offer horror? And what are your thoughts on what should happen with the remake?

A: The original offered a wild, memorable ride with no end in sight and a supernatural edge. It's not something you see on the news. The new flick should offer the same.

Q: What responsibility do the people (directors, actors, studios, etc.) who produce horror remakes have to the original productions?

A: Same—honor the fans of the genre.

Q: Horror films of the '70s and '80s carried strong social, cultural, and moral messages of their eras. Do horror remakes convey any messages to contemporary audiences?

A: None at all, and that's fine. We don't have that in flicks anymore because nobody cares.

Q: A lot of scholars and critics acknowledge *Scream* for changing the face of horror in 1996. Have you seen *Scream 4*, and if so, what are your thoughts on the film?

A: Every 10 or 20 years, someone comes along and shakes things up. I credit *Blair Witch* as much as *Scream*.

Q: The above statement has been made about Hitchcock's *Psycho* in 1960, as well. What are your thoughts on the Gus Van Sant remake in the '90s?

A: An absurd waste of celluloid.

Q: What film would you like to see get the remake treatment and why?
A: If remakes continue at this pace, they should make a new genre. I don't wish for remakes.
Q: Are there any remakes on the horizon that you are anticipating?
A: No.
Q: Where do you see the horror genre venturing in the next decade, and what part would you like to play in its continued development?
A: I just hope that filmmakers use the genre to flex their visual muscles. Not many genres let you go crazy. Most importantly, they need to be scary.

Campbell's critical attention to horror over the years allows him the chance to make strong calls to action for the genre and its participants. His outlook argues that horror has lost some of its power in the fright department, and in making that argument it is his hope that directors, producers, actors and more recognize that this cinematic field has no boundaries; it should be used to create productions that are visual, risky in content, and, all above, scary. Campbell is not alone in his musings on what is and what has happened to horror; the widespread franchising in the '80s created a huge fan-base for the genre and simultaneously lost some of the fear factor. There are a number of new franchises, original creations, and even remakes seeking to revive the fear for 21st century audiences and fans.

Respect seems to be a key factor for Campbell regarding the way in which horror films are created. He understands the use of special effects and the remake movement, but also sees these elements and developments as components of the genre instead of what should dominate a film or the field in general. Although he does not consider the *Psycho* remake to be a great contribution to cinema, it is his hope that *The Evil Dead* remake will give fans a memorable and enjoyable moviegoing experience. Campbell understands that sometimes a movie is just a movie, without need for social, cultural, or moral commentary, and this approach gives the genre a level playing field in which original and remake productions can play with audiences. Horror offers scares, laughs, tears, and much more to help maintain its recognition as a cinematic catchall, and that openness of the genre allows all of these industry minds to come together and comment on its existence.

The panel of interviewees all touch on relevant topics concerning contemporary American horror cinema and its propulsion into the remake zone. Torture porn films where horror elements take a backseat to exploitative depictions of pain, body mutilations, and other visceral presentations come under scrutiny. Films like *The Last House on the Left*, *I Spit on Your Grave*, and the contemporary *A Serbian Film* (2009) were created with intentional meanings relating back to drug culture, gender equality, and widespread genocide. Torture porn horror makes people think the entire contemporary genre overflows with this aesthetic. Stephen Prince says, "Horror films today, arguably, are more disturbing than those produced in earlier periods. In films of the classical Hollywood era, for example, the monsters were reliably killed at the end, and the hero and heroine safely prevailed and went on to lead their ordinary, banal lives" (3). In the remake—indeed, in most contemporary horror films—good does not always win, but it did not always reign victorious in the classic era either. The contemporary American horror film and its remake wave are only "more" disturbing because people generalize about the genre according to elements of torture porn. Current horror leaves little room for viewer imagination to fill in the gaps; classic films provoked fear without being so overt with the subject matter. *The Blair Witch Project* (1999) resonated with many critics because it harkened back to that era of scaring people without showing them the monster's face. Audiences, on the other hand, were split; some appreciated the old sensibility of atmospheric fear while others had become too accustomed to always seeing the killer and wanting to see everything in the open.

Contemporary films labeled as torture porn—the long-lasting *Saw* franchise, *Hostel*, *Hostel II* (2007), *Hostel III* (2011), *Wolf Creek* (2005), *Train* (2008), and others—are categorized as such because they represent glossy productions of violent killings with seemingly no intrinsic film or story value. Moviegoers could also rent the controversial *Faces of Death* series (1978, 1981, 1985, 1990, 1995, 1996), in which they can witness a mixture of faked and real deaths with minimal story content. These movies, and countless remakes like *I Spit on Your Grave*, are not made for cultural significance; they are shock value films that typically bring in good money at the box office. And horror is an all-encompassing genre that allows its audiences the choice to see a film with narrative strength versus a production that highlights scare tactics. It is a genre full of extremes that offers a movie for everyone who enjoys film entertainment.

No one is under the impression that remakes are going away anytime soon, but if the films are going to continue being made at a progressive incremental rate, filmmakers and viewers must ask themselves what makes the movies relevant for the genre. Some of the reasons we see these films being created relates to a filmmaker's desire to present a new attention to detail (social and cultural climates, storytelling, acting), advances in special effects, the popularity of an actor, or the will to utilize the fame of the original to springboard a new career in directing. The remake machine is always gearing up to unleash a horde of "new" films, but we have to wonder if the trend will change anytime soon. Remakes of remakes have already started to filter into the market (see the Remake Catalog, 1931–2013, for a full listing).

8

What's to Come

The contemporary American horror film and the genre's future are in remakes; however, a few novelties remain. Before examining some of these movies, discussion must shift briefly to a technology that came to cinema decades ago and has returned to help horror at the box office: 3D. Examples of this trend include *My Bloody Valentine 3D*, *The Final Destination 3D* (2009), *Piranha 3DD*, and the rumored or in-development projects *Hellraiser*, *Halloween III*, and *Zombieland 2*.

It is true that special effects play a powerful role in attracting patrons to contemporary horror films—hence the large number of movies being remade, with many of them attempting to heighten fear by way of special effects. *My Bloody Valentine* was a film not many younger viewers would know from the 1980s, but remaking it with a 3D edge brings in that crowd to experience fear enhanced by technology. The same can be said about *Piranha* 3D. It is possible that filmmakers are crafting projects to relive the experience of the drive-in where proximity to the unknown was closer at hand; all that separated viewers from the darkness was a glass pane in the form of a car window instead of stadium seating, theater walls, hallways, concession stands, arcade rooms, and lounges. The return of such special effects nostalgically reminds us of the artistic value of horror films.

The idea behind 3D filmmaking began in the 19th century, but its notable applications in horror cinema are typically recognized for productions in the 1950s, like *House of Wax*. The application made a comeback in the 1980s with *Piranha Part Two: The Spawning* (1981), *Friday the 13th Part 3*, and *Jaws 3* (1983), and then seemed to fade away in the early 1990s with *Freddy's Dead: The Final Nightmare*. Other genres have employed the effect quite liberally; it evolved into a staple of 21st century cinema for children and young adults. *Spy Kids 3: Game Over* (2003), *The Adventures of Sharkboy and Lavagirl* (2005), *Monsters vs. Aliens* (2009), and *Coraline* (2009) are just a few contemporary productions that have utilized 3D as a way to attract audiences. Many critics and fans have never considered 3D to be "good" for movies. Moviegoers were already frightened by *L'Arrivée d'un train à La Ciotat* (1896), which presented a steamroller in close proximity to the crowd; the filmmakers did not use a special effect to elicit audience reaction. 3D gave audiences something at which they could marvel or poke fun. Its current application in the remake machine creates movies that audiences can see for extra entertainment value.

As 3D movies are on the rise, the number of horror film parodies is fading. It is not surprising to see a fifth installment in the *Scary Movie* (2013) franchise pop up, somehow related to *Black Swan* (2010), but this series (and offshoots like *Shriek If You Know What I Did Last Friday the Thirteenth* [2000] and *Stan Helsing* [2009]) has started to fade from the genre's radar. When movies such as *Friday the 13th* were the new thing in horror, a parody film was easily created. *Saturday the 14th* is little-known today, but it paved the way for campy horror movies to benefit from the success of original productions. *Repossessed* (1990) may be one of the last big parody horror films before the *Scary Movie* franchise dominated the field. The movie's promotional ads gave the appearance that it was part of *The Exorcist* series; Linda Blair was mentioned, and a shot reminiscent of the original film—her possessed eyes—had fans clamoring for its release. But once it was revealed that Leslie Nielsen would star in the film, audiences quickly understood it would be a spoof. In this respect, *Scary Movie 2* (2001) not only parodied *The Exorcist* but *Repossessed* as well in a blend of metafiction that may be too tangled to fully investigate but clearly contributed to the remake trend.

Although remakes (3D and non–3D) and parodies have caused many people to say true horror no longer exists, at least for American horror, international productions reveal that the genre has plenty of originality left in it. As Badley mentioned earlier, Asian cinema (notably Japanese and Korean, or J-Horror and K-Horror) helped fuel the American remake train with *The Ring*, *The Grudge*, *The Eye*, *The Uninvited* (2009), and other single-article, single-name titles. The remakes continue, but the force of that wave has declined. Asian cinema continues to produce moody, atmospheric films, but they are no longer prominent among the sequels and prequels of movies American cinema has already appropriated into remakes. *L'horreur est maintenant aux mains des Français* (horror is now in the hands of the French). There have been interesting showings of horror from Australia (*Wolf Creek*, 2005), New Zealand (*Black Sheep*, 2006), Spain ([*REC*]), Mexico (*El orfanato* [*The Orphanage*], 2007), the UK (*The Cottage*, 2008), Sweden (*Låt den rätte komma in* [*Let the Right One In*]), Norway (*Død snø* [*Dead Snow*], 2009), and the Netherlands (*The Human Centipede* [*First Sequence*]). Most of these films lean toward comedy, with a foundation in horror, and a few of them are on the remake block ([*REC*] was remade into *Quarantine*); but it is French cinema that continues to create innovative horror true to the genre's visceral nature. Four French films—*Haute tension*, *À l'intérieur* (2007), *Frontières* (2007), and *Martyrs* (2008)—are emblematic of a new movement in horror that could help put a stop to remakes.

What is likely to become known as French New Wave Horror owes much of its contemporary development to Alexandre Aja's second feature film *Haute tension* (*High Tension*). Released initially to mix reviews, it made both critics and viewers take notice of Aja as a talented director. The story follows Marie and Alexia, two college girlfriends (not lovers) taking a trip to visit Alexia's family for school break. A grisly madman murders the family in the dead of night and kidnaps Alexia, and Marie takes the hero role to save her friend. The plot and conflicts are standard horror fare until the film nears its conclusion. In a twist of psychological narration, it is revealed that Marie is the madman; she has multiple, or at least two, personalities. This surprise ending is the predominate reason many panned over the value of the film because they found it to be a parlor trick or a filmic cheat: the way Marie and the madman are depicted in the movie does not seem physically possible. Roger Ebert, longtime critic of horror films, says there are "several crucial events in the movie that would seem to be physically, logically and dramat-

Marie (Cécile De France) is covered in blood and wields a buzz-saw to protect herself from the psychotic, stalking killer in *Haute tension* (*High Tension* 2003); however, Marie has a secret that is not revealed until the end of the film.

ically impossible, but clever viewers will be able to see for themselves that the movie's plot has a hole not only large enough to drive a truck through, but in fact does have a truck driven right through it." His commentary might well be extended to *Hide and Seek* (2005), a film with a similar presentation of mental breakdown. *Haute tension*'s surprise succeeds, however, in shocking viewers and offending some by its premise, but nevertheless leaves audiences with discussions of storytelling and an attempt to decipher Marie's split personality.

Aja is a representative director for this new wave, and he also exemplifies the trend to produce remakes once the director has established a name in the States. After *Haute tension*, his focus turned to *The Hills Have Eyes* and *Mirrors*, two high-profile remakes, and his remake of *Piranha* in 3D. Some argue that *Haute tension* is not original because it is an adaptation of the Dean Koonz novel *Intensity* (2000), but remake films are the subject matter here. What seemed to be a burgeoning career in French horror may have shifted to the remake.

Storyline aside, *Haute tension* fills the screen with visceral killings (the father decapitated by the madman), creepy moments (the madman pleasuring himself with a severed head), and an unrelenting mood of terror that shows the viewer no one—not even a child nor animal (Alexia's sibling and family dog)—escapes alive. What is also interesting about *Haute tension* as a representative film for this new wave of French horror cinema is its concentration on female characters. The movie exposes female sexuality (Marie masturbating), physical strength, mental faculties (endurance and breakdown), and strong characterizations of women as killers and victims.

French cinema has always offered elegant film noir and thrillers with strong female characterizations, like *Les Diaboliques* in 1955 (remade in 1996 as *Diabolique*, with Isabelle Adjani and Sharon Stone). A female lead portrayed as survivor or final girl is nothing new to American cinema, but the French re-imagine the essence of the motif without mocking it. This illustration of woman as simultaneously a merciless torturer and a devastated survivor removes the stereotypical male aggressor, creating a female victim binary. *Haute tension* may not be considered a perfect film, but it complicates women in horror and allows other movies to experiment with the same narrative constructs.

À l'intérieur, a simple story of a pregnant woman (Sarah) and her husband who are involved in a car crash, toys with a surprise ending and female conflict as well. Sarah and her unborn child are the only survivors. A few months pass, and when Sarah expects to deliver, a strange woman (La femme) begins to terrorize her in an attempt to take her baby. La femme is later revealed to be the unseen second party to the car crash that opens the film. Her actions are meant to avenge the miscarriage she suffered from the accident. *À l'intérieur* is a movie about a woman's body as much as *Haute tension* is about a woman's state of mind. Both characters (Marie and La femme) stop at nothing to get to their victims by killing anyone who gets in the way. La femme terrorizes Sarah to the point where she accidentally kills her own mother. *À l'intérieur*'s story structure works like a short film narrative, but its content and visuals (most notably a c-section performed with scissors) remain striking throughout the film's entirety. Along with the French and other international moviemakers leading the way in producing noteworthy films, the American remake influence continues to spread. Jaume Balagueró, director of Spain's [*REC*], has already mentioned the possibility of remaking *À l'intérieur* (McAllister). Balagueró's remake intentions demonstrate that although the U.S. has cornered the market on remakes, other filmmakers across international waters are taking notice to join the movement.

Frontières is a departure from *Haute tension* and *À l'intérieur* in terms of story, but the confrontational/assaulting visual images remain. In the midst of political upheaval and rioting, a group of five friends plan to leave Paris and head for the Amsterdam border with stolen money. The only female in the group (Yasmine) is pregnant to one of the guys, her brother is shot and hospitalized before they can leave the tumultuous streets, and (to make a long but interesting story short) all the characters come to face certain death at the hands of a cannibalistic Nazi family that operates an inn outside Amsterdam. Politics, social climate, pregnancy, theft, sibling love, romantic love, cannibalism, capitalism, incest, and brothel hospitality are just a few elements of the film that allow it to break genre stereotypes. *Frontières* as a title is fitting because the film and its movie peers question the boundaries of human suffering and devotion/love. A lot of this (particularly in *Frontières*) involves eye gouging, bodies drenched in blood, head shaving, scarification, deformity, post-traumatic stress, and other physical and mental maladies. The narrative is extremely original; however, Yasmine is a final girl of sorts, and the Nazi family can be connected to classic crazies in films like *The Texas Chain Saw Massacre*, *Motel Hell*, and *The People Under the Stairs* (1991).

These filmic traits are presented in raw fashion in *Martyrs*. The depictions of physical torture and mental abuse in this film are probably some of the most raw and poignant representations in new French horror. It is another tale of two women (Lucie and Anna) whose friendship is forged after Lucie is brutally tortured as a child. Anna, also a victim of abuse, stands by Lucie through her traumatic hallucinations and personal quest to locate the people who abused her. When Lucie is certain she has identified the woman who held her captive, she murders the entire family, and Anna sweeps in to help clean up the mess. At this time a secret society of people storm into the family's house; they kill Lucie and take Anna prisoner to face the same torture Lucie suffered as a child. Mademoiselle (the female torturer) is the leader of the group whose intentions are to create martyrs via trials of physical and mental abuse.

The way the film visually presents the human body evokes memories of Julia from Clive Barker's *Hellraiser*; Anna's skin eventually resembles Julia's flayed body as a result of body mutilation. *Martyrs* attempts much by taking what most viewers and critics call torture porn and turning it into a philosophical debate concerning the spiritual enlightenment that victims can receive from their oppressors. Its narrative drive overshadows body bondage and flaying. Not many filmmakers would tackle such heady material, and the same can be said for audiences willing to endure the experience.

Films like *Martyrs* challenge critical voices like that of Jonathan Crane who says contemporary horror films "refuse to entertain the unconscious as they, instead, offer meaningless death in response to the terrors of everyday life" (39). "Old horror" does some of the same things "new horror" does, and vice versa. *Martyrs* challenges Crane's statement about the unconscious. This film is certainly one of the most intelligent and academically-informed horror movies in the past two decades, and it is reminiscent of the content in *Dead Ringers* and other Cronenberg films that deal with the body and explore the mind in innovative ways. When moviegoers think about horror, their minds conjure images of axes, bare breasts, darkened forests, creepy houses, and sounds of blood-curdling screams. It is rare, and indeed groundbreaking, to have a horror film offer its audience unstable representations of theology and metaphysical testaments. This is a new direction for horror that is innovative and helps the genre achieve artistic merit; however, critics and filmmakers of the films question their validity.

James Quandt discusses the idea of new French horror cinema in *Art-Forum*. He identifies the components of the films but completely disagrees that a new wave exists. Quandt's words are strongly opinionated, but they must be read in full to appreciate the depth of his argument:

> The critic truffle-snuffing for trends might call it the New French Extremity, this recent tendency to the willfully transgressive by directors like Francois Ozon, Gaspar Noe, Catherine Breillat, Philippe Grandrieux—and now, alas, Dumont. Bava as much as Bataille, Salo no less than Sade seem the determinants of a cinema suddenly determined to break every taboo, to wade in rivers of viscera and spumes of sperm, to fill each frame with flesh, nubile or gnarled, and subject it to all manner of penetration, mutilation, and defilement. Images and subjects once the provenance of splatter films, exploitation flicks, and porn—gang rapes, bashings and slashings and blindings, hard-ons and vulvas, cannibalism, sadomasochism and incest, fucking and fisting, sluices of cum and gore—proliferate in the high-art

environs of a national cinema whose provocations have historically been formal, political, or philosophical (Godard, Clouzot, Debord) or, at their most immoderate (Franju, Bunuel, Walerian Borowczyk, Andrzej Zulawski), at least assimilable as emanations of an artistic movement (Surrealism mostly). Does a kind of irredentist spirit of incitement and confrontation, reviving the hallowed Gallic traditions of the film maudit, of epater les bourgeois and amour fou, account for the shock tactics employed in recent French cinema? Or do they bespeak a cultural crisis, forcing French filmmakers to respond to the death of the ineluctable (French identity, language, ideology, aesthetic forms) with desperate measures?

Quandt is absolutely correct to name rape, bodily fluids, incest, and gore as story elements present in horror films. No one can dispute his assertion; however, to a degree film *is* taboo because it reveals things viewers know about and/or practice but would rather not have on public display. Film, especially French horror cinema, does not create these acts or taboos; penetrations, mutilations, erections, and more have existed before and beyond the scope of any film genre. Quandt also discusses French film as an art form that historically elevated political and philosophical concerns; he separates new French horror films from these same elements, but previous explorations of *Frontières* and *Martyrs* demonstrate that the movies present political and philosophical issues in their innovative narratives.

Quandt is not alone in his criticism. The filmmakers of *À l'intérieur* (Julien Maury and Alex Bustillo) and *Martyrs* (Pascal Laugier) offer perspectives that partially support his argument. Maury does not believe there is anything new about the French films. He says, "This 'new wave' is not really a wave, they're more separate films. It's really hard to find funding because the movies you're talking about like *Frontier(s)* and *Martyrs*—they're not big hits at the box office here. They're not flops, but the audiences are always fairly low" (McAllister). The problem with Maury's statement is that he grounds his argument in box-office returns and not in the quality of film (story and visuals).

Laugier holds a similar opinion in his disregard of a new French horror cinema. In an interview with John White of *HomeCinema*, Laugier says:

> The fact is that we are much more successful in foreign countries and in our homeland it's always the same stuff where you're never a prophet. What I mean is that even the horror fans, the French ones, they are very condescending about French horror films. It's still a hell to find the money, a hell to convince people that we are legitimate to make this kind of movie in France. So I know from an American point of view and probably an English one too, there is a kind of new wave of modern horror film, but it's not true. It's still hell. My country produces almost two-hundred films a year and there are like two or three horror films. It's not even an industry,

French horror cinema is very low budget, it's kinda prototype. I think that a genre really exists when it's industrially produced like the Italians did six-hundred spaghetti westerns. So we can't really say that there is a wave of horror in French Cinema, I don't believe it.

He, too, seems convinced that a new French horror cinema depends on money, but what he says about how many French horror films are produced per year and how genres are created is interesting.

Laugier tackles a classic American debate concerning production: quality versus quantity. A genre does not mean conformity or mass production. Genre is about representative types, and there do not have to be six-hundred films to construct a new French horror genre. If moviegoers are asked to consider the American political documentary, most would name Michael Moore as a representative director, and he has made seven major documentary films—not hundreds. Laugier is trying to not make a big deal of the role he plays in new French horror; he is more than likely being extremely humble. He states, "To be honest, I don't like anything in my job. Writing, I find very hard, when I shoot I find it unbearable, and when I edit it I find it very boring. Sometimes when I am doing a film I am wondering why I have chosen this profession, and when I have finished I am glad it's finished. After one month or two I just can't wait to do another one. It's like a disease" (White). This is an example of tortured artist syndrome, but what he says does provide reasoning behind the subject matter he tackles in *Martyrs*.

Although Laugier does not support a new French horror cinema movement, his words contradict this notion in a discussion of the production and content of *Martyrs*. He tells White:

> It was one of the goals.... To play with the archetypes and codes of the genre, trying to bring something fresh to it.... I wanted to do a film that was as unexpected as possible so that the audience wouldn't leave the film. They would wait for the last few minutes of the film to find out the whole point of the picture. That was my intent. Because the more I was writing it, the more I realised how brutal it was, and, after a while, I realised that the brutality and the violence was the subject of the film itself. Normally, it's there to tell a story but here it's the very point.

Laugier admits to intentionally wanting to create something new for horror by making a film that would play with the rules and regulations of the genre. There is certainly a story to *Martyrs*, but the experience of the film is also important to viewers:

> I understand the debates around the film very well. The film forces the audiences to have a position about it. And I understand it, and I'm not sure as a member of the audience that I would love the film. I'm not sure at all. It's not a very likeable movie, it's an exploration. Once again, I always

understand the horror genre as transgressive, as an experimental one, and I wanted to do a film very far away from actual formulas. I wanted the film to be free, experimental, so that the audience would have some feeling whether that's a love or hate relationship. They would have a strong feeling and an experience.

This is the current development for horror in French cinema, or the "New French Extremity," in which movies are created with connections to traditional/conventional horror, but their subject matter, viewer experience, and visual presentations push the genre outside its boundaries. The films present a progression or fluid spectrum of women: *Haute tension*'s single women explore mono, hetero, and homosexuality, and the fragility of mental states; *À l'intérieur* showcases the classic struggle of a woman fighting for her unborn child's life and another attempting to steal the child; *Frontières* demonstrates the extremes to which a woman would go in order to save her unborn baby; *Martyrs* exhibits the strength of female bonds and the mind's capacity for torture; and *La Meute* (*The Pack*, 2010) displays a mother's relentless efforts to keep her children alive and how troublesome offspring can be after they are born.

The remake machine crosses international borders. *À l'intérieur* and *Martyrs* are already set for remakes. Maury and Bustillo were approached by the Weinsteins to direct a *Hellraiser* remake, but when creative differences surfaced the project passed to Laugier. Before he was attached to the film, Laugier told White, "I don't want to do a remake of *Hellraiser* because the original was so good, you know redoing the original with more money—that's not the point. The point is to bring something new and fresh to the franchise, and still staying very faithful to Clive Barker's work." His comments again speak to a trend concern over franchising, money, and marketing; however, he has since detached himself from the remake production.

Maury and Bustillo were later approached to direct *Halloween II*, but Rob Zombie came on to the project, and they bowed out. Maury says, "And though we'd said we weren't going to go through the same thing again after *Hellraiser*, it was like a dream to film Michael Myers! We couldn't say no! So we began to work on it for a few months, but then Rob Zombie came back—and compared to Rob Zombie we are nothing, so we said bye-bye!" (McAllister). It is interesting that a creative team compares itself so lowly to Rob Zombie, but this demonstrates that the power of Hollywood is strong from an international perspective. French horror is equally as valuable and innovative as American horror; hopefully the roadblocks between the cultures will fall and allow for collaborations that can stimulate the genre even more in the future.

According to Maury, "The battle is now in France, because ... horror and 'fantastique' movies aren't really popular here. The audience does exist—the *Saw* franchise was a big hit with teenagers—but they don't seem to trust French horror films. They're like, 'Horror movies in France? Bah! It's going to be two people talking in a kitchen!' It's a pity, but they just like American horror movies, so we have to convince them" (White). But this should not mean that French filmmakers have to make movies that adhere to American standards. French cinema is celebrated by viewers in America, and if the audiences are not showing up in France, new strategies could be undertaken when the films are promoted overseas to provide wide, international releases.

Contemporary French horror films are approaching a pivotal moment in cinema that represents a revival of what the horror genre was and an exploration of what lies beyond its genre parameters. Linda Badley describes the inception of horror, and her words offer an understanding of where French horror is heading:

> Horror was a bastard: it plundered the media for its iconographies, and for its themes and metaphors it drew on sources from advertising to biochemistry to postmodern philosophy. Soon it had become more than a genre. It was a widespread mythology that informed and constructed mass culture, causing people to think and speak about themselves and their feelings in particular ways. It was awful and it was interesting for precisely that reason [2].

Horror has a long way to go before it is ever accepted as a widely-celebrated presence in society and cinema, but the French have definitely stumbled upon something to cultivate, even if critics or the film directors do not believe in it.

Conclusion

Contemporary American horror has become a genre of remakes, and the originality and creativity of horror films from the 1970s, 1980s, and early 1990s is revisited in their productions. The impressive number of horror remakes has developed into a film movement whose influence is filtering into other genres. Hitchcock's *Psycho* is one of horror's most revered films, and Van Sant's remake has its own historical importance for opening the door for the remake machine to become the important movement it has developed into today. *Halloween, Friday the 13th,* and *A Nightmare on Elm Street* owe their successes to *Pyscho*, and their remakes remind us of the genre's heyday. Original horror films are important because they often reflect social and cultural atmospheres; some remakes do the same, but they also add a concentration on box-office revenue and star power. Horror movies also represent cinematic works of art that are worthy of academic study and historic preservation.

  I grew up watching horror films. This is the story I have told my friends and students for as long as I can remember, but I have never put the words on paper. When I was younger my mother would cover my eyes if a sex scene was onscreen, but if someone were being decapitated I could watch it without restriction because it "wasn't real." I learned a lot about blood and gore films, psychological thrillers, exploitation cinema, and all the subgenres, including zombie, slasher, demon possession, ghost story, serial killer, monster, contagion/infection films, and others. While most kids were reading children's books, I was watching Jef Delman's *Deadtime Stories* and other mature material. I cannot count how many times I watched *A Clockwork Orange* (1971) and *Equus* (1977) as a kid, though I did not know what those movies were about until I was an adult. Here I am today: a normal, functioning member of society who studies children's literature, horror films, and sometimes the link between the two (my Ph.D. areas of concentration), and someone who will always be a fan of innovative horror movies for my personal viewing experience rather than mass audience appeal.

Working on this book has been an exhilarating experience for the horror fan within as well as the academic. It has also conjured up feelings of uncertainty with what directions the genre may soon take. I hope for a swift socioocultural and ecopolicital change in climate to bring about an atmosphere in which horror may appropriate stories that reflect the surrounding times.

It would also be great if production companies re-released original works of horror into theaters. Audiences who remember the great originals and new viewers would have the chance to see novel creations that cannot be easily remade. Long ago we sat near each other in dark theaters as strangers to the movies on the screen. We jumped, screamed, cringed, and averted our eyes from terror by watching some of the best horror had to offer. People lined up around the block to see the *Star Wars* trilogy (1977–1983) return to the silver screen (albeit with remastering and a few additional scenes). People could be equally excited if *Poltergeist* (1982), *The Howling* (1981), *Hellraiser*, and other films are re-released in theaters. *Psycho* can still be re-released, and maybe with Gus Van Sant's version as a double feature. Original horror films should be re-released and new films should be produced; remakes cannot sustain the genre alone.

It sounds as if horror remakes popped up overnight, but they did not; the films grew out of progressive changes in the field. When *Scream* was released, the industry began using star power in horror. When *Psycho* was remade, star power was mixed with director prestige. As more remakes started to appear, more formulae were developed to bring in box-office revenue. Remakes of *The Ring*, *The Grudge*, *The Fog*, and *When a Stranger Calls* all exhibit star power with fresh directors, and were able to make more money by being released in the theaters with PG-13 ratings, thereby allowing younger, larger audiences to see the films rather than just the usual R-rated crowds. The new 3D movies are produced for the viewing experience and added entertainment value, and they draw patrons into movie theaters. Unlike the "old days" in which moviegoers were provided the 3D glasses with movie tickets, the glasses are now purchased, and merchandisers are savvy enough to make them aesthetically pleasing (constructed like sunglasses) so people feel their money has been well spent. All of these marketing methods test well.

Money keeps cinema afloat, and when I spoke to Matt Riddlehoover he suggested remakes were also a part of rejuvenating a fallen economy. When a feature-length remake is released, it sparks interest in consumers to buy/rent the original (the entire franchise if there are sequels and prequels) because they assume the film's predecessor(s) must be good to watch if it is being made a second (or third) time. Money pours into the economy at the box office, in video stores, in chain stores, local retailers, and online enterprises. The economy strengthens on remakes, and the cinematic production cycle is able to continue.

Remakes, of course, are not limited to horror films. Recent productions like *The Karate Kid* (2010) and *Death at a Funeral* (2010) have been remade from a past American franchise and an original British film, respectively. The movies are representative types for the remake machine because *Death* was remade only three years after its original, which shows how quickly the films are being made and how they cross international borders. *Karate Kid* demonstrates how important revenue is for remakes because it took in over $175 million domestically (over $180 million internationally) in box-office sales, with a production budget of $40 million. The remake machine largely created by contemporary horror productions is spreading into other genres. Sam Peckinpah's *Straw Dogs* (1971), with Dustin Hoffman, was remade in 2011 by Rod Lurie; Craig Brewer remade *Footloose* (2011) from the 1984 Kevin Bacon hit; the musical drama *Sparkle* (1976) was remade in 2012 with the late Whitney Houston; and Hitchcock's *Rebecca* (1940) is awaiting a makeover treatment. There is also industry talk, gossip, and rumor of reboots and remakes of *Child's Play* (1988), *It* (1990), and *Starship Troopers* (1997)— to name a few from a long list of titles. Thrillers and sci-fi action films join comedies and dramas in the wave of remakes.

As a fan of horror and a scholar of film, I watch remakes and I do my best to keep up with what is being turned out. Although my entire discussion represents a simple investigation into the horror remake movement, I can admit that *Dawn of the Dead*, *The Texas Chainsaw Massacre*, and *The Crazies* are my favorites of the trend. *Dawn* and *Chainsaw* are a part of the early wave of remakes and are aesthetically pleasing and relevant. This does not mean they are "pretty" films; the filmmakers worked together to demonstrate that remakes can have cultural and social value. Zack Snyder directed the *Dawn* remake, and although he had previously directed two music videos, he was basically an unknown; he has to be given credit for making George Romero's original fitting for the 21st century. The remake showcased contemporary American consumerism, race relations, single-parenting, and fear of bodily decay and death.

Chainsaw, on the other hand, is a little different and maybe more interesting to watch because it is the first film from Michael Bay's production line of remakes. It represents a major turning point in remake production in which the actors were from popular television shows and the camera work shifted the film from horror to action. Bay's partnership with Nispel as the director resulted in a film with a style that matched content. The movie entertains some of Tobe Hooper's original vision; the aesthetics highlight rural decay and poverty, and the content revisits subject matter such as the dangers of picking up a hitchhiker and small-town justice.

The Crazies, yet another Romero remake, offers a mix of elements from other films in the current wave, but it is a solid film. There are no noticeable special effects (minus one scene in which a window breaks that showcases computer-generated glass), the acting and directing are in tune with action on the screen, and the social significance of government involvement in the lives of private citizens still resonates from the original film. An interesting development is that Breck Eisner, the film's director, has become a remake director. He was relatively unknown before directing *The Crazies*, but the success of the film put him in negotiations to helm 21st century remakes of *The Brood* (1979), *Flash Gordon* (1980), and *Escape from New York* (1981)—all projects of which *IMDb* recently removed his name. This demonstrates how a single remake can be both a positive contribution to horror and a career path for a director.

These standout films are rare in the remake movement. Earlier films—Kaufman's *Invasion of the Body Snatchers*, Carpenter's *The Thing*, and Cronenberg's *The Fly*—are excellent examples that demonstrate remakes can contribute strong directing, acting, dialogue, special effects, and social commentaries to the horror genre. The contemporary American horror film, however, is still on a downward spiral, with originality, relevance, fear, and artistic value in decline (see the Remake Catalog for a full listing, 1931–2013). I expect (and would be interested) to see remakes of *Candyman* (1992), *Rawhead Rex* (1986), *Madman* (1982), and *Phantasm* (1979). It is surprising these films have not already been remade because they are all strong, cult horror, but it is probably only a matter of time. If the remake trend holds long enough, I definitely welcome these productions.

As a self-proclaimed visual person, I understand that all forms of art are inspired by various media. Homage is due those considered masters of their crafts, and the catchphrase "imitation is the sincerest form of flattery" makes sense, but it is also my hope to see individual expression in American society create more original horror films to complement the remake features. Directors such as Michael Haneke and Takashi Shimizu remade their own original films. Haneke directed *Funny Games* in 1997 and 2007, and Shimizu directed *Ju-on* in 2000 and 2002 (as *The Grudge*). Both movies were remade into American films, which again shows border-crossing influence, and Shimizu remade *Ju-on* only two years after its original production.

Several contemporary films that keep the American horror genre vital are worth mentioning: *Behind the Mask: The Rise of Leslie Vernon* (2006), *Feast* (2006), *Hatchet* (2006), *Slither* (2006), *The Ruins* (2008), *Splinter* (2008), *Drag Me to Hell* (2009), *The Hills Run Red* (2009), *The House of the Devil* (2009), *Jennifer's Body* (2009), and *Zombieland* (2009). *Feast* and *Slither* pay homage to creature features, but add in modern humor with quirky acting

Brenda (Brenda James) is transformed into a monstrous blob that is ready to give birth to hundreds of alien slugs, as Bill (Nathan Fillion), Wally (Don Thompson), and Margaret (Jennifer Copping) try to figure out her condition in *Slither* (2006).

and meta-commentary to make the films resonate with audiences. The special effects are not polished, but the acting and atmosphere of the movies work well. *Hatchet*, *Behind the Mask*, and *The Hills Run Red* are excellent slasher films for the 21st century because they introduce new villains to the subgenre. Each film incorporates elements of classic slasher horror but offers original stories, good acting, innovative kills, and a mix of fear with humor and suspense.

Jennifer's Body and *The House of the Devil* are completely different movies, but both contain intelligent writing that speaks directly to horror audiences. With its quick-witted pop culture references, *Jennifer's Body* shows viewers the turmoil of being a contemporary teenager, and *House of the Devil* uses 1980s nostalgia (feathered hair and no cell phones) to show horror as an art form. *Zombieland*, on the other hand, is a mainstream horror film, but zombie culture (defined by George Romero) has always been connected to consumerism and the social masses. It is a movie with crisp cinematography, makeup effects, and zombie rules-of-survival that fans appreciate. Sam Raimi's *Drag Me to Hell* is funny and utilizes the gross-out factor by showing what happens to the human body via old age, death, or while under the influence of a Gypsy curse. The filmmaking is reminiscent of *The Evil Dead*, and fans of that movie are able to see the same camera techniques that made it a cult favorite.

A lot of contemporary horror succeeds because of the restriction of camera space to one location, which heightens the constructs of fear and suspense: *Feast* takes place in a bar, *The Ruins* is filmed atop a Mayan temple, *The House of the Devil* has its protagonist take a babysitting job in a creepy house, and *Splinter* is filmed inside a gas station convenience store. *Pontypool* (2009) is a Canadian film, but it deserves honorable mention for turning the zombie/infection film upside down by focusing on rhetoric (how language becomes poison) instead of diseased monkeys, bacterial infections from meat, or a supernatural occurrence that awakens the dead. Horror is a smart genre, and these films demonstrate its creativity.

Each decade of American horror has at least one representative film that stands out as a "moment" to be remembered. Kendall Phillips says:

> This history of the horror film, at least as I've tried to understand it, is as much about American culture as it is about film. These films emerge at particular points in time, and in my reading, it is their relationships to the cultural moments that has energized their reception. In this way, the successful, groundbreaking horror film tells us a great deal about the culture that reacts to it, about its fears and dreams, its anxieties and aspirations. Read in this way, the horror film is an important barometer for the national mood and an important cultural space to which citizens may retreat to engage and examine the tendencies in their culture and to make choices about how to interpret and react to them. In the final analysis, the lesson of the history of the American horror film is clear: the things that we fear, and the ways that we express this fear, tell a great deal about us [198].

The 21st century recently supplied a film that may not have had a stellar presence at the box office, but contains one scene that sums up American horror for the past decade. In 1996, Wes Craven's *Scream* changed the face of horror with a new take on the slasher movie. Its cast was young, the killer(s) was unique, and the story offered commentary on horror itself. Two sequels, lots of kills, box-office gold, and 15 years later, the director returned with writer Kevin Williamson to make *Scream 4*. It reunited audiences with Sidney (Neve Campbell), Gale (Courtney Cox), and Dewey (David Arquette), and a host of young acting talent that includes Emma Thompson (Julia Roberts's niece), Hayden Panettiere (*Heroes* [NBC 2006–2010]), Anna Paquin (*True Blood*), and Kristen Bell (*Veronica Mars* [UPN 2004–2006, CW 2006–2007]).

Sidney returns to Woodsboro to promote her book about overcoming fear, and Ghostface murders and mayhem return soon after. It is the formula of cat-and-mouse whodunit killings Craven used for the previous films, and again the killer(s) is revealed to be the result of Sidney's existence. The film was made for approximately $40 million and pulled in just under $100 million worldwide, which makes it the least monetarily successful entry in the franchise. Although the movie features recognizable actors, has a masterful production team, and exhibited high production values, one scene explains why it may not have fared well in ticket sales or have had the same cultural impact as the original, and it also defines the state of contemporary American horror. Ghostface asks Kirby (Panettiere) to "name the remake of the groundbreaking horror movie in which the villain..." and before the statement is complete, she responds, "*Halloween*, uh, *Texas Chainsaw, Dawn of the Dead, The Hills Have Eyes, Amityville Horror*, uh, *Last House on the Left, Friday the 13th, A Nightmare on Elm Street, My Bloody Valentine, When a Stranger Calls, Prom Night, Black Christmas, House of Wax, The Fog*, uh, *Piranha*.... It's one of those, right? Right? I got it right. I was fucking right."

And Kirby is completely right; her words poignantly express to us that contemporary American horror is creating a new legacy for itself from remakes, and Craven's film—as a sequel—is not a part of the movement. Although *The Cabin in the Woods* (2011) offers critique of the horror genre and its reflexive nature in an innovative manner, it is also not a part of the movement. Steven C. Miller's *Silent Night* (2012) is an overhauled homage to *Silent Night, Deadly Night* from 1984, and it is more representative of horror's current development. Franck Khalfoun's *Maniac* (2012) is a remake of William Lustig's gritty original film from 1980, with Alexandre Aja attached to the project as writer and producer. The wave continues to rise in 2013 with these films, the upcoming *Carrie* and *Evil Dead* remakes, and many other movies in early planning and filming stages. Audience members will simply have to decide if they wish to weather the ride or jump ship as the trend progresses into the future.

I have not included discussion of films such as Freddy vs. Jason *because "versus films" (hybrids) are their own branch of entertainment. Like* AVP: Alien vs. Predator *(2004), these films are neither original sequels nor remakes; they are creations from comic books, video games, and fan-appreciation movies that are typically made to rejuvenate the separate franchises.*

Remake Catalog, 1931–2013

The following is a listing of horror films, chronicled from original productions starting in 1931 and their remake counterparts into 2013. Data has been gathered from the *Internet Movie Database* (IMDb.com) and verified with *Box Office Mojo* (boxofficemojo.com) in an effort to eliminate any discrepancies. The films are in order by production date, not alphabetical order, and although not all of the films originate in the United States, the remakes are being produced in America. Only domestic box-office results are presented, and only films with theatrical releases are listed, with a few exceptions that are recognized titles in horror (i.e. the miniseries *It* [1990], based on Stephen King's novel, is being remade into a feature-length film). Other films, such as *Rosemary's Baby* (1968), do not appear on the list because their remakes continue to live in rumor, and no concrete deals have been made to produce them.

Each original film is detailed on the left side of the column list by its title, release date, MPAA rating (or earlier Production Code rating, depending on the year of release), budget, and box-office revenue, where information is available; its remake appears on the right with the same information. If a film has been remade more than once, the second and/or third remakes appear below the original, following the same left-to-right format. In some cases, film ratings were revised or petitioned, and the changes are noted with a "/" separating the modifications from left to right.

The list demonstrates changes in MPAA rating categories, remake acquisitions from international territories, trends in budgetary spending and box-office revenue, and the rapidly increasing response time for filmmakers to create remakes from original productions. It should also be noted that some budget and box-office figures have been approximated due to currency exchange rates from international locations.

Original Title Release Date Rating Budget / Box Office	Remake Title Release Date Rating Budget / Box Office
Frankenstein 1931 UR $291,000 / $12 million	*Frankenstein* 1994 R $45 million / $22,006,296
Island of Lost Souls 1932 UR N/A / N/A	*The Island of Dr. Moreau* 1977 PG $6 million / NA
The Island of Dr. Moreau 1996 PG-13 $40 million / $27,663,982	*The Island of Lost Souls* (in development) 20xx NA N/A / N/A
Mystery of the Wax Museum 1933 UR N/A / N/A	*House of Wax* 1953 Approved $658,000 / N/A
	House of Wax 2005 R $30 million / $32,048,809
King Kong 1933 Approved $670,000 / $1.7 million	*King Kong* 1976 PG $24 million / $52,614,445
	King Kong 2005 PG-13 $207 million / $218,080,025
Bride of Frankenstein 1935 Approved $397,000 / N/A	*The Bride* 1985 PG-13 N/A / $3,558,669
The Wolf Man 1941 Approved $180,000 / N/A	*The Wolfman* 2010 R $85 million / $61,937,495
Cat People 1942 Approved $134,000 / $4 million	*Cat People* 1982 R $18 million / $5,694,940

The Beast with Five Fingers
1946
Approved
N/A / N/A

The Thing from Another World
1951
Approved
N/A / N/A

Invaders from Mars
1953
Approved
$290,000 / N/A

Creature from the Black Lagoon

1954
Approved
N/A / $1.3 million

Gojira
1954
UR
$1 million / $412,520

Godzilla
1998
PG-13
$130 million / $136,314,294

Invasion of the Body Snatchers
1956
Approved
$417,000 / N/A

Body Snatchers
1993
R
$13 million / $428,868

The Blob
1958
N/A
$240,000 / N/A

The Fly
1958
UR
$700,000 / N/A

The Hand
1981
R
$6.5 million / $2,447,576

The Thing
1982
R
$15 million / $13,782,838

The Thing
2011
N/A
$35 million / N/A

Invaders from Mars
1986
PG
$12 million / $4,884,663

Creature from the Black Lagoon
(in development)
20xx
N/A
$750,000 / N/A

Gojira
1984
PG
$200,000 / $4,116,395

Godzilla
2014
N/A
N/A / N/A

Invasion of the Body Snatchers
1978
PG
$3.5 million / $24,946,533

The Invasion
2007
PG-13
$80 million / $15,071,514

The Blob
1988
R
$19 million / $8,247,943

The Fly
1986
R
$15 million / $40,456,565

Original Title Release Date Rating Budget / Box Office	Remake Title Release Date Rating Budget / Box Office
House on Haunted Hill 1959 UR $200,000 / N/A	*House on Haunted Hill* 1999 R $19 million / $40,846,082
Psycho 1960 Approved / M / R $806,947 / $32 million	*Psycho* 1998 R $25 million / $21,456,130
13 Ghosts 1960 Approved N/A / N/A	*Thir13en Ghosts* 2001 R $20 million / $41,867,960
Village of the Damned 1960 UR $200,000 / N/A	*Village of the Damned* 1995 R $22 million / $9,417,567
The Birds 1963 Approved / PG-13 $2.5 million / $11,403,529	*The Birds* (in development) 20xx N/A N/A / N/A
The Haunting 1963 Approved / G $1.4 million / N/A	*The Haunting* 1999 PG-13 $80 million / $91,411,151
Two Thousand Maniacs 1964 UR $65,000 / N/A	*2001 Maniacs* 2005 R $3 million / N/A
Night of the Living Dead 1968 UR $114,000 / $12 million	*Night of the Living Dead* 1990 R $4.2 million / $5,835,247
	Night of the Living Dead 3D 2006 R $750,000 / $215,000
The Wizard of Gore 1970 NR $60,000 / N/A	*The Wizard of Gore* 2007 R N/A / N/A

Remake Catalog, 1931–2013

The Last House on the Left
1972
R
$90,000 / $3.1 million

Don't Be Afraid of the Dark
1973
UR
N/A / N/A

The Crazies
1973
R
$275, 000 / N/A

The Forgotten
1973
R
N/A / N/A

The Wicker Man
1973
R
N/A / N/A

Black Christmas
1974
R
$686,000 / $4,053,000

Deathdream
1974
PG
$235,000

It's Alive
1974
PG
N/A / N/A

The Texas Chain Saw Massacre
1974
R
$83,532 / $30,859,000

The Rocky Horror Picture Show

1975
R
$1.2 million / $139,876,417

Carrie
1976
R
$1.8 million / $33.8 million

The Last House on the Left
2009
R
N/A / $32,721,635

Don't Be Afraid of the Dark
2010
R
$12.5 million / N/A

The Crazies
2010
R
$12 million / $39,123,589

Don't Look in the Basement!
2011
N/A
N/A / N/A

The Wicker Man
2006
PG-13
$40 million / $23,643,531

Black Christmas
2006
R
$9 million / $16,235,293

Zero Dark Thirty
2010
N/A
N/A / N/A

It's Alive
2008
R
$10 million / N/A

The Texas Chainsaw Massacre
2003
R
$9.2 million / $80,571,655

The Rocky Horror Picture Show
(in development)
20xx
N/A
N/A / N/A

Carrie
2002
N/A
N/A / N/A

Original Title Release Date Rating Budget / Box Office	Remake Title Release Date Rating Budget / Box Office
	Carrie 2013 N/A N/A / N/A
The Omen 1976 R $2.8 million / $4,273,886	*The Omen* 2006 R $25 million / $54,607,383
The Hills Have Eyes 1977 X / R $230,000 / N/A	*The Hills Have Eyes* 2006 NC-17 / R $15 million / $41,778,863
Suspiria 1977 R N/A / N/A	*Suspiria* (in development) 20xx N/A $13 million / N/A
Dawn of the Dead 1978 R $650,000 / N/A	*Dawn of the Dead* 2004 R $28 million / $59,020,957
Faces of Death 1978 NR $450,000 / $35 million	*Faces of Death* 2011 N/A N/A / N/A
Halloween 1978 R $320,000 / $47 million	*Halloween* 2007 R $15 million / $58,272,029
I Spit on Your Grave 1978 X / R N/A / N/A	*I Spit on Your Grave* 2009 N/A $1.5 million / $572,809
Long Weekend 1978 N/A N/A / N/A	*Long Weekend* 2008 R N/A / N/A
Piranha 1978 R $600,000 / N/A	*Piranha 3D* 2010 N/A $24 million / $25 million

The Fury
1978
R
$5.5 million / $24 million

The Toolbox Murders
1978
R
$185,000 / N/A

The Amityville Horror
1979
R
N/A / $86,432,520

When a Stranger Calls
1979
R
$740,000 / $21,411,158

Friday the 13th
1980
R
$550,000 / $39,754,601

Prom Night
1980
R
$1.6 million / $14,796,236

Mother's Day
1980
UR
$150,000 / N/A

The Fog
1980
R
$1 million / $21,378,000

The Shining
1980
R
$22 million / $44,017,374

My Bloody Valentine
1981
R
$2.3 million / $5,672,031

The Evil Dead
1981
NR
$375,000 / $2,400,000

The Fury (in development)
20xx
N/A
N/A / N/A

Toolbox Murders
2004
R
N/A / N/A

The Amityville Horror
2005
R
$19 million / $65,233,369

When a Stranger Calls
2006
PG-13
$15 million / $47,860,214

Friday the 13th
2009
R
$19 million / $64,997,188

Prom Night
2008
PG-13
$20 million / $43,869,350

Mother's Day
2010
NR
$11 million / N/A

The Fog
2005
PG-13
$18 million / $29,511,112

The Shining
1997
UR
$25 million / N/A

My Bloody Valentine 3D
2009
R
$15 million / $51,545,952

The Evil Dead
2013
N/A
N/A / N/A

Original Title Release Date Rating Budget / Box Office	Remake Title Release Date Rating Budget / Box Office
Poltergeist 1982 R / PG $10.7 million / $76,606,280	*Poltergeist* (in development) 20xx N/A N/A / N/A
The House on Sorority Row 1983 R $425,000 / $4,330,028	*Sorority Row* 2009 R $16 million / $11,915,856
Children of the Corn 1984 R $3 million / $14,568,989	*Children of the Corn* 2009 UR $2 million / N/A
A Nightmare on Elm Street 1984 R $1.8 million / $25,504,513	*A Nightmare on Elm Street* 2010 R $35 million / $63,005,877
Fright Night 1985 R N/A / $24,922,237	*Fright Night* 2011 R $30 million / $18,302,607
The Hitcher 1986 R $6 million / $5,844,868	*The Hitcher* 2007 R N/A / $16,472,961
Angustia 1987 R $228,789 / N/A	*Anguish* 2011 N/A N/A / N/A
Hellraiser 1987 R $1 million / $14,564,027	*Hellraiser* (in development) 20xx N/A N/A / N/A
The Stepfather 1987 R N/A / $2,488,740	*The Stepfather* 2009 PG-13 N/A / $28,802,131
Child's Play 1988 R $9 million / $33,244,684	*Child's Play* (in development) 2014 N/A N/A / N/A

Night of the Demons
  1988
  R
  $1.2 million / $3,109,904
They Live
  1988
  R
  $4 million / $13,008,928
Pet Semetary
  1989
  R
  $11.5 million / $57,469,179
It
  1990
  NR
  N/A / N/A
Joyû-rei
  1996
  UR
  N/A / N/A
Funny Games
  1997
  UR
  N/A / N/A
Ringu
  1998
  UR
  $1.2 million / N/A
Honogurai mizu no soko kara
  2002
  PG-13
  N/A / N/A
Kairo
  2001
  R
  N/A / $49,046
Gin gwai
  2002
  R
  $3.2 million / $503,714
Janghwa, Hongryeon
  2003
  R
  N/A / N/A

Night of the Demons
  2009
  R
  $10 million / N/A
They Live (in development)
  20xx
  N/A
  N/A / N/A
Pet Semetary (in development)
  2013
  N/A
  N/A / N/A
It (in development)
  20xx
  N/A
  N/A / N/A
Don't Look Up
  2009
  R
  N/A / N/A
Funny Games
  2007
  R
  $15 million / $1,294,640
The Ring
  2002
  PG-13
  $48 million / $128,579,698
Dark Water
  2005
  PG-13
  $30 million / $25,473,352
Pulse
  2006
  R / PG-13
  $20 million / $20,259,297
The Eye
  2008
  PG-13
  $12 million / $31,418,697
A Tale of Two Sisters
  2009
  PG-13
  N/A / $28,573,173

Original Title Release Date Rating Budget / Box Office	Remake Title Release Date Rating Budget / Box Office
Ju-on 2002 R N/A / $325,661	*The Grudge* 2004 PG-13 $10 million / $110,175,871
Die Nacht der lebenden Loser 2004 UR $4.3 million / N/A	*Night of the Living Dorks* 2010 N/A N/A / N/A
Shutter 2004 NR $3.38 million / N/A	*Shutter* 2008 PG-13 N/A / $25,926,543
Sigaw 2004 N/A $350,000 / N/A	*The Echo* 2008 R $5 million / N/A
Al final del espectro 2006 N/A $838,926 / N/A	*At the End of the Spectra* 2010 N/A N/A / N/A
Gwoemul 2006 R $11 million / $2,201,412	*The Host* 2010 N/A N/A / N/A
Myortvye docheri 2007 N/A $1.2 million / N/A	*Dead Daughters* 2010 N/A N/A / N/A
[Rec] 2007 R $1,845,300 / N/A	*Quarantine* 2008 R $12 million / $31,691,811
Låt den rätte komma in 2008 Rated R N/A / $2,122,065	*Let Me In* 2010 N/A N/A / N/A

Works Cited

À l'intérieur (Inside). Dir. Alexandre Bustillo and Julien Maury. The Weinstein Company, 2007. Film.

The Abyss. Dir. James Cameron. Twentieth Century–Fox Film Corporation, 1989. Film.

The Adventures of Sharkboy and Lavagirl. Dir. Robert Rodriguez. Dimension Films, 2005. Film.

Alice in Wonderland. Dir. Tim Burton. Walt Disney Studios Motion Pictures, 2010. Film.

Alien. Dir. Ridley Scott. Twentieth Century–Fox Film Corporation, 1979. Film.

Aliens. Dir. James Cameron. Twentieth Century–Fox Film Corporation, 1986. Film.

Altered States. Dir. Ken Russell. Warner Bros. Pictures, 1980. Film.

American Nightmare. Dir. Adam Simon. Independent Film Channel (IFC), 2000. Film.

An American Werewolf in London. Dir. John Landis. Universal Pictures, 1981. Film.

The Amityville Horror. Dir. Stuart Rosenberg. American International Pictures (AIP), 1979. Film.

The Amityville Horror. Dir. Andrew Douglas. MGM, 2005. Film.

April Fool's Day. Dir. Fred Walton. Paramount Pictures, 1986. Film.

Armageddon. Dir. Michael Bay. Buena Vista Pictures, 1998. Film.

Army of Darkness. Dir. Sam Raimi. Universal Pictures, 1992. Film.

L'Arrivée d'un train à La Ciotat. Dir. Auguste Lumière and Louis Lumière. Lumière, 1896. Film.

The Arsenio Hall Show. Paramount Television, 1989–1994. Television.

Assault on Precinct 13. Dir. John Carpenter. Turtle Releasing, 1976. Film.

Avatar. Dir. James Cameron. Twentieth Century–Fox Film Corporation, 2010. Film.

AVP: Alien vs. Predator. Dir. Paul W. S. Anderson. Twentieth Century–Fox Film Corporation, 2004. Film.

AVPR: Alien vs. Predator: Requiem. Dir. Colin and Greg Strause. Twentieth Century–Fox Film Corporation, 2007. Film.

Bad Boys. Dir. Michael Bay. Columbia Pictures, 1995. Film.

Bad Boys II. Dir. Michael Bay. Columbia Pictures, 2003. Film.

Bad Dreams. Dir. Andrew Fleming. Twentieth Century–Fox Film Corporation, 1988. Film.

The Bad Seed. Dir. Mervyn LeRoy. Warner Bros. Pictures, 1956. Film.

Badley, Linda. Film, Horror, and the Body Fantastic. Westport: Greenwood Press, 1995. Print.

_____. "Recycled Fear: The Contemporary Horror Remake as American Cinema Industry Standard." Dissertation Comment. 1 July 2010.

Bayer, Samuel, dir. A Nightmare on Elm Street. New Line Cinema, 2010. Film.

The Beast with Five Fingers. Dir. Robert Florey. Warner Bros. Pictures, 1946. Film.

The Beast Within. Dir. Philippe Mora. United Artists, 1982. Film.

The Bees. Dir. Alfredo Zacarias. New World Pictures, 1978. Film.

Behind Enemy Lines. Dir. John Moore. Twentieth Century–Fox Film Corporation, 2001. Film.

Behind the Mask: The Rise of Leslie Vernon. Dir. Scott Glosserman. Anchor Bay Entertainment, 2006. Film.

Big Business. Dir. Jim Abrahams. Buena Vista Pictures, 1988. Film.

Big Love. HBO, 2006–2011. Television.

Big Trouble in Little China. Dir. John Carpenter. Twentieth Century–Fox Film Corporation, 1986. Film.

Black Christmas. Dir. Bob Clark. Warner Bros. Pictures, 1974. Film.

Black Christmas. Dir. Glen Morgan. Metro-Goldwyn-Mayer (MGM), 2006. Film.

Black Sheep. Dir. Jonathan King. IFC Films, 2007. Film.

Black Swan. Dir. Darren Aronofsky. Fox Searchlight Pictures, 2010. Film.

Blade. New Line Cinema, 1998, 2002, 2004. Film.

The Blair Witch Project. Dir. Daniel Myrick and Eduardo Sanchez. Aristan Entertainment, 1999. Film.

The Blob. Dir. Irvin S. Yeaworth, Jr. Paramount Pictures, 1958. Film.

The Blob. Dir. Chuck Russell. TriStar Pictures, 1988. Film.

Block, Melissa. "Film Historian: *Psycho* Altered Ideas on Censorship." NPR.org. 11 Jul 2010. Web. http://www.npr.org/templates/story/story.php?storyId=127937275

Blood for Dracula. Dir. Paul Morrissey. Bryanston Distributing, 1974. Film.

Body Snatchers. Dir. Abel Ferrara. Warner Bros. Pictures, 1993. Film.

Bones. Fox Network, 2005. Television.

Boogie Nights. Dir. Paul Thomas Anderson. New Line Cinema, 1997. Film.

Box office / business for Friday the 13th *(1980)*. IMDB.com. 11 Jul 2010. Web. http://www.imdb.com/title/tt0080761/business

Box office / business for Friday the 13th *(2009)*. IMDB.com. 11 Jul 2010. Web. http://www.imdb.com/title/tt0758746/business

Box office / business for Halloween *(1978)*. IMDB.com. 11 Jul 2010. Web. http://www.imdb.com/title/tt0077651/business

Box office / business for Halloween *(2007)*. IMDB.com. 11 Jul 2010. Web. http://www.imdb.com/title/tt0373883/business

Box office / business for Karate Kid, The *(2010)*. IMDB.com. 11 Jul 2010. Web. http://www.imdb.com/title/tt1155076/business

Box office / business for New Nightmare *(1994)*. IMDB.com. 11 Jul 2010. Web. http://www.imdb.com/title/tt0111686/business

Box office / business for Scream *(1996)*. IMDB.com. 11 Jul 2010. Web. http://www.imdb.com/title/tt0117571/business

Box office / business for Scream 2 *(1997)*. IMDB.com. 11 Jul 2010. Web. http://www.imdb.com/title/tt0120082/business

Box office / business for Scream 3 *(2000)*. IMDB.com. 11 Jul 2010. Web. http://www.imdb.com/title/tt0134084/business

Brain Damage. Dir. Frank Henenlotter. Manson International Pictures, 1988. Film.

The Bride. Dir. Franc Roddam. Columbia Pictures, 1985. Film.

Bride of Frankenstein. Dir. James Whale. Universal Pictures, 1935. Film.

Bringing Out the Dead. Dir. Martin Scorsese. Paramount Pictures, 1999. Film.

The Brood. Dir. David Cronenberg. New World Pictures, 1979. Film.

Brottman, Mikita. *Offensive Films: Toward*

an *Anthology of Cinema Vomitif.* Westport: Greenwood Press, 1997. Print.

Buffy the Vampire Slayer. The WB Television Network, 1997–2001. Television.

Buffy the Vampire Slayer. United Paramount Network (UPN), 2001–2003. Television.

The 'Burbs. Dir. Joe Dante. Universal Pictures, 1989. Film.

Burn Notice. USA Network, 2007. Television.

The Burning. Dir. Tony Maylam. Filmways Pictures, 1981. Film.

Busta Rhymes. "Gimme Some More." *E.L.E. (Extinction Level Event): The Final World Front.* Flipmode/Elektra Records, 1998. CD.

The Cabin in the Woods. Dir. Drew Goddard. Lionsgate, 2011. Film.

Campbell, Bruce. Email Interview. 1 March 2012.

Campbell, John W., Jr. "Who Goes There?" *Astounding Stories*, 1938. Print.

Candyman. Dir. Bernard Rose. TriStar Pictures, 1992. Film.

Cantor, Joanne, and Mary Beth Oliver. "Developmental Differences in Responses to Horror." In *The Horror Film*, edited by Stephen Prince, 224–241. New Brunswick: Rutgers University Press, 2004. Print.

Carpenter, John, dir. *Halloween.* Compass International Pictures, 1978. Film.

Carrie. Dir. Brian De Palma. United Artists, 1976. Film.

Carrie. Dir. David Carson. NBC, 2002. Television.

La Casa Muda. Dir. Gustavo Hernández. Tokio Films, 2010. Film.

Cash, Johnny. "The Man Comes Around." *American IV: The Man Comes Around.* Lost Highway, 2000. CD.

Castle Freak. Dir. Stuart Gordon. Full Moon Entertainment, 1995. Film.

Cat People. Dir. Jacques Tourneur. RKO Radio Pictures, 1942. Film.

Cat People. Dir. Paul Schrader. Universal Pictures, 1982. Film.

The Cell. Dir. Tarsem Singh. New Line Cinema, 2000. Film.

Charlie and the Chocolate Factory. Dir. Tim Burton. Warner Bros. Pictures, 2005. Film.

Charlie's Angels. ABC, 1976–1981. Television.

Charmed. The WB Television Network, 1998–2006. Television.

Children of the Corn. Dir. Fritz Kiersch. New World Pictures, 1984. Film.

Children of the Corn. Dir. Donald P. Borchers. Syfy, 2009. Television.

Child's Play. Dir. Tom Holland. United Artists, 1988. Film.

Cigarette Burns. Dir. John Carpenter. Showtime Networks, 2005. Film.

A Clockwork Orange. Dir. Stanley Kubrick. Warner Bros. Pictures, 1971. Film.

Cloverfield. Dir. Matt Reeves. Paramount Pictures, 2008. Film.

Clueless. ABC, 1996–1997. Television.

Clueless. United Paramount Network (UPN), 1997–1999. Television.

Columbo. NBC, 1971–1990. Television.

Coraline. Dir. Henry Selick. Universal Pictures, 2009. Film.

The Cottage. Dir. Paul Andrew Williams. Screen Gems, 2008. Film.

Crane, Jonathan Lake. *Terror and Everyday Life: Singular Moments in the History of the Horror Film.* London: Sage Publications, 1994. Print.

Craven, Wes. Dir. *A Nightmare on Elm Street.* New Line Cinema, 1984. Film.

The Crazies. Dir. George A. Romero. Cambist Films, 1973. Film.

The Crazies. Dir. Breck Eisner. Overture Films, 2010. Film.

Creed, Barbara. *The Monstrous-Feminine: Film, Feminism, Psychoanalysis.* London: Routledge, 1993. Print.

Creepshow. Dir. George A. Romero. Warner Bros. Pictures, 1982. Film.

Creepy, Uncle. "Colin Farrell on *Fright Night* Remake." DreadCentral.com (2011). Web. 13 July 2011. http://www.dreadcentral.com/news/41904/colin-farrell-fright-night-remake

Critters 4. Dir. Rupert Harvey. New Line Cinema, 1992. Film.
CSI: NY. CBS, 2004. Television.
Cujo. Dir. Lewis Teague. Warner Bros. Pictures, 1983. Film.
Cunningham, Sean S. Dir. *Friday the 13th*. Paramount Pictures, 1980. Film.
Curse of the Fly. Dir. Don Sharp. Twentieth Century–Fox Film Corporation, 1965. Film.
Damien: Omen II. Dir. Don Taylor. Twentieth Century–Fox Film Corporation, 1978. Film.
Dawn of the Dead. Dir. George A. Romero. United Film Distribution Company (UFDC), 1978. Film.
Dawn of the Dead. Dir. Zack Snyder. Universal Pictures, 2004. Film.
Day of the Animals. Dir. William Girdler. Film Ventures International (FVI), 1977. Film.
Day of the Dead. Dir. George A. Romero. United Film Distribution Company (UFDC), 1985. Film.
Day of the Dead. Dir. Steve Miner. Millennium Films, 2008. Film.
The Day of the Triffids. Dir. Steve Sekely. Allied Artists Pictures, 1962. Film.
The Day of the Triffids. Dir. Ken Hannam. British Broadcasting Corporation (BBC), 1981. Television.
The Day of the Triffids. Dir. Nick Copus. Power, 2009. Television.
The Day the Earth Stood Still. Dir. Robert Wise. Twentieth Century–Fox Film Corporation, 1951. Film.
The Day the Earth Stood Still. Dir. Scott Derrickson. Twentieth Century–Fox Film Corporation, 2008. Film.
Dead Man. Dir. Jim Jarmusch. Miramax Films, 1996. Film.
Dead Ringers. Dir. David Cronenberg. Anchor Bay Entertainment, 1988. Film.
Deadtime Stories. Dir. Jef Delman. Cinema Group, 1986. Film.
Death at a Funeral. Dir. Neil LaBute. Screen Gems, 2010. Film.
Death Proof. Dir. Quentin Tarantino. Dimension Films, 2007. Film.

Deep Red. Dir. Dario Argento. Rizzoli Film, 1975. Film.
Delman, Jef. Email Interview. 12 May 2010.
Derry, Charles. "More Dark Dreams: Some Notes on the Recent Horror Film." In *American Horrors: Essays on the Modern American Horror Film*. Urbana: University of Illinois Press, 1987. Print.
The Devil's Rejects. Dir. Rob Zombie. Lions Gate Films, 2005. Film.
Diabolique. Dir. Jeremiah S. Chechik. Warner Bros. Pictures, 1996. Film.
Diaboliques, Les. Dir. Henri-Georges Clouzot. Janus Films, 1955. Film.
Dial M for Murder. Dir. Alfred Hitchcock. Film. Warner Bros. Pictures, 1954. Film.
Diary of the Dead. Dir. George A. Romero. Third Rail Releasing, 2007. Film.
Diff'rent Strokes. NBC, 1978–1985. Television.
Diff'rent Strokes. ABC, 1985–1986. Television.
Disturbed. "Down with the Sickness." *Sickness*. Giant Records, 2000. CD.
Død snø (Dead Snow). Dir. Tommy Wirkola. IFC Films, 2009. Film.
Don't Be Afraid of the Dark. Dir. Troy Nixey. FilmDistrict, 2010. Film.
Dracula. Dir. Todd Browning. Universal Pictures, 1931. Film.
Dracula. Dir. John Badham. Universal Pictures, 1979. Film.
Dracula. Dir. Francis Ford Coppola. American Zoetrope, 1992. Film.
Dracula: Dead and Loving It. Dir. Mel Brooks. Castle Rock Entertainment, 1995. Film.
Dracula 2000. Dir. Patrick Lussier: 2000, 2003, 2005. Film.
Drag Me to Hell. Dir. Sam Raimi. Universal Pictures, 2009. Film.
Dreamscape. Dir. Joseph Ruben. Twentieth Century–Fox Film Corporation, 1984. Film.
Ebert, Roger. "High Tension." *RogerEbert.Suntimes.com*. 9 June 2005. Web. 8 December 2009.

Ed Wood. Dir. Tim Burton. Buena Vista Pictures, 1994. Film.

Edward Scissorhands. Dir. Tim Burton. Twentieth Century–Fox Film Corporation, 1990. Film.

Englund, Robert. Email Interview. 30 May 2010.

The Entity. Dir. Sidney J. Furie. Twentieth Century–Fox Film Corporation, 1982. Film.

Equus. Dir. Sidney Lumet. United Artists, 1977. Film.

Eraserhead. Dir. David Lynch. Libra Films International, 1976. Film.

Escape from New York. Dir. John Carpenter. AVCO Embassy Pictures, 1981. Film.

The Evil Dead. Dir. Sam Raimi. New Line Cinema, 1981. Film.

The Evil Dead. Dir. Fede Alvarez. TriStar Pictures, 2013. Film.

Evil Dead II. Dir. Sam Raimi. Rosebud Releasing Corporation, 1987. Film.

The Exorcist. Dir. William Friedkin. Warner Bros. Pictures, 1973. Film.

The Eye. Dir. David Moreau and Xavier Palud. Lionsgate, 2008. Film.

Faces of Death. Dir. John Alan Schwartz. Gorgon Video: 1978, 1981, 1985, 1990, 1995, 1996. Film.

The Faculty. Dir. Robert Rodriguez. Dimension Films, 1998. Film.

Family Guy. Fox Network, 1999. Television.

Family Matters. ABC, 1989–1997. Television.

Family Matters. CBS, 1997–1998. Television.

Fangoria magazine, 1979–2010. Print.

Fatal Attraction. Dir. Adrian Lyne. Paramount Pictures, 1987. Film.

Fear No Evil. Dir. Frank LaLoggia. AVCO Embassy Pictures, 1981. Film.

Feast. Dir. John Gulager: 2005, 2008, 2009. Film.

Fiend Without a Face. Dir. Arthur Crabtree. MGM, 1958. Film.

The Final Destination 3D. Dir. David R. Ellis. Warner Bros. Pictures, 2009. Film.

Finney, Jack. "The Body Snatchers." *Colliers Magazine*, 1954. Print.

Firestarter. Dir. Mark L. Lester. Universal Pictures, 1984. Film.

Flash Gordon. Dir. Mike Hodges. Universal Pictures, 1980. Film.

Flesh for Frankenstein. Dir. Paul Morrissey and Antonio Margheriti. Bryanston Distributing, 1973. Film.

Flight of the Phoenix. Dir. John Moore. Twentieth Century–Fox Film Corporation, 2004. Film.

The Fly. Dir. Kurt Neumann. Twentieth Century–Fox Film Corporation, 1958. Film.

The Fly. Dir. David Cronenberg. Twentieth Century–Fox Film Corporation, 1986. Film.

The Fly II. Dir. Chris Walas. Twentieth Century–Fox Film Corporation, 1989. Film.

The Fog. Dir. John Carpenter. AVCO Embassy Pictures, 1980. Film.

The Fog. Dir. Rupert Wainwright. Columbia Pictures, 2005. Film.

Footloose. Dir. Hebert Ross. Paramount Pictures, 1984. Film.

Footloose. Dir. Craig Brewer. Paramount Pictures, 2011. Film.

Frankenstein. Dir. James Whale. Universal Pictures, 1931. Film.

Frankenstein. Dir. Kenneth Branagh. TriStar Pictures, 1994. Film.

Freaky Friday. Dir. Mark Waters. Buena Vista Pictures, 2003. Film.

Freddy's Dead: The Final Nightmare. Dir. Rachel Talalay. New Line Cinema, 1991. Film.

Freddy vs. Jason. Dir. Ronny Yu. New Line Cinema, 2003. Film.

Freeway. Dir. Matthew Bright. Roxie Releasing, 1996. Film.

Friday the 13th (franchise). Wikipedia.org. 9 July 2010. Web. http://en.wikipedia.org/wiki/Friday_the_13th_(franchise)

Friday the 13th Part 2. Dir. Steve Miner. Paramount Pictures, 1981. Film.

Friday the 13th Part III. Dir. Steve Miner. Paramount Pictures, 1982. Film.

Friday the 13th: The Final Chapter. Dir. Joseph Zito. Paramount Pictures, 1984. Film.

Friday the 13th: A New Beginning. Dir. Danny Steinmann. Paramount Pictures, 1985. Film.

Friday the 13th Part VI: Jason Lives. Dir. Tom McLoughlin. Paramount Pictures, 1986. Film.

Friday the 13th Part VII: The New Blood. Dir. John Carl Buechler. Paramount Pictures, 1988. Film.

Friday the 13th Part VIII: Jason Takes Manhattan. Dir. Rob Hedden. Paramount Pictures, 1989. Film.

Fright Night. Dir. Tom Holland. Columbia Pictures, 1985. Film.

Fright Night. Dir. Craig Gillespie. Walt Disney Studios Motion Pictures, 2011. Film.

Fright Night 2. Dir. Tommy Lee Wallace. New Century Vista Film Company, 1988. Film.

Frogs. Dir. George McCowan. American International Pictures, 1972. Film.

From Dusk Till Dawn. Dir. Robert Rodriguez. Dimension Films, 1996. Film.

Frontières. Dir. Xavier Gens. After Dark Films, 2007. Film.

Funny Games. Dir. Michael Haneke. Attitude Films, 1997. Film.

Funny Games. Dir. Michael Haneke. Warner Independent Pictures, 2007. Film.

The Fury. Dir. Brian De Palma. Twentieth Century–Fox Film Corporation, 1978. Film.

Gilmore Girls. The WB Television Network, 2000–2007. Television.

Ginger Snaps. Dir. John Fawcett. Motion International, 2000. Film.

Godzilla. Dir. Ishirô Honda and Terry O. Morse. Embassy Pictures Corporation, 1956. Film.

Godzilla. Dir. Roland Emmerich. TriStar Pictures, 1998. Film.

Going to Pieces: The Rise and Fall of the Slasher Film. Executive Producer Michael Baker. thinkfilm, 2006. DVD.

Gojira. Dir. Ishirô Honda. Toho Film Co. Ltd., 1954. Film.

The Good Son. Dir. Joseph Ruben. Twentieth Century–Fox Film Corporation, 1993. Film.

The Goonies. Dir. Richard Donner. Warner Bros. Pictures, 1985. Film.

Grahame-Smith, Seth. *How to Survive a Horror Movie: All the Skills to Dodge the Kills.* Philadelphia: Quirk Books, 2007. Print.

Grant, Barry Keith, ed. *The Dread of Difference: Gender and the Horror Film.* Austin: Utah University Press, 1996. Print.

Gremlins. Dir. Joe Dante. Warner Bros. Pictures, 1984. Film.

Grindhouse. Dir. Robert Rodriguez and Quentin Tarantino. Dimension Films, 2007. Film.

Growing Pains. ABC, 1985–1992. Television.

The Grudge. Dir. Takashi Shimizu. Columbia Pictures, 2004. Film.

Halloween (1978). IMDB.com. 11 July 2010. Web. http://www.imdb.com/title/tt0077651/

Halloween (1978 film). Wikipedia.org. 11 July 2010. Web. http://en.wikipedia.org/wiki/Halloween_(1978_film)

Halloween: A Cut Above the Rest. Executive Producer Steven Burns. Anchor Bay Entertainment, 2003. DVD.

Halloween II. Dir. Rick Rosenthal. Universal Pictures, 1981. Film.

Halloween II. Dir. Rob Zombie. Dimension Films, 2009. Film.

Halloween III: Season of the Witch. Dir. Tommy Lee Wallace. Universal Pictures, 1982. Film.

Halloween III. Dir. Patrick Lussier. Dimension Films, 2012. Film.

Halloween 4: The Return of Michael Myers. Dir. Dwight H. Little. Galaxy International Releasing, 1988. Film.

Halloween 5. Dir. Dominique Othenin-Girard. Galaxy International Releasing, 1989. Film.

Halloween: The Curse of Michael Myers.

Dir. Joe Chappelle. Dimension Films, 1995. Film.

Halloween H20: 20 Years Later. Dir. Steve Miner. Dimension Films, 1998. Film.

Halloween: Resurrection. Dir. Rick Rosenthal. Dimension Films, 2002. Film.

HalloweenMovies: The Official Website of Michael Myers. "Rob Zombie's Halloween: Interview with Rob." HalloweenMovies.com. 16 June 2006. Web. 2 May 2010. http://www.halloweenmovies.com/h9_lobby.html

The Hand. Dir. Oliver Stone. Orion Pictures Corporation, 1981. Film.

The Hand That Rocks the Cradle. Dir. Curtis Hanson. Buena Vista Pictures, 1992. Film.

Happy Birthday to Me. Dir. J. Lee Thompson. Columbia Pictures, 1981. Film.

Hard Candy. Dir. David Slade. Vulcan Productions, 2005. Film.

Harry Potter and the Order of the Phoenix. Dir. David Yates. Warner Bros. Pictures, 2007. Film.

Hatchet. Dir. Adam Green. Anchor Bay Entertainment, 2006. Film.

Hatchet III. Dir. B.J. McDonnell. Dark Sky Films, 2013. Film.

The Haunting. Dir. Robert Wise. MGM, 1963. Film.

The Haunting. Dir. Jan de Bont. DreamWorks Distribution, 1999. Film.

Haute Tension (High Tension). Dir. Alexandre Aja. Lions Gate Films, 2003. Film.

Hell Night. Dir. Tom DeSimone. Compass International Pictures, 1981. Film.

Hellboy. Dir. Guillermo del Toro. Columbia Pictures, 2004. Film.

Hellraiser. Dir. Clive Barker. New World Pictures, 1987. Film.

Hellraiser: Bloodline. Dir. Kevin Yagher and Alan Smithee. Miramax Films, 1996. Film.

Heroes. NBC, 2006–2010. Television.

Hide and Seek. Dir. John Polson. Twentieth Century–Fox Film Corporation, 2005. Film.

The Hills. MTV, 2006–2010. Television.

The Hills Have Eyes. Dir. Wes Craven. Vanguard, 1977. Film.

The Hills Have Eyes. Dir. Alexandre Aja. Fox Searchlight Pictures, 2006. Film.

The Hills Have Eyes Part II. Dir. Wes Craven. Anchor Bay Entertainment, 1985. Film.

The Hills Have Eyes II. Dir. Martin Weisz. Fox Atomic, 2007. Film.

The Hills Run Red. Dir. Dave Parker. Dark Castle Entertainment, 2009. Film.

His Name Was Jason: 30 Years of Friday the 13th. Dir. Daniel Farrands. Anchor Bay Entertainment, 2009. DVD.

The Hitcher. Dir. Robert Harmon. TriStar Pictures, 1986. Film.

The Hitcher. Dir. Dave Meyers. Rogue Pictures, 2007. Film.

Hodder, Kane. Email Interview. 15 February 2012.

Holes. Dir. Andrew Davis. Buena Vista Pictures, 2003. Film.

Horror Hotel. Dir. John Llewellyn Moxey. Trans Lux, 1962. Film.

Horror of Dracula. Dir. Terence Fisher. Universal Pictures, 1958. Film.

The Host. Dir. Joon-ho Bong. Chungeorahm Film, 2006. Film.

Hostel. Dir. Eli Roth. Lionsgate, 2005. Film.

Hostel. Dir. Scott Spiegel. Raw Nerve, 2011. DVD.

Hostel: Part II. Dir. Eli Roth. Lionsgate, 2007. Film.

House of 1000 Corpses. Dir. Rob Zombie. Lions Gate Films, 2003.

House of the Dead. Dir. Uwe Boll. Artisan Entertainment, 2003. Film.

The House of the Devil. Dir. Ti West. Magnet Releasing, 2009. Film.

House of Wax. Dir. André De Toth. Warner Bros. Pictures, 1953. Film.

House of Wax. Dir. Jaume Collet-Serra. Warner Bros. Pictures, 2005. Film.

House on Haunted Hill. Dir. William Castle. United Artists, 1959. Film.

House on Haunted Hill. Dir. William Malone. Warner Bros. Pictures, 1999. Film.

Houston, Whitney. "I Will Always Love

You." *The Bodyguard: Original Soundtrack Album.* Arista, 1992. CD.

The Howling. Dir. Joe Dante. AVCO Embassy Pictures, 1981. Film.

The Human Centipede (First Sequence). Dir. Tom Six. IFC Films, 2009. Film.

The Human Centipede II (Full Sequence). Dir. Tom Six. Bounty Films, 2011. Film.

The Human Centipede III (Final Sequence). Dir. Tom Six. 2013. Film.

I Spit on Your Grave. Dir. Meir Zarchi. Cinemagic, 1978. Film.

I Spit on Your Grave. Dir. Steven R. Monroe. Anchor Bay Entertainment, 2010. Film.

I Was a Teenage Werewolf. Dir. Gene Fowler, Jr. American International Pictures, 1957. Film.

In Dreams. Dir. Neil Jordan. DreamWorks Distribution, 1999. Film.

Interview with the Vampire. Dir. Neil Jordan. Geffen Pictures, 1994. Film.

Into the Dark: Exploring the Horror Film. Dir. Johanna Wartio McEvoy and Paul Davis. Blaze Films, 2012. Film.

Into the Mirror. Dir. Sung-ho Kim. Key Plus Pictures, 2003. Film.

Invaders from Mars. Dir. William Cameron Menzies. Twentieth Century–Fox Film Corporation, 1953. Film.

Invaders from Mars. Dir. Tobe Hooper. Cannon Pictures, 1986. Film.

The Invasion. Dir. Oliver Hirschbiegel. Warner Bros. Pictures, 2007. Film.

Invasion of the Body Snatchers. Dir. Don Siegel. Allied Artists Pictures, 1956. Film.

Invasion of the Body Snatchers. Dir. Philip Kaufman. United Artists, 1978. Film.

The Island of Dr. Moreau. Dir. Don Taylor. American International Pictures, 1977. Film.

The Island of Dr. Moreau. Dir. John Frankenheimer. New Line Cinema, 1996. Film.

Island of Lost Souls. Dir. Erle C. Kenton. Paramount Pictures, 1932. Film.

It. Dir. Tommy Lee Wallace. ABC, 1990. Television.

It's Alive. Dir. Larry Cohen. Warner Bros. Pictures, 1974. Film.

It's Alive. Dir. Josef Rusnak. Alive Productions, 2008. Film.

Jack Brooks: Monster Slayer. Dir. Jon Knautz. Anchor Bay Entertainment, 2007. Film.

Jack Frost. Dir. Michael Cooney. Image Entertainment, 1997. Film.

Jamie Lee Curtis. IMDB.com. 11 July 2010. Web. http://www.imdb.com/name/nm0000130/

Jason Goes to Hell: The Final Friday. Dir. Adam Marcus. New Line Cinema, 1993. Film.

Jason X. Dir. James Issac. New Line Cinema, 2001. Film.

Jaws. Dir. Steven Spielberg. Universal Pictures, 1975. Film.

Jaws 3. Dir. Joe Alves. Universal Pictures, 1983. Film.

Jeepers Creepers. Dir. Victor Salva. United Artists, 2001. Film.

Jennifer's Body. Dir. Karyn Kusama. Twentieth Century–Fox Film Corporation, 2009. Film.

John Carpenter. IMDB.com. 11 July 2010. Web. http://www.imdb.com/name/nm0000118/

Jones, Darryl. *A Thematic History in Fiction and Film.* London: Arnold, 2002. Print.

Jungfrukällan (The Virgin Spring). Dir. Ingmar Bergman. Janus Films, 1960. Film.

Ju-on. Dir. Takashi Shimizu. Toei Video Company, 2002. Film.

Jurassic Park. Universal Pictures: 1993, 1997, 2001. Film.

Just Before Dawn. Dir. Jeff Lieberman. Picturmedia, 1981.

Just the Ten of Us. ABC, 1988–1990. Television.

The Karate Kid. Dir. Harald Zwart. Columbia Pictures, 2010. Film.

The Keep. Dir. Michael Mann. Paramount Pictures, 1983. Film.

Kill Bill: Vol 1. Dir. Quentin Tarantino. Miramax, 2003. Film.

King Kong. Dir. Merian C. Cooper and Ernest B. Schoedsack. RKO Radio Pictures, 1933. Film.

King Kong. Dir. John Guillermin. Paramount Pictures, 1976. Film.

King Kong. Dir. Peter Jackson. Universal Pictures, 2005. Film.

Kingdom of the Spiders. Dir. John Cardos. Dimension Pictures, 1977. Film.

Kondom des Grauens (*Killer Condom*). Dir. Martin Walz. Troma Entertainment, 1996. Film.

Koonz, Dean. *Intensity*. New York: Bantam, 2000. Print.

Kristeva, Julia. *Powers of Horror: An Essay on Abjection*. New York: Columbia University Press, 1982. Print.

Krull. Dir. Peter Yates. Columbia Pictures, 1983. Film.

L.A. Gothic. Dir. John Carpenter. Principal Entertainment, 2010. Film.

Laguna Beach: The Real Orange County. MTV, 2004–2006. Television.

Land of the Dead. Dir. George Romero. Universal Pictures, 2005. Film.

Lars and the Real Girl. Dir. Craig Gillespie. Metro-Goldwyn-Mayer, 2007. Film.

The Last House on the Left. Dir. Wes Craven. Hallmark Releasing Corp., 1972. Film.

The Last House on the Left. Dir. Dennis Iliadis. Rogue Pictures, 2009. Film.

Låt den rätte komma in (*Let the Right One In*). Dir. Tomas Alfredson. Magnet Releasing, 2008. Film.

Leatherface: The Texas Chainsaw Massacre III. Dir. Jeff Burr. New Line Cinema, 1990. Film.

Legend of the Guardians: The Owls of Ga'Hoole. Dir. Zack Snyder. Warner Bros. Pictures, 2010. Film.

Leprechaun. Dir. Mark Jones. Trimark Pictures, 1993. Film.

Leprechaun 4: In Space. Dir. Brian Trenchard-Smith. Trimark Pictures, 1997. Film.

Let Me In. Dir. Matt Reeves. Overture Films, 2010. Film.

The Little Shop of Horrors. Dir. Roger Corman. The Filmgroup, 1960. Film.

Lone Star. Dir. John Sayles. Columbia Pictures Corporation, 1996. Film.

Lord of the Rings. Dir. Peter Jackson. New Line Cinema: 2001, 2002, 2003. Film.

Lost. ABC, 2004–2010. Television.

The Lost Boys. Dir. Joel Schumacher. Warner Bros. Pictures, 1987. Film.

Lost Boys: The Tribe. Dir. P.J. Pesce. Warner Premiere, 2008. Film.

Lost Boys: The Thirst. Dir. Dario Piana. Warner Home Video, 2010. Film.

Lost Highway. Dir. David Lynch. October Films, 1997. Film.

The Lost World: Jurassic Park. Dir. Steven Spielberg. Universal Pictures, 1997. Film.

Machete. Dir. Ethan Maniquis and Robert Rodriguez. Twentieth Century–Fox Film Corporation, 2010. Film.

Mad Max Beyond Thunderdome. Dir. George Miller and George Ogilvie. Warner Bros. Pictures, 1985. Film.

Madman. Dir. Joe Giannone. Jensen Farley Pictures, 1982. Film.

MadTV. Fox Television, 1995–2009. Television.

Magnum, P.I. CBS, 1980–1988. Television.

The Man Who Knew Too Much. Dir. Alfred Hitchcock. Paramount Pictures, 1956. Film.

The Man Who Wasn't There. Dir. Joel Coen. USA Films, 2001. Film.

Maniac. Dir. William Lustig. Analysis Film Releasing Corporation, 1980. Film.

Maniac. Dir. Franck Khalfoun. IFC Midnight, 2012. Film.

Martin. Dir. George A. Romero. Libra Films International, 1977. Film.

Martyrs. Dir. Pascal Laugier. The Weinstein Company, 2008. Film.

Maximum Overdrive. Dir. Stephen King. De Laurentiis Entertainment Group, 1986. Film.

McAllister, Matt. "Julien Maury: *Inside Man*." *TotalSciFiOnline.com*. 9 October 2009. Web. 9 December 2009. http://totalscifionline.com/interviews/4083-julien-maury-inside-man

McFerrin, Bobby. "Don't Worry, Be Happy." *Simple Pleasures*. Capitol, 1990.

Medium. NBC, 2005–2009. Television.

Medium. CBS, 2009. Television.

Melrose Place. CW Television Network, 2009–2010. Television.

Metropolis. Dir. Fritz Lang. Paramount Pictures, 1927.

La Meute (The Pack). Dir. Franck Richard. Indomina Releasing, 2010. Film.

Milk. Dir. Gus Van Sant. Focus Features, 2008. Film.

Mirrors. Dir. Alexandre Aja. Twentieth Century–Fox Film Corporation, 2008. Film.

Missing in Action. Dir. Joseph Zito. Cannon Film Distributors, 1984. Film.

Mr. Woodcock. Dir. Craig Gillespie. New Line Cinema, 2007. Film.

Monsters vs. Aliens. Dir. Rob Letterman and Conrad Vernon. DreamWorks Distribution, 2009. Film.

Morgan, Jack. *The Biology of Horror: Gothic Literature and Film*. Carbondale: Southern Illinois University Press, 2002. Print.

The Most Dangerous Game. Dir. Irving Pichel and Ernest B. Schoedsack. RKO Radio Pictures, 1932. Film.

Motel Hell. Dir. Kevin Connor. United Artists, 1980. Film.

Mother's Day. Dir. Charles Kaufman. United Film Distribution Company, 1980. Film.

Mother's Day. Dir. Darren Lynn Bousman. The Genre Co., 2010. Film.

My Bloody Valentine. Dir. George Mihalka. Paramount Pictures, 1981. Film.

My Bloody Valentine 3D. Dir. Patrick Lussier. Lionsgate, 2009. Film.

Mystery of the Wax Museum. Dir. Michael Curtiz. Warner Bros. Pictures, 1933. Film.

Nelson, Daniel, and Seth Nelson. "Killing His Contemporaries: Dissecting The Musical Worlds Of John Carpenter." *Perfect Sound Forever* (2002). Web. 18 May 2010. http://www.furious.com/perfect/johncarpenter.html

The Nest. Dir. Terence H. Winkless. Concorde Pictures, 1988. Film.

New Nightmare. Dir. Wes Craven. New Line Cinema, 1994. Film.

New Year's Evil. Dir. Emmett Alston. Cannon Film Distributors, 1980. Film.

Night of the Demons. Dir. Kevin Tenney. International Film Marketing, 1988. Film.

Night of the Demons. Dir. Adam Gierasch. Cold Fusion Media Group, 2010. Film.

Night of the Living Dead. Dir. George A. Romero. Walter Reade Organization, 1968. Film.

Night of the Living Dead. Dir. Tom Savini. Columbia Pictures, 1990. Film.

Night of the Living Dead 3D. Dir. Jeff Broadstreet. Midnight Movies, 2006. Film.

Nightmare Café. NBC, 1992. Television.

A Nightmare on Elm Street Part 2: Freddy's Revenge. Dir. Jack Sholder. New Line Cinema, 1985. Film.

A Nightmare on Elm Street 3: Dream Warriors. Dir. Chuck Russell. New Line Cinema, 1987. Film.

A Nightmare on Elm Street 4: The Dream Master. Dir. Renny Harlin. New Line Cinema, 1988. Film.

A Nightmare on Elm Street: The Dream Child. Dir. Stephen Hopkins. New Line Cinema, 1989. Film.

90210. CW Television Network, 2008. Television.

Nispel, Marcus, dir. *Friday the 13th*. New Line Cinema, 2009. Film.

Nix. "Rob Zombie Says No to Halloween Sequels." *BeyondHollywood.com*. 11 July 2010. Web. http://www.beyondhollywood.com/rob-zombie-says-no-to-halloween-sequels/

North by Northwest. Dir. Alfred Hitchcock. MGM, 1959. Film.

North Shore. Fox Network, 2004–2005. Television.

Nosferatu. Dir. F.W. Murnau. Jofa-Atelier Berlin-Johannisthal, 1922. Film.

The O.C. Fox Network, 2003–2007. Television.

Oliver, Mary Beth, and Meghan Sanders. "The Appeal of Horror and Suspense," in *The Horror Film*, edited by Stephen Prince, 242–260. New Brunswick: Rutgers University Press, 2004. Print.

The Omen. Dir. Richard Donner. Twentieth Century–Fox Film Corporation, 1976. Film.

The Omen. Dir. John Moore. Twentieth Century–Fox Film Corporation, 2006. Film.

Omen III: The Final Conflict. Dir. Graham Baker. Twentieth Century–Fox Film Corporation, 1981. Film.

Omen IV: The Awakening. Dir. Jorge Montesi and Dominique Othenin-Girard. Fox Network, 1991. Television.

The 100 Scariest Movie Moments. Bravo Cable, 2004. Television.

One Tree Hill. The WB Television Network, 2003–2006. Television.

One Tree Hill. CW Television Network, 2006. Television.

Operation Petticoat. ABC, 1977–1979. Television.

El Orfanato (The Orphanage). Dir. Juan Antonio Bayona. Picturehouse Entertainment, 2007. Film.

Orphan. Dir. Jaume Collet-Serra. Warner Bros. Pictures, 2009. Film.

Paranormal Activity. Dir. Oren Peli. Paramount Pictures, 2007. Film.

Parton, Dolly. "I Will Always Love You." *Jolene.* RCA, 1974. LP.

Passion Fish. Dir. John Sayles. Atchafalaya, 1992. Film.

Pearl Harbor. Dir. Michael Bay. Buena Vista Pictures, 2001. Film.

The People Under the Stairs. Dir. Wes Craven. Universal Pictures, 1991. Film.

Phantasm. Dir. Don Coscarelli. AVCO Embassy Pictures, 1979.

Phillips, Kendall R. *Projected Fears: Horror Films and American Culture.* Westport: Praeger, 2005. Print.

Picart, Caroline J.S., and David A. Frank. "Horror and the Holocaust: Genre Elements in *Schindler's List* and *Psycho*," in *The Horror Film*, edited by Stephen Prince, 206–223. New Brunswick: Rutgers University Press, 2004. Print.

Pinedo, Isabel Cristina. "Postmodern Elements of the Contemporary Horror Film," in *The Horror Film*, edited by Stephen Prince, 85–117. New Brunswick: Rutgers University Press, 2004. Print.

Piranha. Dir. Joe Dante. New World Pictures, 1978. Film.

Piranha Part Two: The Spawning. Dir. James Cameron. Columbia Pictures, 1981. Film.

Piranha 3D. Dir. Alexandre Aja. Dimension Films, 2010. Film.

Piranha 3DD. Dir. John Gulager. Dimension Films, 2012. Film.

Pirates of the Caribbean. The Walt Disney Company: 2003, 2006, 2007, 2011. Film.

Planet Terror. Dir. Robert Rodriguez. Dimension Films, 2007. Film.

Poison Ivy. Dir. Katt Shea. New Line Cinema, 1992. Film.

Poltergeist. Dir. Tobe Hooper. MGM/UA Entertainment Company, 1982. Film.

Pontypool. Dir. Bruce McDonald. IFC Films, 2009. Film.

Predator. Dir. John McTiernan. Twentieth Century–Fox Film Corporation, 1987. Film.

Predator 2. Dir. Stephen Hopkins. Twentieth Century–Fox Film Corporation, 1990. Film.

Primeval. Dir. Michael Katleman. Buena Vista Pictures, 2007. Film.

Prince, Stephen, ed. *The Horror Film.* New Brunswick: Rutgers University Press, 2004. Print.

Prom Night. Dir. Paul Lynch. AVCO Embassy Pictures, 1980. Film.

Prom Night. Dir. Nelson McCormick. Screen Gems, 2008. Film.

Prophecy. Dir. John Frankenheimer. Paramount Pictures, 1979. Film.

The Prophecy. Dir. Gregory Widen. Dimension Home Video, 1995. Film.

The Prophecy 3: The Ascent. Dir. Patrick Lussier. Dimension Films, 2000. Film.

Psych. USA Network, 2006. Television.

Psycho. Dir. Alfred Hitchcock. Paramount Pictures, 1960. Film.

Psycho. Dir. Gus Van Sant. Universal Pictures, 1998. Film.

Punky Brewster. NBC, 1984–1988. Television.

The Puppet Masters. Dir. Stuart Orme. Buena Vista Pictures, 1994. Film.

Quandt, James. "Flesh & Blood: Sex and Violence in Recent French Cinema." *ArtForum*. February 2004. Web. 9 December 2009. http://findarticles.com/p/articles/mi_m0268/is_6_42/ai_113389507/?tag=content;col1

Quarantine. Dir. John Erick Dowdle. Screen Gems, 2008. Film.

Rawhead Rex. Dir. George Pavlou. Empire Pictures, 1987. Film.

Re-Animator. Dir. Stuart Gordon. Empire Pictures, 1985. Film.

Rear Window. Dir. Alfred Hitchcock. Paramount Pictures, 1954. Film.

Rebecca. Dir. Alfred Hitchcock. United Artists, 1940. Film.

[REC]. Dir. Jaume Balaguero and Paco Plaza. Sony Pictures Home Entertainment, 2007. Film.

Red Riding Hood. Dir. Catherine Hardwicke. Warner Bros. Pictures, 2011. Film.

Red Scorpion. Dir. Joseph Zito. Shapiro-Glickenhaus Home Video, 1989. Film.

Repossessed. Dir. Bob Logan. New Line Cinema, 1990. Film.

Resident Evil. Dir. Paul W.S. Anderson. Screen Gems, 2002. Film.

Return of the Fly. Dir. Edward Bernds. Twentieth Century–Fox Film Corporation, 1959. Film.

Richard Cheese and Lounge Against the Machine. "Down with the Sickness." *Tuxicity*. Ideatown, 2002. CD.

Riddlehoover, Matt. Email Interview. 17 May 2010.

The Ring. Dir. Gore Verbinski. DreamWorks Distribution, 2002. Film.

Robot Chicken. Adult Swim, 2005. Television.

The Rock. Dir. Michael Bay. Buena Vista Pictures, 1996. Film.

Romeo + Juliet. Dir. Baz Luhrmann. Twentieth Century–Fox Film Corporation, 1996. Film.

The Ruins. Dir. Carter Smith. Paramount Pictures, 2008. Film.

Santas, Constantine. *Responding to Film*. Lanham, MD: Rowman and Littlefield Publishers, Inc., 2002. Print.

_____. "The Remake of *Psycho* (Gus Van Sant, 1998): Creativity or Cinematic Blasphemy?" *senses of cinema* (2000). Web. 3 February 2010. http://archive.sensesofcinema.com/contents/00/10/psycho.html

Saturday the 14th. Dir. Howard R. Cohen. New World Pictures. 1981. Film.

Saw. Lions Gate Films: 2004, 2005, 2006, 2007, 2008, 2009, 2010. Film.

Scanners. Dir. David Cronenberg. AVCO Embassy Pictures, 1981. Film.

Scary Movie. Dimension Films: 2000, 2001, 2003, 2006, 2013. Film.

Scenes from a Gay Marriage. Dir. Matt Riddlehoover. Made It Myself Pictures, 2012. Film.

Schindler's List. Dir. Steven Spielberg. Universal Pictures, 1993. Film.

Scream. Dir. Wes Craven. Dimension Films, 1996. Film.

Scream 2. Dir. Wes Craven. Dimension Films, 1997. Film.

Scream 3. Dir. Wes Craven. Dimension Films, 2000. Film.

Scream 4. Dir. Wes Craven. Dimension Films, 2011. Film.

A Serbian Film. Dir. Srdjan Spasojevic. Jinga Films, 2009. Film.

The Serpent and the Rainbow. Dir. Wes Craven. Universal Pictures, 1988. Film.

7th Heaven. The WB Television Network, 1996–2006. Television.

7th Heaven. CW Television Network, 2006–2007. Television.
Shakespeare, William. *The Tragedy of Hamlet, Prince of Denmark*. *The Riverside Shakespeare, 2nd Edition*. Eds. G. Blakemore Evans and J.J.M. Tobin. Boston: Houghton Mifflin Company, 1996. Print.
Shark. CBS, 2006–2008. Television.
Shaun of the Dead. Dir. Edgar Wright. Focus Features, 2004. Film.
Sherwood, Mary Martha. *The History of the Fairchild Family; or, the Child's Manual*. 1818. Print.
The Shining. Dir. Stanley Kubrick. Warner Bros. Pictures, 1980. Film.
The Shining. Dir. Mick Garris. ABC, 1997. Television.
Shriek If You Know What I Did Last Friday the Thirteenth. Dir. John Blanchard. USA Network, 2000. Film.
The Silence of the Lambs. Dir. Jonathan Demme. Orion Pictures Corporation, 1991. Film.
Silent House. Dir. Chris Kentis and Laura Lau. Open Road Films (II), 2011. Film.
Silent Night. Dir. Steven C. Miller. Anchor Bay Films, 2012. Film.
Silent Night, Deadly Night. Dir. Charles E. Sellier, Jr. TriStar Pictures, 1984. Film.
Silver Bullet. Dir. Daniel Attias. Paramount Pictures, 1985. Film.
The Simple Life. Fox Network, 2003–2007. Television.
The Simpsons. Fox Network, 1989. Television.
Single White Female. Dir. Barbet Schroeder. Columbia Pictures, 1992. Film.
Six Days Seven Nights. Dir. Ivan Reitman. Buena Vista International, 1998. Film.
Six Feet Under. HBO, 2001–2005. Television.
Sleeping with the Enemy. Dir. Joseph Ruben. Twentieth Century–Fox Film Corporation, 1991. Film.
Sleepy Hollow. Dir. Tim Burton. Paramount Pictures, 1999. Film.
Slither. Dir. James Gunn. Universal Pictures, 2006. Film.

Slovenko, Ralph. *Psychiatry in Law / Law in Psychiatry*. New York: Routledge, 2009. Print.
Slugs. Dir. Juan Piquer Simón. New World Pictures, 1988. Film.
Smallville. The WB Television Network, 2001–2006. Television.
Smallville. CW Television Network, 2006–2011. Television.
Snakes on a Plane. Dir. David R. Ellis. New Line Cinema, 2006. Film.
South Park. Comedy Central, 1997. Television.
Sparkle. Dir. Sam O'Steen. Warner Bros. Pictures, 1976. Film.
Sparkle. Dir. Salim Akil. TriStar Pictures, 2012. Film.
Splice. Dir. Vincenzo Natali. Warner Bros. Pictures, 2009. Film.
Splinter. Dir. Toby Wilkins. Magnet Releasing, 2008. Film.
Spy Kids 3: Game Over. Dir. Robert Rodriguez. Miramax Films, 2003. Film.
Squirm. Dir. Jeff Lieberman. American International Pictures, 1976. Film.
Sssssss. Dir. Bernard L. Kowalski. Universal Pictures, 1973. Film.
Stan Helsing. Dir. Bo Zenga. Anchor Bay Entertainment, 2009. Film.
Stand by Me. Dir. Rob Reiner. Columbia Pictures, 1986. Film.
Star Wars. Twentieth Century–Fox Film Corporation: 1977, 1980, 1983. Film.
Starman. Dir. John Carpenter. Columbia Pictures, 1984. Film.
Starship Troopers. Dir. Paul Verhoeven. TriStar Pictures, 1997. Film.
The Stepfather. Dir. Joseph Ruben. New Century Vista Film Company, 1987. Film.
The Stepfather. Dir. Nelson McCormick. Screen Gems, 2009. Film.
The Stepford Wives. Dir. Bryan Forbes. Columbia Pictures, 1975. Film.
The Stepford Wives. Dir. Frank Oz. Paramount Pictures, 2004. Film.
Stevenson, Robert Louis. *Strange Case of Dr. Jekyll and Mr. Hyde*. UK: Longmans, Green, and Co., 1886. Print.

Stigmata. Dir. Rupert Wainwright. Metro-Goldwyn-Mayer, 1999. Film.
Straw Dogs. Dir. Sam Peckinpah. Cinerama Releasing Corporation, 1971. Film.
Straw Dogs. Dir. Rod Lurie. Screen Gems, 2011. Film.
Strays. Dir. John McPherson. USA Network, 1991. Television.
Student Bodies. Dir. Mickey Rose. Paramount Pictures, 1981. Film.
Sunshine State. Dir. John Sayles. Sony Pictures Classics, 2002. Film.
Superman. Warner Bros. Pictures: 1978, 1980, 1983, 1987. Film.
Supernatural. The WB Television Network, 2005–2006. Television.
Supernatural. CW Television Network, 2006. Television.
Survival of the Dead. Dir. George A. Romero. Magnet Releasing, 2009. Film.
Suspiria. Dir. Dario Argento. International Classics, 1977. Film.
Swamp Thing. Dir. Wes Craven. Embassy Pictures Corporation, 1982. Film.
A Tale of Two Sisters. Dir. Jee-woon Kim. B.O.M. Film Productions, Co., 2003. Film.
Teeth. Dir. Mitchell Lichtenstein. Roadside Attractions, 2007. Film.
Telotte, J.P. "Through a Pumpkin's Eye: The Reflexive Nature of Horror," in *American Horrors: Essays on the Modern American Horror Film*. Urbana: University of Illinois Press, 1987. Print.
The Tenant. Dir. Roman Polanski. Paramount Pictures, 1976. Film.
Terror Train. Dir. Roger Spottiswoode. Twentieth Century–Fox Film Corporation, 1980. Film.
The Texas Chain Saw Massacre. Dir. Tobe Hooper. Bryanston Distributing, 1974. Film.
The Texas Chainsaw Massacre. Dir. Marcus Nispel. New Line Cinema, 2003. Film.
The Texas Chainsaw Massacre Part 2. Dir. Tobe Hooper. Cannon Films, 1986. Film.
The Texas Chainsaw Massacre: The Next Generation. Dir. Kim Henkel. New Line Cinema, 1994. Film.
The Texas Chainsaw Massacre: The Beginning. Dir. Jonathan Liebesman. New Line Cinema, 2006. Film.
Texas Chainsaw Massacre 3D. Dir. John Luessenhop. Lionsgate, 2013. Film.
Thanksgiving. Dir. Eli Roth. Dimension Films, 2007. Film.
That '70s Show. Fox Network, 1998–2006. Television.
Them! Dir. Gordon Douglas. Warner Bros. Pictures, 1954. Film.
The Thing. Dir. John Carpenter. Universal Pictures, 1982. Film.
The Thing. Dir. Matthijs van Heijningen, Jr. Universal Pictures, 2011. Film.
The Thing from Another World. Dir. Christian Nyby. RKO Radio Pictures, 1951. Film.
13 Ghosts. Dir. William Castle. Columbia Pictures, 1960. Film.
Thir13en Ghosts. Dir. Steve Beck. Warner Bros. Pictures, 2001. Film.
300. Dir. Zack Snyder. Warner Bros. Pictures, 2006. Film.
Thriller. Dir. John Landis. Vestron Video, 1983. Television.
Timpone, Tony. Email Interview. 12 May 2010.
Titanic. Dir. James Cameron. Paramount Pictures, 1997. Film.
To a Tee. Dir. Matt Riddlehoover. Made It Myself Pictures, 2006. Film.
The Toolbox Murders. Dir. Dennis Donnelly. Cal-Am Artists, 1978. Film.
Toolbox Murders. Dir. Tobe Hooper. Lions Gate Films, 2004. Film.
Total Recall. Dir. Paul Verhoeven. TriStar Pictures, 1990. Film.
Total Recall. Dir. Len Wiseman. Columbia Pictures, 2012. Film.
The Toxic Avenger. Dir. Michael Herz and Lloyd Kaufman. Troma Entertainment, 1984. Film.
Trading Places. Dir. John Landis. Paramount Pictures, 1983. Film.
Train. Dir. Gideon Raff. Lionsgate Home Entertainment, 2008. Film.

Transformers. Dir. Michael Bay. Paramount Pictures: 2007, 2009, 2011. Film.

Tremors. Dir. Ron Underwood. Universal Pictures, 1990. Film.

Troll. Dir. John Carl Buechler. Vestron Video, 1986. Film.

Tromeo and Juliet. Dir. Lloyd Kaufman. Troma Entertainment, 1996. Film.

True Blood. HBO, 2008. Television.

True Lies. Dir. James Cameron. Twentieth Century–Fox Film Corporation, 1994. Film.

28 Days Later. Dir. Danny Boyle. DNA Films, 2002. Film.

28 Weeks Later. Dir. Juan Carlos Fresnadillo. Fox Atomic, 2007. Film.

24. Fox Network, 2001–2010. Television.

21 Jump Street. Fox Network, 1987–1991. Television.

Twilight. Dir. Catherine Hardwicke. Summit Distribution, 2008. Film.

The Twilight People. Dir. Eddie Romero. Dimension Pictures, 1973. Film.

The Twilight Saga. Summit Entertainment: 2008, 2009, 2010, 2011, 2012. Film.

Twin Peaks: Fire Walk with Me. Dir. David Lynch. New Line Cinema, 1992. Film.

Twitchell, James B. *Dreadful Pleasures: An Anatomy of Modern Horror.* New York: Oxford University Press, 1985. Print.

Two Guys, a Girl and a Pizza Place. ABC, 1998–2001. Television.

2001 Maniacs. Dir. Tim Sullivan. Lions Gate Films, 2005. Film.

2012. Dir. Roland Emmerich. Columbia Pictures, 2009. Film.

Two Thousand Maniacs! Dir. Herschell Gordon Lewis. Box Office Spectaculars, 1964. Film.

Underworld. Dir. Len Wiseman. Screen Gems, 2003. Film.

The Uninvited. Dir. Charles Guard and Thomas Guard. Paramount Pictures, 2009. Film.

United States of Tara. Showtime Networks, 2009–2011. Television.

V. NBC, 1984–1985. Television.

V: The Original Miniseries. NBC, 1983. Television.

The Vampire Diaries. CW Television Network, 2009. Television.

Veronica Mars. UPN, 2004–2006. Television.

Veronica Mars. CW, 2006–2007. Television.

Vertigo. Dir. Alfred Hitchcock. Paramount Pictures, 1958. Film.

Village of the Damned. Dir. Wolf Rilla. Metro-Goldwyn-Mayer, 1960. Film.

Village of the Damned. Dir. John Carpenter. Universal Pictures, 1995. Film.

The Virgin Spring. Dir. Ingmar Bergman. Janus Films, 1960. Film.

The Walking Dead. AMC, 2010. Television.

Waller, Gregory A. *American Horrors: Essays on the Modern American Horror Film.* Urbana: University of Illinois Press, 1987. Print.

The Ward. Dir. John Carpenter. Echo Lake Productions, 2010. Film.

Warlock. Dir. Steve Miner. Trimark Pictures, 1989. Film.

Watchmen. Dir. Zack Snyder. Warner Bros. Pictures, 2009. Film.

Wells, H.G. *The Island of Dr. Moreau.* UK: Heinemann, Stone, and Kimball, 1896. Print.

Werewolf Women of the S.S. Dir. Rob Zombie. Dimension Films, 2007. Film.

When a Stranger Calls. Dir. Fred Walton. Columbia Pictures, 1979. Film.

When a Stranger Calls. Dir. Simon West. Screen Gems, 2006. Film.

When a Stranger Calls Back. Dir. Fred Walton. Showtime Networks, 1993. Television.

White, John. "Interview with Pascal Laugier (Director of *Martyrs*)." *HomeCinema.TheDigitalFlix.co.uk*. 13 April 2009. Web. 9 December 2009. http://homecinema.thedigitalfix.co.uk/content/id/70486/interview-with-pascal-laugier-director-of-martyrs.html

White Noise 2: The Light. Dir. Patrick Lussier. Universal Pictures, 2007. Film.

The Wicker Man. Dir. Neil LaBute. Warner Bros. Pictures, 2006. Film.

Williams, Tony. *Hearths of Darkness: The Family in the American Horror Film*. New Jersey: Fairleigh Dickinson University Press, 1996. Print.

The Wizard of Gore. Dir. Herschell Gordon Lewis. Mayflower Pictures, 1970. Film.

The Wizard of Gore. Dir. Jeremy Kasten. Open Sky Entertainment, 2007. Film.

Wolf. Dir. Mike Nichols. Columbia Pictures, 1994. Film.

Wolf Creek. Dir. Greg Mclean. Dimension Films, 2005. Film.

The Wolf Man. Dir. George Waggner. Universal Pictures, 1941. Film.

The Wolfman. Dir. Joe Johnston. Universal Pictures, 2010. Film.

Wrong Turn 2: Dead End. Dir. Joe Lynch. Twentieth Century–Fox Home Entertainment, 2007. Film.

The X-Files. Fox Network, 1993–2002. Television.

Youth in Revolt. Dir. Miguel Arteta. Dimension Films, 2009. Film.

The Zombie Diaries. Dir. Michael Bartlett and Kevin Gates. Bleeding Edge Films, 2006. Film.

Zombie, Rob, dir. *Halloween*. Dimension Films, 2007. Film.

Zombie Strippers! Dir. Jay Lee. Stage 6 Films, 2008. Film.

Zombieland. Dir. Ruben Fleischer. Columbia Pictures, 2009. Film.

Index

À l'intérieur (Inside) 166–168, 170, 172
Aja, Alexandre 3–4, 129–131, 144, 166–167
Aliens 5, 68, 92, 97, 131, 143
aliens 20, 77, 85–87, 91–94
Altered States 17
An American Werewolf in London 84
The Amityville Horror (1979) 120, 143
The Amityville Horror (2005) 5, 57, 143, 181
Anderson, Paul Thomas 28
April Fool's Day 44, 72
Argento, Dario 17, 39, 114; Asia 112
Army of Darkness 161
art 3, 5, 8, 15–17, 19, 23, 25, 32, 38, 47, 169–170, 175, 178–179
Australian horror 5
AVP: Alien vs. Predator see hybrid horror
AVPR: Alien vs. Predator: Requiem see hybrid horror

Badley, Linda 2, 9, 16–17, 165, 173
Bay, Michael 5–6, 57, 123–125, 177
Bayer, Samuel 4, 57, 72, 76–77, 157
Bacon, Kevin 55, 177
Bad Dreams 72
The Bad Seed 126
Bates, Norman 20–23, 27–31, 51, 121, 156; mother 21, 27–29, 41, 48, 51
The Beast with Five Fingers 77, 143
The Beast Within 17
The Bees 79
Behind the Mask: The Rise of Leslie Vernon 21, 178–179
Big Business 91
Black Christmas (1974) 119–121, 134, 157
Black Christmas (2006) 121, 181
Blade series 78
The Blair Witch Project 158, 161, 163
The Blob (1958) 4, 94, 97
The Blob (1988) 99
Block, Melissa 19
blood 2, 12, 25, 31, 33, 38–39, 41, 46, 57, 67–68, 71, 85–87, 97, 108, 119, 129, 132, 136, 141, 143, 166, 168, 175

Blood for Dracula 143
Body Snatchers 92–93
The Bride 143
Bride of Frankenstein 77, 143
The Brood 178
Buffy the Vampire Slayer 24, 124
The Burning 56
Burton, Tim 71
Bustillo, Alex 170, 172

The Cabin in the Woods 181
Cameron, James 27, 131
Campbell, Bruce 146, 152, 160–162
Campbell, Neve 70, 180
Candyman 107, 178
Carpenter, John 4, 7, 33, 36–37, 39–45, 47, 49, 54, 56, 60–61, 77, 86–87, 103, 136–137, 151, 178
Carrie (1976) 61, 135, 143
Carrie (2002) 143
Carrie (2013) 143
La Casa muda 145
Cash, Johnny 110
Castle Freak 17
Cat People (1942) 77, 143
Cat People (1982) 143
The Cell 72
Cheese, Richard 110
childhood 4, 37, 64, 69, 73, 74, 84, 93, 121, 147, 156
children 12, 13, 14, 60, 67, 69, 72–74, 116, 125, 127, 134–135, 142, 147, 164, 172
Children of the Corn (1984) 142
Children of the Corn (2009) 142
children's literature 147, 175
Child's Play 66, 177
class 20–21
A Clockwork Orange 175
Clover, Carol 6
Cloverfield 79
contagion 78, 110, 118, 175
Coraline 164
The Cottage 165

Index

Crane, Jonathan 10–11, 14–17, 55, 169
Crane, Marion 19–23, 25–31, 38–39, 148
Craven, Wes 60–63, 65–71, 74, 114–115, 117, 127, 129, 155, 180, 181
The Crazies (1973) 118, 154
The Crazies (2010) 58, 118–119, 153, 177–178
creature features 79
Creed, Barbara 6
Critters 4 51
Cronenberg, David 77, 95, 97, 169, 178
Cujo 79
culture 9, 20, 23, 25, 31, 67, 78, 80, 84, 105, 172–173, 180; drug 163; popular 21, 71, 85, 106, 149–150, 179; queer 31; teen 20, 25; zombie 108, 179
Cunningham, Sean S. 48, 54, 56, 59, 61, 114
Curse of the Fly 95
Curtis, Jamie Lee 36, 40, 43, 47, 55, 137

Damien: Omen II 126
Dawn of the Dead (1978) 17, 106, 108, 112
Dawn of the Dead (2004) 17, 119, 153, 155, 177, 181
Day of the Animals 79
Day of the Dead (1985) 106, 110, 112
Day of the Dead (2008) 111
The Day of the Triffids (1962) 79
The Day of the Triffids (1981) 79
The Day of the Triffids (2009) 79
The Day the Earth Stood Still (1951) 20, 86
The Day the Earth Stood Still (2008) 86
Dead Ringers 169
Deadtime Stories 147, 175
Death Proof 44
Deep Red 114
Delman, Jef 146–150, 175
demons 10, 38, 84; possession 36, 62, 126, 142, 175
Depp, Johnny 70–71
The Devil's Rejects 4, 44
Les Diaboliques (1955) 167
Les Diaboliques (1996) 167
Dial M for Murder 25
Diary of the Dead 113
Disturbed *see* Cheese, Richard
Død snø (*Dead Snow*) 165
Don't Be Afraid of the Dark 144
Dracula (1931) 77–78, 143
Dracula (1979) 143
Dracula (1992) 143
Dracula: Dead and Loving It 143
Dracula 2000 138, 143
Drag Me to Hell 178–179
Dreamscape 61

Ebert, Roger 52, 166
Englund, Robert 65, 71, 146, 150–152
Equus 175
Eraserhead 17

Escape from New York 178
The Evil Dead (1981) 145, 160–161, 179
The Evil Dead (2013) 160–162
Evil Dead II 161
The Exorcist 10, 14, 40, 126, 158, 165
exploitation 75, 137, 169, 175; rape-revenge 46, 61
The Eye 144, 165

Faces of Death 163
The Faculty 91
Feast 131, 178, 180
Feldman, Corey 55
Fiend Without a Face 154
Finney, Jack 90
Firestarter 61
Flesh for Frankenstein 143
The Fly (1958) 94–95
The Fly (1986) 77, 95–97, 178
The Fly II 97
The Fog (1980) 39, 43, 136
The Fog (2005) 137, 176, 181
Footloose (1984) 177
Footloose (2011) 177
Frank, David A. 9–10
Frankenstein (1931) 77–78
Frankenstein (1994) 143
Frankenstein monster 13, 78, 104
Freddy vs. Jason see hybrid horror
Freeway 85
French horror 3, 5, 8, 123, 129, 153, 165–173
Friday the 13th series 48–59, 62–65, 71, 112, 147, 164
Friday the 13th series (1980) 6, 8, 44, 61–63, 67, 69, 120, 121, 135, 138, 165, 175
Friday the 13th series (2009) 3, 5–6, 72, 77, 136, 139, 155, 157, 159, 181
Fright Night (1985) 139–140
Fright Night (2011) 140–142
Fright Night 2 140
Frogs 79
Frontières 166, 168, 170, 172
Funny Games (1997) 156, 178
Funny Games (2007) 156, 178
The Fury 61

Gein, Ed 10, 20, 33, 121
gender 63, 93, 139, 163
ghosts 99, 101–103, 136–137, 143; stories 48, 175
Ginger Snaps 85
Godzilla 3, 20, 77, 79, 143
Gojira 77, 143
The Good Son 126
gore 85, 87, 103, 121, 146, 169–170, 175
Grahame-Smith, Seth 52
Gremlins 130
Grindhouse 44
The Grudge 77, 144, 165, 176, 178

Index

Halloween series 33–47, 52, 62, 65, 112, 164, 172
Halloween series (1978) 4, 7–8, 21, 48–51, 54, 61–63, 66–67, 69, 120–121, 138, 175
Halloween series (2007) 4, 7, 57, 64, 72, 77, 139, 157–158, 181
The Hand 143
The Hand That Rocks the Cradle 137
Happy Birthday to Me 44, 145
Hard Candy 85
Harry Potter and the Order of the Phoenix 85
Hatchet 71, 159, 178–179
Hatchet III 158
The Haunting (1963) 102
The Haunting (1999) 2, 17, 103–104
Haute tension 3–4, 129, 166–168, 172
Heche, Anne 24–31, 154, 156
Hell Night 145
Hellboy 137
Hellraiser series 51, 145, 164, 169, 172, 176
Hide and Seek 167
The Hills Have Eyes (1977) 61, 127–129, 154
The Hills Have Eyes (2006) 3, 129–130, 167, 181
The Hills Have Eyes Part II (1985) 70
The Hills Have Eyes Part II (2007) 92
The Hills Run Red 178–179
Hitchcock, Alfred 7–8, 10, 19–20, 23–26, 29–30, 32–33, 43, 102, 121, 148–150, 153–154, 156, 159, 161, 175, 177
The Hitcher (1986) 139
The Hitcher (2007) 139
HIV/AIDS 5, 68, 97,
Hodder, Kane 55, 146, 157–160
Hooper, Tobe 17, 121, 123–124, 143, 177
Horror of Dracula 143
The Host 79
Hostel series 116, 163
House of 1000 Corpses 4, 44, 123,
House of the Dead 152
The House of the Devil 135, 178–180
House of Wax (1953) 87–88
House of Wax (2005) 58, 88–90
House on Haunted Hill (1959) 98–102
House on Haunted Hill (1999) 17, 101–103
Houston, Whitney 32, 177
The Howling 85
The Human Centipede series 82, 165
hybrid horror 71, 92, 160, 181

I Spit on Your Grave (1978) 132–133, 162
I Spit on Your Grave (2010) 133, 163
I Was a Teenage Werewolf 85
In Dreams 72
infection *see* contagion
Interview with the Vampire 78
Into the Mirror 144; *see also* Mirrors
Invaders from Mars (1953) 77, 143
Invaders from Mars (1986) 91, 143

The Invasion 93–94
Invasion of the Body Snatchers (1956) 90–91
Invasion of the Body Snatchers (1978) 92–93, 148, 178
The Island of Dr. Moreau (1896) 79
The Island of Dr. Moreau (1977) 80–81, 87
The Island of Dr. Moreau (1996) 80–81, 85
Island of Lost Souls 79–80
It 121, 177, 183
It's Alive (1974) 5, 143–144
It's Alive (2008) 143–144

Jack Brooks: Monster Slayer 71
Japanese horror 2, 5, 165
Jaws series 19, 40, 48, 130, 164
Jeepers Creepers 89
Jennifer's Body 178–179
Jungfrukällan 61, 115
Ju-on 178
Jurassic Park 92; *see also* creature features
Just Before Dawn 56

The Karate Kid 177
The Keep 154
Kill Bill 38
King Kong (1933) 78–79, 87, 143
King Kong (1976) 143
King Kong (2005) 79
Kingdom of the Spiders 145
Koonz, Dean 167
Korean horror 2, 5, 165
Kristeva, Julia 6
Krueger, Fred/Freddy 17, 52, 58, 60, 63–76, 114, 138, 150, 156, 158, 160, 164, 181

Lake Placid 79
Land of the Dead 78, 112–113
Langenkamp, Heather 62–63, 65, 70
The Last House on the Left (1972) 61, 114–117, 162
The Last House on the Left (2009) 54, 115–117, 155, 181
Låt den rätte komma in (Let the Right One In) 144, 165
Laugier, Pascal 170–172
Leatherface 122–125
Leatherface: The Texas Chainsaw Massacre III 122
Leigh, Janet 19, 22, 27–29, 43, 137, 154
Leprechaun series 51, 66
Let Me In 78, 144
The Little Shop of Horrors 131
Lord of the Rings 38
The Lost Boys series 55, 78

Mad Max Beyond Thunderdome 112
Madman 178
The Man Who Knew Too Much 25
The Man Who Wasn't There 25

Maniac (1980) 181
Maniac (2012) 181
Martin 17
Martyrs 166, 168–172
Maury, Julien 170, 172–173
Maximum Overdrive 145
McAllister, Matt 168, 170, 172
McFerrin, Bobby 110
Metropolis 11
La Meute 172
Milk 29
Mirrors 131, 144, 167
Moore, Julianne 24, 28, 31
Mortensen, Viggo 25, 30–31, 122
Motel Hell 123, 168
Mother's Day (1980) 44, 137
Mother's Day (2010) 137
My Bloody Valentine (1981) 138
My Bloody Valentine (2009) 138
Myers, Michael 17, 33–37, 39–41, 43–47, 50, 52–53, 55, 65, 67, 71, 138, 172
Mystery of the Wax Museum 87–88

Nelson, Daniel 40
Nelson, Seth 40
The Nest 79
New Year's Evil 44, 119
Night of the Demons (1988) 142
Night of the Demons (2010) 142
Night of the Living Dead (1968) 5, 37, 102, 104–106, 108, 112, 114, 154
Night of the Living Dead (1990) 106–107
Night of the Living Dead (2006) 108
Nightmare Café 71
A Nightmare on Elm Street series 60–76, 150, 164
A Nightmare on Elm Street series (1984) 8, 21, 48, 52, 120–121, 175
A Nightmare on Elm Street series (2010) 4–5, 57, 77, 136, 153, 155, 157, 181
Nispel, Marcus 3–4, 6, 56–58, 72, 77, 88, 123, 125, 127, 157, 177
North by Northwest 25
Nosferatu 78

The Omen (1976) 125–126
The Omen (2006) 126
Omen III: The Final Conflict 126
Omen IV: The Awakening 126
El Orfanato 165
Orphan 126
The Orphanage 165

The Pack 172
Paranormal Activity series 8, 154, 158
Parton, Dolly 32
The People Under the Stairs 168
Perkins, Anthony 19, 22, 27–28, 30, 32, 154
Phantasm 178

Phillips, Kendall R. 7, 17, 19–20, 180
Picart, Caroline J.S. 9–10
Pinhead 17
Piranha (1978) 130–131
Piranha (2010) 131, 167, 181
Piranha Part Two: The Spawning 131
Piranha 3DD 131, 164
Planet Terror 44
Poltergeist 176
Pontypool 180
possession 143
Predator 92
Predator 2 92
Primeval 79
Prince, Stephen 9–10, 16–17, 163
Prom Night (1980) 142
Prom Night (2008) 142
Prophecy 154
The Prophecy series 66, 138
Psycho (1960) 7, 9–10, 16, 19–33, 36–39, 41, 43, 45, 48, 51–52, 62–63, 87, 102, 121, 148–151, 153–154, 156, 175–176
Psycho (1998) 7, 19–32, 77, 148, 150, 153–154, 156, 159, 161, 162, 175–176
psychological 2, 25, 45–46, 166, 175
The Puppet Masters 91

Quandt, James 169–170
Quarantine 144, 165
queer 30–32

race 67–68, 105, 108, 177; African American 2, 55
rape *see* exploitation
ratings 8, 12, 176, 183; MPAA 8, 38
Rawhead Rex 17, 178
Re-Animator 82
Rear Window 25
Rebecca 177
[REC] 165, 168
Red Riding Hood 85
Repossessed 165
Resident Evil 114
Return of the Fly 95, 97
Riddlehoover, Matt 146, 155–157, 176
The Ring 2, 77, 134, 144, 165, 176
Romero, George A. 17, 78, 104, 106–107, 109–114, 118–119, 152, 177–179
The Ruins 178, 180

Santas, Constantine 24–27, 32
Saturday the 14th 56, 165
Saw series 8 11, 98, 116–117, 121, 134, 163, 173
Scanners 61
Scary Movie series 44, 165
Schindler's List 9–10, 25
Scream series 66, 70–71, 134, 159, 161, 165, 176, 180

Index

A Serbian Film 163
serial killers 121, 139, 175
The Serpent and the Rainbow 70
sex 14, 33, 42, 49, 61, 75, 105, 116, 133, 146, 175; incest 121; intercourse 41
sexuality 75; female 167; homosexuality 68–69, 172; teenage 74–76
Shakespeare, William 148, 151
Shatner, William 36–37, 53, 67, 138
Shaun of the Dead 14, 78, 114
The Shining (1980) 142
The Shining (1997) 142
Shriek If You Know What I Did Last Friday the Thirteenth 165
The Silence of the Lambs 21, 121, 129
Silent House 145
Silent Night 181
Silent Night, Deadly Night 44, 119, 181
Silver Bullet 85, 140
Six Days Seven Nights 26
slasher 7–8, 11, 13, 21, 33, 36, 38, 41–42, 44, 48, 51–52, 59, 61–63, 65–67, 69, 71–74, 136, 147, 157, 175
Sleeping with the Enemy 44
Sleepy Hollow 70
Slither 79
Slovenko, Ralph 69
Slugs 79
Snakes on a Plane 79
society 5, 9, 20, 21, 24, 33, 37, 52, 69, 76, 80, 84, 105–106, 108–109, 111–113, 115, 117, 122, 139, 144, 173, 175, 178; capitalist 47; secret 168
Sparkle (1976) 177
Sparkle (2012) 177
Splice 153
Splinter 178, 180
Squirm 79
Sssssss 79
Stan Helsing 165
The Stepfather (1987) 142
The Stepfather (2009) 142
The Stepford Wives (1975) 143
The Stepford Wives (2004) 143
Stevenson, Robert Louis 82
Stigmata 126
Straw Dogs (1971) 177
Straw Dogs (2011) 177
Strays see creature features
Strode, Laurie 33–36, 39–40, 43–46, 55, 65
Student Bodies 44
Supernatural 4, 57, 88, 138
Survival of the Dead 113–114
Suspiria 17, 39
Swamp Thing 61

A Tale of Two Sisters 144
Teen Wolf 85
teenage/teenager 12, 20, 34, 41–42, 48–51, 59–61, 63–64, 72–76, 98, 104, 113, 115, 138, 173, 179
The Tenant 161
Terror Train 43
The Texas Chain Saw Massacre (1974) 121–124, 153 168
The Texas Chain Saw Massacre (2003) 123–125, 127, 153, 177, 181
The Texas Chainsaw Massacre Part 2 122
The Texas Chainsaw Massacre: The Beginning 125
The Texas Chainsaw Massacre: The Next Generation 122
Texas Chainsaw 3D 125
Thanksgiving 44, 119
Them! see creature features
The Thing (1982) 43, 77, 86–87
The Thing (2011) 87
The Thing from Another World 20, 85–87
13 Ghosts 21, 102
Thir13en Ghosts 17, 103
Thompson, Nancy 60, 62–67, 70–71, 73–75
Thriller 85
Timpone, Tony 41, 44, 146, 152–154
The Toolbox Murders (1978) 143
The Toolbox Murders (2004) 143
Total Recall (1990) 142
Total Recall (2012) 142
The Toxic Avenger 137
Train 163
Tremors 66
Troll 54
True Blood 13, 84, 180
28 Days Later 78, 114, 150
28 Weeks Later 92
The Twilight People 81–82
The Twilight Saga 13, 78, 84, 142
Twitchell, James B. 12–14, 16
2001 Maniacs 143
Two Thousand Maniacs! 143

Underworld 13, 84
The Uninvited 144, 165

V 71
The Vampire Diaries 13, 84
vampires 13, 38, 78, 84–85, 139–143
Vaughn, Vince 24, 27–30, 72, 154, 156
Vertigo 25
Village of the Damned (1960) 21, 103
Village of the Damned (1995) 103, 104
The Virgin Spring 61, 115
Voorhees, Jason 6, 17, 48–59, 67–68, 71, 114, 138, 157–160, 181
Voorhees, Pamela 48–51, 54, 58–59

The Walking Dead 114
Warlock 66
Wells, H.G. 79, 81–82

Werewolf Women of the S.S. 44
werewolves 13, 38, 82–85, 140
Whedon, Joss *see The Cabin in the Woods*
When a Stranger Calls (1979) 133–135
When a Stranger Calls (2006) 135
When a Stranger Calls Back 136
White, John 170–173
White Noise 2: The Light 138
The Wicker Man 144
The Wizard of Gore (1970) 143
The Wizard of Gore (2007) 143
Wolf 84

Wolf Creek 163, 165
The Wolf Man (1941) 77–78, 82–84–85
The Wolf Man (2010) 13, 84–85, 87
Wrong Turn 2: Dead End 53

Zombie, Rob 4, 7, 44–47, 64, 72, 77, 157, 158, 172
The Zombie Diaries 114
Zombie Strippers! 71
Zombieland 78, 164, 178, 179
zombies 38, 71, 78, 102, 104–114, 118, 164, 175, 178–180